AF605049

The Big Trial

The Big Trial

Law as Public Spectacle

Lawrence M. Friedman

University Press of Kansas

Published by the University Press of Kansas (Lawrence, Kansas 66045), which was organized by the Kansas Board of Regents and is operated and funded by Emporia State University, Fort Hays State University, Kansas State University, Pittsburg State University, the University of Kansas, and Wichita State University

Library of Congress Cataloging-in-Publication Data
Friedman, Lawrence M. (Lawrence Meir), 1930– author.
The big trial : law as public spectacle / Lawrence M. Friedman.
pages cm
Includes bibliographical references and index.
ISBN 978-0-7006-2077-7 (cloth : alk. paper)—ISBN 978-0-7006-2078-4 (ebook)
1. Trials—United States—History. I. Title.
KF220.F75 2015
347.73'709—dc23
2014045937

British Library Cataloguing-in-Publication Data is available.

Printed in the United States of America

10 9 8 7 6 5 4 3 2 1

The paper used in this publication is recycled and contains 30 percent postconsumer waste. It is acid free and meets the minimum requirements of the American National Standard for Permanence of Paper for Printed Library Materials Z39.48-1992.

To: *Leah, Jane, Amy, Sarah, David, Lucy, and Irene*

Contents

Acknowledgments

I would like to thank William Havemann, Mark Hernandez, Dante O'Connell, Vivek Vijay Tata, and David Oyer for their assistance in the research on this book. I would also like to thank George Fisher for his extremely helpful comments and Charles Myers, of the University Press of Kansas, and two anonymous reviewers for their valuable suggestions. As always, I owe a great deal to the enormously helpful and skillful staff of the Stanford Law Library and its director, Paul Lomio.

The Big Trial

1

Law and Its Audience

On October 3, 1995, the whole United States, it seemed, was holding its breath. O. J. Simpson—sports hero, movie star—had been on trial for murder. Now a verdict was about to be announced. Millions of people put their lives on hold, as they waited for the news. At my school, faculty and students crowded into lounges where the TV sets were on, so as not to miss this event. This scene was repeated in homes, bars, and institutions all over the country, and elsewhere as well. The Los Angeles County courthouse was ringed with police. Fear of riots hung in the air like a dark, fetid cloud. Volume dropped on the stock exchange. The president of the United States stopped work to listen to the news.

At 10 a.m. the jury's verdict came, and it was a sensation: not guilty.[1] Sixteen months had gone by since Nicole Brown Simpson, the defendant's ex-wife, and a friend of hers, Ronald L. Goldman, had been found, slashed to death, in the front yard of Nicole Simpson's condominium. From that moment on, the case was a total sensation. A great deal of evidence pointed to Simpson. The trial was televised, to an audience of millions, here and abroad. Everyone involved in the case—the judge, the witnesses, the lawyers—became celebrity figures. The courtroom battle went on, month after month. In the end, the jury reached its verdict quickly. But the case did not end with its verdict. True, Simpson went free. But a burning question remained: Was justice done?

The Simpson case was a prime example of what we might call "headline trials," the subject of this book. By this I mean criminal trials that make the headlines, and often the front page, in the daily newspaper, that claim a share of attention in the evening news, and that, in any event, evoke intense public interest. Like many people, I find these trials quite fascinating. Many of these big trials have kept their fascination over the years. The Lizzie Borden trial, in the 1890s, has in a real sense never died. Among other things, this book tries to answer the question: Why? What was it about this trial that gave it such powers of survival?

Big, notorious trials like the Simpson trial are, of course, in no way typical of criminal trials in the United States. Yet that trial had a number of traits that are hardly unique; these traits are, in fact, to be found in quite a few of these headline trials. It was, to begin with, a *celebrity* trial: Simpson was a celebrity defendant. There have also been celebrity victims: Stanford White, the country's leading architect, shot down by Harry K. Thaw; President Garfield, assassinated by Charles Guiteau. And, like many other big trials, by the time the Simpson trial had ended, the judge, the witnesses, and everybody involved in the case had themselves become celebrities. Also, like many headline trials, the Simpson trial was left enveloped in a fog of mystery and uncertainty: Did he or did he not do it? Also, one can ask (as we mentioned) whether justice had in fact been done. Simpson was black; his ex-wife was white; and the trial developed strong political overtones, polarizing white and black opinion about what happened and why. The undertone of sexuality and sexual jealousy made it also what we might call a "*tabloid* trial"—that is, a trial that flowed out of a sensational and lurid crime.

As these last paragraphs make clear, headline trials come in various sizes, shapes, and types. The types overlap, of course.

What they all have in common is their sheer notoriety. They are public theater: The events take place in public and before a public audience (real and virtual) in a dramatic, theatrical way. All dramas have messages, of course; hence, headline trials can be labeled, if you wish, as didactic theater.

But what makes them so dramatic? What is it about society that gives them their fascination? And how has the social meaning and importance of these trials changed over time? These, too, are themes of this book. Why do these cases capture the imagination of the public? Are the headline trials of our period different from those of a century or two ago? And what do we learn from these trials about the nature of our society, past and present?

To tame this rather unruly subject, I have classified headline trials—divided them into distinctive types. The types, to be sure, tend to overlap. Some trials (like O. J. Simpson's) can fall into several categories. One obvious type of headline trial is the *political* trial: trials for treason, spy trials, trials of dissenters and radicals, among others. Trials for *corruption and fraud* are an important subcategory of the political trial.

Perhaps all trials have at least a certain amount of political relevance. This is particularly true of trials that leave people asking, was justice done? Some of these trials call the whole legal process into question. The O. J. Simpson trial began as a straightforward murder trial and morphed into something rather different. It also had elements of two other categories, which we mentioned in connection with the case: tabloid trials and celebrity trials. When we come to discuss celebrity trials, we will need to explore exactly what we mean by "celebrity." Headline trials also, as we said, *create* celebrities. *Whodunit* trials, another category, are trials whose fascination consists, at least in part, of the sheer element of mystery surrounding the events in question. We know who killed President Garfield, but are we sure about O. J. Simpson? Claus von Bulow, defendant in a sensational trial, was accused of acts that sent his wife, Sunny, into an irreversible coma. But did he actually do it?

I group an especially interesting type of trial under the phrase "worm in the bud." These cases seem, somehow, to put society itself on trial, to raise fundamental social questions that probe beneath the surface, suggesting hidden and secret pathologies. These are among the most unsettling cases. The classic example is Lizzie Borden, which we will deal with later. Did Lizzie really commit the brutal axe-murders she was charged with? What made the case so notorious, then and later, was the notion of a worm in the bud, the idea that an unmarried, straitlaced, churchgoing woman from polite, bourgeois society was capable of such an awful crime. Finally, a small but important group of cases flows out of moral panic. The classic example is the Salem witch trials, but there are some significant recent examples as well.

Not much ties all of these trials together; indeed, one point of this book is to establish how many *different* types there are. They all do have, however, a few gross commonalities. One we have already mentioned: all are examples of *didactic theater.* Also, increasingly, they reflect and depend on the mass media. In a sense, the mass media gave birth to the headline trial, and the role of the media has been vital to the progress (if that is the word) of headline trials. Lastly, headline trials, for the most part, raise a question about *identity*: Who is this person on trial? Is he or she a villainous killer or an innocent, caught unfairly in a web? As we will argue, modern society, with its intense mobility and where there are always strangers among us, is also a world in which identity has become problematic in ways that were not so pronounced before. Big trials reflect this aspect of modern society.

You might think that headline trials must have produced a huge literature. And in a way they have. Oceans of ink were spilled over the case of Lizzie Borden in its day, and the case continues to resonate to this day. The trial of O. J. Simpson was in the news constantly; it was perhaps the greatest television drama of them all. No doubt every year or so some trial catches the public's fancy and makes big news. In the 1950s, it was the trial of Dr. Sam Sheppard for killing his wife. In the summer of 2013, it was the trial in Florida of George Zimmerman, who was accused of killing a young black man, Trayvon Martin. Zimmerman's trial generated enormous heat, and controversy. It absorbed huge amounts of space in the press and on TV.

There are many books, articles, and television programs about some of these trials, and sometimes about groups of trials. But, oddly enough, very little has been written about big trials *in general*—about their nature, how it has changed, and what it all means. This short book is a modest attempt to fill in a few of the gaps and to add something to our general understanding of these trials. The period in question is roughly that of American independence. There were fascinating trials in ancient history—the trial of Socrates, for example, and in the Middle Ages, the trial of Joan of Arc—and probably in every society. But, for the most part, I will stick to the modern period, and to the United States.

In Public

What all of these trials have in common is that they were public events. Secret trials are not supposed to exist in our system.[2] Trials have always been open to the public. Of course, a public event today is not the same as a public event of the nineteenth century, or even of the first half of the twentieth century. At one time, "the public" was the small group of people who actually attended the trials and those who heard about it from neighbors. This was no doubt true for the Salem witch trials, in the seventeenth century. These trials made a great stir in their day, to be sure, and in their community; but news about these trials spread very slowly.

The modern world is entirely different. Telling the story of headline trials is also telling the story of the rise of the mass media. In the nineteenth century, cheap, popular newspapers broke through to a mass audience. The whole country could and did read about Lizzie Borden. Next came radio, then television, and now, in the twenty-first century, the Internet: all have vastly increased the number of people who watch, listen, or care about headline trials. More recent trials—O. J. Simpson being a prime example—reached audiences that would have been unthinkable in the past. The O. J. Simpson trial was, for a while, the most popular and prominent television show in America.

Nobody was forced to watch the O. J. Simpson trial on TV. People watched because they wanted to, because it was fascinating—it was, in other words, prime entertainment. They might have watched a baseball game or a quiz program or a reality show or tended to their rose garden. Instead, they became, as it were, spectators at a criminal trial.

Clearly, people enjoyed the trial. It fascinated them. Did they also learn something? Even pure entertainment gives off messages, overt and covert. Criminal trials carry messages as well. They can tell us about society's norms and values. As Emile Durkheim long ago pointed out, criminal justice defines the normative boundaries of society. It expresses what is and what is not allowed, in an overt, dramatic way. Political trials are often meant to send an explicit message. A lurid murder trial sends a less obvious message, but in every case, some sort of message, some lesson, some idea, is there, hidden perhaps in the dense legal shrubbery or disguised by the overt drama.

The big criminal trial is historically important precisely because of the mixture of what fascinates people and what instructs them. This is one of the theses of this book: Headline trials have, and have always had, two distinct social tasks. One is to instruct, to teach, to send a message. The other is to entertain. But the exact mixture of the two varies from type to type and has varied over time. In the age of mass media, the mixture is not the way it was in the age of the Salem witch trials. But big trials are always a kind of social drama—didactic theater, as we called it. And these trials have always been, in a sense, public debates. They tell a story (or, more often, two conflicting stories). And they carry messages. To be sure, the stories and messages come out in complicated ways, because procedural rules tie trials up in legal knots. And the messages can be false or misleading, or misreported.

In a big trial, lawyers on both sides appeal to popular justice, in the broadest sense of that phrase. The stories they tell have to be plausible, sympathetic, and persuasive. In a jury trial, they have to give the jury something reasonable, something familiar, something they can carry with them into the jury room. This makes these trials important social documents. The media, too, must be able to tap into and exploit norms and attitudes that are already out there in the ocean of society. For this reason, trials can shed light on social norms that might otherwise be obscure. Arguments and strategies in jury trials are windows into social stereotypes and norms, into what people think and believe. They can help show us which norms, ideas, and attitudes pack the most social punch, at various points in history. The evidence is rough; it is hardly rigorous and systematic, but sometimes this is the best we can do.

Patterns of jury decisions also tell a story. Jurors do not normally talk about their decisions. They come out of their locked room and utter a few gnomic words. Their reasoning can only be inferred. The jury room is the blackest of black boxes.

Besides, as we know, *both* sides are at work, trying to concoct a coherent story. The stories are usually in conflict. It is often hard to tell, for jurors or outsiders, what is true (whatever "truth" might mean). Sometimes neither story makes total sense; sometimes neither side is playing with a full deck. But the stories themselves are revealing. And the patterns of decisions can make clear what individual trials do not.

As we said, headline trials are above all *public.* They are open, on display. Big trials are, and always have been, *public* in a quite literal sense. For the big trials, people line up eagerly for a chance to watch the show. At the trial in 1879 of the Reverend Herbert Hayden, a married Methodist minister with children, who was accused of killing a young woman he had impregnated, people lined up early in the morning, waiting for the doors to open. People "pushed, shoved, and trampled each other to get in and the deputies had quite a time of it to close the doors on the hundreds who were unsuccessful."[3] These "unsuccessful" people, of course, could read the newspapers: Since the dawn of the mass-circulation press, big trials have also been public in this wider sense. They were broadcast, as it were, to a vast audience outside of the courtroom. When Harry K. Thaw was on trial for murdering Stanford White in 1907—we shall have more to say about this trial later on—the general public had to be satisfied with this kind of vicarious attendance. The courtroom was jammed with lawyers, family, and friends of the defendant; more than one hundred reporters with press passes filled seats in the courtroom. But, though the public had no chance to get into the room, thanks to newspaper coverage, the trial was "reported to the ends of the civilized globe."[4]

That the process is and should be open is a rule for democratic societies. These societies are committed to the rule of law—the idea that legal institutions are or ought to be impartial, transparent, and independent and that legal process should be orderly, regular, and fair.[5] Policy in democratic societies is supposed to be made in the open, in the sunshine. Secrecy is disfavored. Statutes like the Freedom of Information Act[6] are supposed to make government an open book. The Administrative Procedure Act tells government agencies that they must, generally speaking, give the public notice, and a chance to be heard, before they issue rules and regulations.[7] If the Food and Drug Administration (FDA) wants to specify what dyes can be used to turn cucumbers green and tomatoes red, it must (in theory at least) let the public know what it plans to do, publish its proposals in the Federal Register, and throw the process open to comments and suggestions. Very likely chemical companies will demand to be heard, if the FDA intends to ban some sort of chemical additive. Various consumer groups might have a thing or two to say as well.

So much for theory. Transparency and participation are ideals, not realities. The very text of the Administrative Procedure Act opens the door to exceptions: for "good cause," an agency can bypass requirements of notice. Some agencies are very good at discovering these "good causes." The Freedom of Information Act is peppered with exceptions. Government in the modern world is staggeringly complex. So is the legal system. There are rooms within rooms within rooms, locked doors and secret panels. What goes on, every day, in thousands of offices and bureaus, is for the most part totally opaque. Laws are made the way some sort of giant sausage might be made. Mysterious ingredients are ground up and stirred in the pot, and a gaggle of cooks and sub-cooks mix and stir, add and subtract, boil and steam and fry. Courts, legislatures, regulatory bodies, members of the Executive staff, and even the president himself are part of the law-making process. And on other levels, governors, mayors, city officials, police officers, wardens of prisons, commissioners of agencies, members of zoning boards and boards of education, people who license doctors and plumbers, and so on and so forth: All are busily engaged in making and enforcing rules. In addition, members of the public, by voting, making campaign contributions, writing letters, and nagging and demonstrating and protesting, leave their mark on the system as well. Some—for example, big donors—leave more of a mark than others.

In practice, there are more closed doors than open doors. Many aspects of the process are totally and officially closed to the public. There is no right to know, for example, how to put together a hydrogen bomb, or what dirty secrets the Central

Intelligence Agency (CIA) keeps in its breast. You cannot use the Freedom of Information Act to ferret out contingency plans for dealing with a crisis in China or Pakistan, or to learn the names of our spies in other countries. A modern, complex government has to keep secrets, and it has to do a lot of its work in secret. In the summer of 2013, the government was outraged when a whistle-blower, Edward Snowden, revealed dirty secrets about actions of his government. To avoid arrest and trial, he felt forced to flee the country.[8]

That the dirty tricks of the CIA are secret goes without saying. But in fact, law-making and rule-making go on *mostly* behind closed doors; the process is informal and, in the main, below the radar screen. A citizen can hardly expect to see the wheels actually turning. She cannot expect to eavesdrop on people in the State Department arguing about policy or debates in the Department of Agriculture about crop subsidies.

And, for most of us, whatever the theory, most of what government does might as well be labeled "top secret." Of the work of the millions of civil servants, from the president on down to the local postal clerk, only the tiniest fragment gets broadcast to a wider audience. Most government action is visible, if at all, only to a small, select group. Of course, as we mentioned, regulations, executive orders, and drafts of regulations have to be published in the Federal Register. This is Leviathan's diary. It is hardly bedside reading; it runs to tens of thousands of pages each year. It is, however, meat and drink for lobbyists and interest groups. They make it their business to know what the Register says—at least those parts that affect their clients. But even the thousands of pages of the Federal Register are only part of the story. Not everything that is supposed to be there is actually printed; and in any event, for most of us nonlobbyists, and for all of us in many ways, government operates quietly and without publicity. Leviathan hides in the murky depths of an ocean of law.

What is *public*, then, is in fact exceptional. The president's press conferences, debates in the halls of Congress: These are prominent examples. And trials—our subject—are another. Trial personnel are government employees; and, in criminal cases, the government (state or federal) is nominally the plaintiff. Trials, as we said, are open to the public.[9] Most trials and proceedings, to be sure, run their course without an audience, except for family and friends. But when the case makes headlines, people—and reporters—crowd the courtroom. Headline trials are thus extremely visible. They are actually, legitimately, and blatantly public.

Another point: Today especially, headline trials are creatures of the *media.* So much so that we can ask whether it is the media that makes them what they are. The media mediate; they sit squarely in the middle, between legal agencies and institutions, on the one hand, and the general public, on the other. The government brings the cases, but then in a sense the media take over. They report the news about trials and other events, but they also make the news. They turn a whisper into a roar. To say that the media simply report "facts" is naïve; in a real sense, they *make* the facts (within limits, of course). Often enough, the noise from the media is far from rational. It is more like a street scene in the metropolis: a welter of screams, screeches, and sirens.

Increasingly, "public" means what the newspapers report, what is shown on TV, or what is blogged and tweeted about. The media expose headline trials to the public. Before the radio, there were no "broadcasts," but the newspapers did their share. Now, with radio, television, and the Internet, ours has become a broadcast society. The "broadcasting" of trials, literally and figuratively, is essential to any understanding of the trials and their place in society. The story of headline trials is also the story of headlines.

In the next chapter, we will explore in more detail what it means for a trial to be public and look at how the public nature of trials has changed over the years. We will also look briefly at two forms of nonofficial trials: lynchings and vigilante action.

In chapters 3 through 9, we will take up the various types of headline trials and discuss them in order. We will also discuss what makes these trials significant, or notorious, or both; these issues will be discussed in chapters 10 through 14. Headline trials emerge from a specific social milieu. They are rooted in modern society—a society of mobility, in which, more than ever before, a person's very *identity* can be at issue. And in more recent times, these trials have reflected the development of what we have called a *celebrity* society. Many of these trials, as we said, have celebrity defendants or celebrity victims (think of the trial of Charles Guiteau, for example, who shot President Garfield). And, as we said, big trials also *create* celebrities; if the trial makes enough of a splash, the participants all become celebrities themselves.

These then are the main themes of this book; they will be explored and expanded in the coming chapters.

2

Open to the Public
The Headline Trial

The subject of this book is the sensational or headline trial.[1] Mostly, this book is about the sensational *common law* trial, and mostly as the common law trial unfolded and unfolds in the United States, with a few examples from England and other societies thrown in.

The common law trial is dramatic in a quite literal sense. We have used the phrase "didactic theater." Trials are, or can be, a kind of stage play, with a definite story or plot—usually, in fact, *two* stories or plots that stand in sharp contrast to each other and that the lawyers spin out and shape through evidence, testimony, and cross-examination. The general shape of a common law trial is familiar to anyone who studies law and, indeed, to anyone who reads books, sees movies, or watches TV. We can picture, in our mind's eye, the courtroom. Here is the raised bench, where the judge is going to sit; he or she can look down from that height on the courtroom. There, to the side, sits the jury in the jury box. Next to the judge is the witness stand. The defendant is seated next to his lawyer. The judge files in. All rise. The jury enters and takes its place in the jury box. The trial begins. The lawyers on both sides make opening statements. Both sides work to get their story out, to present their case to judge and jury. Witnesses are cross-examined. Evidence is submitted. At the end of the trial, the lawyers sum matters up. Then, the judge instructs the jury, that is, he gives it a lesson on the relevant points of law. The jury is supposed to decide the facts of the case and apply the law to those facts. Whether jurors actually do this, and whether they understand the instructions at all, is often fairly unclear. At any rate, after the instructions, the jury retires to its private room. In a big trial, this part of the drama is full of suspense: the defendant, the prosecutors, and perhaps the world all wait anxiously for the jury to make up its mind. Then comes the climactic moment. After hours, or days, or occasionally weeks, the jury is ready to report; the members of the jury file back into the courtroom, and the foreman announces the verdict to judge, defendant, prosecution, and the world.

The common law trial can be intensely dramatic. A lot of the drama depends on the principle of *orality*. In the classic civil law trial, in Europe or Latin America, judges, lawyers, and other officials shuffle documents and pieces of paper. In the common law trial, on the other hand, the spoken word is king. The trial itself is, by tradition, a kind of stage production. Dialog is all, as so many movies, books, plays, and television dramas tell us. What the lawyers say, what the witnesses say, cross-examination, oral arguments: Always the spoken word. The judge's instructions to the jury are oral. Even the final, climactic scene is oral: the jury tells the defendant his fate, in a few dramatic words.

Of course, in real-life trials come in many shapes and forms. Civil cases are more common than criminal cases. There are civil trials of enormous significance: massive tort cases, huge class actions, mighty lawsuits pitting one corporate giant against another, like the battle between Apple and Samsung, not to mention constitutional cases that may affect millions of people. Or, once in a while, a sensational divorce case, or a struggle over inheritance, piques curiosity and interest. But on the whole, civil trials do not catch the eyes and ears of the public. This is not to say that a civil case cannot act as didactic theater: consider, for example, cases on civil rights and race relations. Nor is it to say that the media do not or cannot play a role in shaping these cases, or at least their public images. Indeed, it is a major theme of some current scholarship that the media report, and distort, some issues in civil trials: a prime example was the suit against McDonald's that began with a spilled cup of very hot coffee and that the media came to portray (unjustly) as a symptom of a tort system that had gone amok.[2] Still, civil trials on the whole do not make much of a splash; and their didactic purpose is not usually so direct. Nor do they raise the issue of disputed identity or implicate the celebrity society, as big trials do. In any event, it is these trials, the big criminal trials, that I will concentrate on.

A big criminal trial is familiar in shape, largely because it is everywhere in popular culture.[3] Criminal justice, in the broadest sense, fills the pages of thousands of books, newspapers, and magazine articles; criminal justice is beamed to the world in thousands of movies and television shows. There is no way to count how many movies, plays, or television dramas, real and fictional, have focused on a criminal trial or featured a criminal trial as part of the news or the story line. One reason these trials are socially important is because they figure so massively in popular culture. A headline trial is, in a way, a cousin of modern "reality" shows on TV. And it is even closer to the ubiquitous dramas of popular culture—except that the courtroom figures are real people, not actors.

Criminal justice is a complex system. It includes, first of all, the criminal law itself: the criminal code or body of rules, a catalog of forbidden actions containing everything from overtime parking to serial murder. Each state, the federal government, and every foreign country has its own version of a criminal code. These are typically extremely bulky, with hundreds of individual sections. The California Penal Code, to take one example, runs to more than a thousand pages.

Without the criminal justice *system,* the penal code, of course, would be nothing but words on paper. The criminal justice *system* has the job of putting the code into effect: finding violators, bringing them to justice, and dealing with them if they are found guilty. The system includes police officers and detectives, judges, prosecutors, defense attorneys, juries, probation officers, prison guards, wardens, forensic scientists, and many others. A lot of the work is unobtrusive. A lot of it is routine. Every year, the police arrest tens of thousands of men and women for one offense or another. Most of these men and woman—the vast majority, in fact—will never go to trial. This is true even of people accused of felonies, that is, of serious crimes.[4] A man puts on a ski mask, tries to rob a convenience store, gets caught, and ends up in the hands of the police. This might be, say, his fourth offense. He is extremely unlikely to go to trial; instead, he will "cop a plea." Plea bargaining will settle the fate of nine out of ten of these defendants.[5] Prosecution and defense strike a deal. The defendant pleads guilty—to something, though not necessarily the original charge. The prosecution will drop some charges, or promise a lighter sentence or some other benefit, in exchange for the guilty plea. At that point, the case is over: No trial will take place.

We live, in fact, in the age of the "vanishing trial."[6] In fact, trials have been vanishing for more than a century. Not that big, full-scale trials were ever common. Headline trials were never the norm, even before the age of the plea bargain. In, say, the early nineteenth century, most serious criminal cases did go to trial; but the "trials" in many places were short, routine, even slapdash. Juries were selected in a hurry. The same panel sat in on a whole series of cases. In some courthouses, the typical "trial" probably took less than a day to run its course; sometimes much less than a day.[7] And in many of these trials, no lawyer appeared for the defendant.[8] The jury, perhaps, might reach a verdict without leaving the room.

In the aggregate, to be sure, these cases were important. Individually, however, they were not. Even today, such trials exist:

routine, cut and dried, coming out of minor offenses such as vagrancy, drunkenness, fights in taverns, moving violations. For these, the courtroom is almost empty, except for the people immediately involved. No reporters come to listen and watch. No television cameras cast their beady eye on these courtrooms. These trials are short and hopefully sweet. They are the plankton of the sea of criminal justice. Public order depends on them. But no one case, or even a dozen, is of consequence or attracts public attention.

A rare handful of trials have a different trajectory. These are our trials, the headline trials. Everything takes place in the glaring spotlight of the media. The jury is carefully selected; the selection process might take days of wrangling and arguing. Both sides, of course, have lawyers. During the trial, they make elaborate arguments. They cross-examine witnesses. Procedures are meticulously followed. The trial itself may stretch out over days or weeks or even months, and in exceptional cases even longer. From start to finish, the O. J. Simpson case consumed more than a year. Even longer was the McMartin day-care trial; it stretched on for more than two years. These cases are rare. But their rarity does not make them insignificant. These trials—headline trials —are important far beyond their numbers.

In every period, in the United States and other common law countries, there have been trials of this sort. There is no way to count them accurately—or even, in fact, to define exactly what we mean by "big." Roughly, these are trials that make a splash in the media. But a trial might make headlines in Wichita, Kansas, and nowhere else. Others, like the trial of O. J. Simpson, seem to set the whole country ablaze; it resonated even beyond the borders of the United States.[9] For want of a better term, and a better definition, I refer to these trials as "big trials" or "headline trials" and define them crudely as trials that attract major public attention. "Major public attention" means, basically, newspaper and other media coverage, including books, movies, TV shows, and (today) exposure on the Internet. Indeed, as we said, these trials have two defining traits: They are *public* and they attract the *media.*

Open to the Public

The modern headline trial is a survivor, in a way, of a system that used to be far more central to criminal justice. Trials and punishments were once *public* in the most literal sense. In colonial America, in the seventeenth century, in small towns and villages, not only were trials open to the public but so too were the punishments.[10] In the colonial period, the normal punishment for serious crime was not imprisonment but public whipping. The whipping post stood in the public square. Colonial law also deployed a stock of punishments meant to shame or embarrass offenders; violators of norms had to sit in the stocks or suffer other humilities. In Essex County, Massachusetts, in 1681, Anstis Maning and Margret Maning, accused of incest, were ordered to "stand or sit upon a high stool" in the "open middle alley of the meeting house, with a paper upon each of their heads, with their crime written in capital letters."[11]

Sometimes punishment was public in another sense: offenders carried with them, for the rest of their lives, visible signs of their crimes and punishments. The key device in Nathaniel Hawthorne's famous novel, *The Scarlet Letter*, was not something Hawthorne invented. It was reality. Under a New Hampshire law of 1701, adulterers were ordered to wear "for ever after . . . a Capitall Letter: A: . . . Sewed upon their Upper Garments."[12] In Kent County, Delaware, in 1699, John Burton, convicted of stealing "Three pounds and one halfe of Cotton Spun," was ordered to "weare a romane T upon the out side of his left arme for the space of Six months of a different Couler from his upper garment;" Burton also got "three Lashes on his beare back well Laid on."[13] Punishment for a burglar, under the Laws and Liberties of Massachusetts (1648), was branding "on the forehead with the letter (B)." If the burglar committed the crime on a Sunday, "he shal for the first offence have one of his ears cut off"; for a second offence, "he shal loose his other ear."[14] This was not a dead letter. One Thomas West, in 1657, in Massachusetts, convicted of burglary and stealing on a Sunday, was duly branded in the forehead; and he indeed lost one of his ears.[15]

Actual trials were significant as ritual and drama, and punishments even more so. Hanging a condemned man was a significant public event. Thousands could and would gather to see the criminal launched into eternity. Often, on Sunday before an execution, the minister would comment in his sermon on the coming execution and explain what lessons the community might learn from it. The condemned man himself might give a speech and point to a lesson, as he stood in the shadow of the gallows. More than thirty-five examples of these supposed last speeches survive from the eighteenth century; to be sure, ministers or other officials might have written them out in advance.[16] Whatever their source, these speeches were meant to point a moral; they were sermons, in effect, preached to the local audience. So, for example, "poor Julian," executed for murder in 1733, told the crowd about his history of drunkenness and Sabbath-breaking. His criminal career began with these offenses, and he then slid down the slippery slope, leading, in the end, "to this great Sin for which I now die. . . . O take warning by me all of you, I intreat you . . . turn from your evil ways."[17] Not every condemned man was willing to play this role. When Ephraim Wheeler was hanged in Massachusetts in 1806 for raping his own daughter, a minister gave an impassioned speech hours before the execution. Wheeler was there, sitting on a coffin. He refused to speak. He was hoisted by "grim-faced deputies," together with his coffin, and carted off to the gallows. A crowd of some five thousand watched him die, stubbornly unrepentant.[18] More pliant was Esther Rodgers, who delivered an "emotional statement of warning" just before she was hanged for infanticide in 1701: "Let me beg of all Young Ones, be not Disobedient, go not with Bad Company, O my dear Friends—Take Warning by Me." She spoke, supposedly, before a crowd of some four or five thousand spectators.[19]

Trials, punishments, and executions were public; they were truly didactic theater. They were meant to teach. It would be cynical to call them entertainment; but in a sense they also filled this role. The very size of the audiences suggests as much. Puritan magistrates and clergy considered this kind of show a useful, powerful way to teach the public that the wages of sin were death. Yet by the early nineteenth century, public execution had lost its luster. Hanging in the public square no longer seemed to be effective moral theater. What worked in the small towns of colonial New England, in small, deeply religious, theologically homogeneous face-to-face communities, lost its magic in big, raucous cities like New York, Baltimore, Philadelphia, and Boston. The seaport cities were full of transient, deracinated, noisy, and disreputable people. These cities had a rich supply of crude waterfront saloons, slums, brothels, and seedy theaters; an atmosphere of drink, sin, disorder, and rioting. To hang somebody in front of this kind of crowd, in public, meant something quite different from hangings in the public square of Puritan villages. Public hangings, arguably, simply appealed to the worst instincts of a jeering mob, feeding their blood-lust and arousing an appetite for licentious violence. Executions, in the view of respectable people, had become "festivals of disorder that subverted morals, increased crimes, and excited sympathy with the criminal."[20]

In reaction, punishment went private. States passed laws to get rid of these spectacles. No more hangings in the public square, no more sermons and speeches from the gallows.[21] Under Pennsylvania law, in the 1830s, executions were to take place within the "walls or yard of the jail," in the county where the criminal had been convicted. The sheriff could select a number of witnesses—a doctor, the attorney general, and "twelve reputable citizens."[22] But the public was not allowed to bear witness—except, that is, for those who climbed up trees or peeked at the show from the roofs of nearby houses.[23] It was still sometimes possible for sizeable crowds to see a hanging. When three Italians went to the gallows in Chicago, on November 14, 1885, for murdering another Italian and stashing his body in a trunk, as many as two thousand people jammed into the place where the gallows was located.[24]

By this time, punishments that inflicted stigma and shame—the stocks, the scarlet letter—had long since been abandoned. Shaming is a technique that works best, if it works at all, in small, homogeneous communities. It depends on an audience of like-minded people. Big cities were the wrong venue for stigma and shame. States also got rid of the whipping post. A conviction arose that bodily punishments were barbaric. Meanwhile, in the first half of the century, first the northern states, and then the rest of the states, erected "penitentiaries": huge, tightly guarded buildings, with massive walls and cellblocks.[25] Here, prisoners were kept totally out of sight (and largely out of mind). And that wonderful invention, the electric chair, in the late nineteenth century, finally succeeded in making executions truly private. Now the condemned died deep in the bowels of the prison, away from the masses, unseen except by a handful of people.[26] The only witnesses, under Pennsylvania law, for example, were to be the warden, a "qualified physician," six "reputable adult citizens" chosen by the warden, a "spiritual adviser" (if the condemned man wanted one), up to six reporters, and such prison officials as the warden might select.[27] William Kemmler of New York, in 1890, had the dubious distinction of being the first to go to his death in the electric chair.[28]

And yet, even though executions were closed to the public, the public could attend vicariously, thanks to the popular press, which reported on executions, sometimes in gruesome detail. Here, too, Kemmler was one of the pioneers. The *New York Times* reported in gross, horrifying prose how he died: it recorded his last words, as eleven leather straps bound him to the fatal chair; explained how long it took to kill him and how he was still alive after the first massive jolt of electricity; described what his body looked like at that stage and how it took another huge jolt to kill him.[29] The *Times* also reported that a "throng" had gathered in front of the prison. Young men "climbed telephone poles and gazed eagerly toward the vine-clad prison"; the platform of the railway station across the street was "black with people."[30] In 1899, Mrs. Martha Place entered history as the first woman to be electrocuted. The *National Police Gazette* eagerly provided details: she was dressed "in a black gown with big sleeves" and with "russet slippers" on her feet; she clutched at a Bible; her hair was clipped to make room for the electrodes.[31] The urge to take part, to be present, to observe, was still alive among members of the public. Since the public was excluded, the popular press worked hard to fill in the gap. Officially, executions were no longer theater. Unofficially, the media made sure that they were.

Nonetheless, formally, punishment was supposed to be a closed book. And in many ways it was. Inside the penitentiaries, men were whipped, punished, shamed. In the cities, inside station houses, the police could and did beat and brutalize men they arrested. None of this was officially "punishment" of course. But on the whole few people knew what went on behind the high stone walls or in the cellars of police stations; and even fewer people cared.

Formal theory, then, dictated that only the trial was open to the public. Whatever lessons were to be learned had to come from the trial itself, which remained didactic theater. Yet, in a real sense, public punishment lived on as didactic theater, long after it was supposedly dead. It took the form of lynching in the South and of vigilante action in the West. Like colonial executions, these were public events, sometimes performed before huge audiences; they were anything but private and discreet. And in some cases of vigilante action (hardly ever in the case of lynch law), they occasionally included something vaguely resembling a trial.

The dreadful practice of lynching was confined mostly to the Southern states. It was mainly associated with a particularly virulent form of white supremacy. Most victims of lynch mobs in the South were black. In Kentucky, for example, between 1865 and 1899, 197 blacks were lynched as compared to 80 whites.[32] And few whites, one imagines, were lynched simply because there were vague suspicions against them, and certainly never because they were deemed too insolent or uppity or economically successful.

Lynching was a violent and brutal way of putting to death men (and a few women) accused of serious crimes. Lynching took place in the open, sometimes in front of huge audiences.[33] The details are often extremely sadistic—cruel and barbaric to a degree hard to believe today. But there was a twisted kind of logic behind them. Lynchings were (like colonial executions) meant to teach a lesson. To be sure, Southern justice in the late nineteenth century was itself an instrument of white supremacy. A black man accused of a crime against a white man, or woman, had almost no hope of success at trial. The trial would be short, perfunctory, one-sided. No blacks served on these juries. A verdict of guilty was a foregone conclusion. But perhaps because these trials *were* so perfunctory, they did not deliver the right amount of warning, the right symbolic message, the right dose of terror. They were not severe enough, not sufficiently horrible, to drive the message of white supremacy home in its cruelest, most naked form. Only lynching had that power.

The public display of sadism makes this point crystal clear. As Leon Litwack has remarked, to "kill the victim was not enough;

the execution needed to be turned into a public ritual"; the victim had to be tortured and mutilated. Luther Holbert and his wife were charged with killing their white employer in Mississippi in 1904. A thousand people watched as they were lynched. Their fingers were chopped off and handed out as souvenirs, a corkscrew was bored into their flesh; they were then burned to death.[34] The horrors of lynch law lasted deep into the twentieth century.[35] There was nothing secret about lynching or lynchers; yet members of the lynch mobs were almost never brought to trial, and certainly almost never punished. Indeed, they were proud of what they had done. They took photographs and kept souvenirs.

Vigilante movements go far back in American history, but this form of popular justice exploded in the second half of the nineteenth century. The Vigilance Committees of San Francisco, which flourished in the 1850s, probably helped give rise to the term "vigilante." Vigilante actions were on the whole a Western phenomenon; they flourished in California, Montana, Nevada, and neighboring states.[36]

No two vigilante movements or actions were exactly the same. Sometimes, these "movements" were nothing more than loose aggregations, mobs, ad hoc groups that formed, took hold of local villains (or men they assumed were villains), and let them dangle at the end of a rope, without much further ado. In Virginia City, Montana, for example, this was the fate of one Captain Slade. Slade was notorious for his outrageous behavior, his defiant and lawless ways, his flouting of authority. Finally, enough was enough: A group of men seized him, dragged him off, and hanged him. Slade's wife, on their ranch, heard what was in store for him; she mounted her horse and rode desperately to town but arrived too late to save him.[37] Other vigilante actions required a certain amount of planning. Occasionally, there was something more or less like a trial, though without the niceties of formal legal procedure; this "trial," too, (such as it was) took place in the open. In Virginia City, for example, three men who had committed a murder were brought before a "people's court" to face a "trial by the people *en masse.*" Arguments were heard, and then the "question was submitted to the people, 'Guilty, or not Guilty.'" "Guilty" was the almost unanimous decision; and on the question of punishment, "a chorus of voices from all parts of the vast assembly shouted 'Hang them.'"[38] Like colonial hangings, these "trials" (and vigilante punishment in general) acted as didactic theater. The point was not only to get rid of desperadoes, rustlers, and hell-raisers but also to warn their fellow travelers to behave, and to aim a moral lesson at the general public.

Vigilante justice was, in essence, a form of lynching. At bottom, the vigilante movements depended on a feeling that ordinary justice, ordinary process, was simply not up to the task. It was impotent or did not send a strong enough message. And, in fact, formal justice did break down in some parts of the West. Some local sheriffs and deputies were corrupt or worked hand in hand with crooks. But at other times, and in other places, vigilante justice had more complex roots; it sometimes represented a kind of culture clash or a struggle for power between two elements of the population. In towns like Virginia City or San Francisco, members of the elite—merchants, civic leaders—acted as leaders of vigilante movements. Thomas Dimsdale, in Montana, who wrote a book praising the vigilantes, complained that juries—who were, after all, chosen from among ordinary folks—acquitted the wrong people and decided on the basis of a defective moral code: "if the criminal is well liked in the community," a verdict of not guilty is almost certain, he wrote.[39] The author of a study of "urban vigilantes" in Tampa, Florida, in the late nineteenth and early twentieth centuries came to a similar conclusion: leaders of the local business community (rather than ordinary folk) were behind vigilante actions, which were virulently antilabor.[40]

Vigilante action, like lynching, was often a form of didactic theater. But the message was, in general, law and order, rather than white supremacy. Ordinary justice was defective; it simply did not deliver a strong enough lesson. Hanging in public, especially when done in the white heat of passion, was more vivid, more compelling—and quicker, too. In 1881, a band of several hundred men in Bodie, California, intervened in the trial of one Joseph DeRoche. DeRoche was in jail and on trial for shooting an innocent man in the back. The band of men decided that De Roche had "had enough justice." No doubt the jury would have found DeRoche guilty. But that was not enough to satisfy community outrage. The men of Bodie took DeRoche from the jail and hanged him then and there, in front of a blacksmith shop.[41]

Vigilante leaders in the West, like leaders of lynch mobs, operated in the bright light of day and without any sense of shame. Vigilantes, too, were almost never punished for their actions. In Bodie, after DeRoche was lynched, a coroner's jury reached the ironic (and disingenuous) verdict that he met his death "at the hands of persons unknown."[42] Vigilante leaders were on the whole quite proud of what they had done. Dr. John E. Osborne, of Wyoming, had been a prominent vigilante during the wild and wooly days of his state. He took part in killing an outlaw, Big Nose George Parrott. This was no secret; the good doctor skinned the corpse and openly exhibited objects made from the skin, including a pair of shoes. Nobody thought of prosecuting Osborne. Indeed, he was later elected governor of Wyoming.[43]

Today, very few people, if any, would have a kind word to say about lynching in the South; one might as well praise Adolf Hitler. This seems only just: lynching was brutal, inhuman, sadistic, and racist to the core.[44] The vigilantes, on the other hand, have always had mixed reviews. In the West, at the time, they were widely praised. Vigilantes were an "absolute necessity," according to Thomas J. Dimsdale, writing about Montana vigilantes. "Law-loving" men, he wrote, had the right, indeed, the duty, to "unite for mutual protection and for the salvation of the community";

this was, after all, war against "gangs of murderers, desperadoes, and robbers."[45] A newspaper account in the *San Francisco Chronicle* (1894) insisted the vigilantes were not a "mob" but a "self-constituted internal police," protecting people and property from "scoundrels and human beasts of prey."[46] Hubert Bancroft's well-known book *Popular Tribunals*, published in 1887, is also full of ringing praise for these noble roughnecks.

Both lynching and vigilantism were forms of popular justice. Even when they were supported, or led, by members of the elite—merchants, civic leaders—they tried to appeal to popular sentiments. Crowds carried them out, and other crowds served as a willing and eager audience. Of course, the line between ordinary rioters and vigilantes or lynch mobs could sometimes be fairly indistinct. Michael Feldberg, who studied the disorders of the Jacksonian period, developed a typology of riots. "Preservatist" riots were political in nature; they "were attempts by groups that held some degree of . . . power to maintain their privileged position." In this category he placed riots against Catholics or African Americans or against the Mormons in Missouri and Illinois.[47] Other riots were "expressive" or "recreational."[48] Some riots had a kind of vigilante flavor. They aimed to enforce rules that the law did not or would not enforce. In Vicksburg, Mississippi, a mob lynched professional gamblers in 1835. In many cities, there were so-called brothel riots. In 1825, a big crowd, which "included clergymen and other substantial citizens," chased women and johns out of the local brothels and destroyed the buildings.[49]

Riots, vigilante action, lynch mobs: These seem far removed from due process and the world of the formal trial. We can arrange forms of open, public "justice" along a continuum, with mob action and lynching on one end and big, formal trials on the other. But even in big, formal trials, carefully run with meticulous attention to process, the mass public can have an influence, in both subtle and unsubtle ways. The crowd inside a courtroom or milling about on the streets may cast a long shadow over what goes on at the trial. So can the reporters and the mass media they work for. The big trials are, in a sense, forms of "popular justice"—to use the term in the broadest sense—and popular justice is at the heart of the legal system, at least in open societies.[50]

Lynching has, happily, become obsolete; and vigilante action, at least on the scale of the late nineteenth century, is also history. In a sense, this marks a kind of triumph of formal justice. The headline trial survives. Trials—especially political trials—perhaps satisfy enough of the demand for popular justice. Before the age of the mass media, there was, perhaps, more of a need to "broadcast" messages about law and order. But even today, riots, demonstrations, and mass actions persist. A grim history of race riots lasted well into the twentieth century. Tulsa was the scene of a horrendous riot in 1921, in which rampaging mobs killed many African Americans (the actual number of deaths is disputed and unclear) and destroyed a flourishing black community. There were race riots in other cities too—very notably, in Detroit, in 1943 and 1967.[51] When enough people feel that justice has badly miscarried—when a headline trial comes out the wrong way—"popular justice" rises from its grave. Riots broke out in San Francisco in May 1979 after the trial of Dan White, a former supervisor who assassinated the mayor of the city, George Moscone; he also killed Harvey Milk, the first gay city official and a hero to the gay community.[52] The trial was politically fraught, and the jury's verdict (manslaughter, rather than murder) outraged many people in San Francisco. A jury acquitted the police officers who beat Rodney King, an African American man, despite the fact that the beating was captured on video tape; the verdict led to serious rioting.[53] In our times, riots of this type are, in a way, the functional equivalent of vigilante action. They have no hope of overturning the verdict; the point is political—and expressive.

Modern riots often begin and end as political acts, as forms of protest. Mob action, though, is almost by nature infectious. Riots spread the way a fire spreads in dried out grass, on a hot summer day, after somebody carelessly flips a match. As the riot expands, it attracts people whose motives are hardly political: gangs of young people, say, who loot stores and help themselves to plunder. Paradoxically perhaps, both lynch mobs and vigilante crowds were subject to much more control.

Public punishment died in the nineteenth century; lynching and vigilantism (mostly) died in the twentieth century. The headline trial remains. It continues to serve as a bold public event, enhanced and magnified by media coverage. These trials still give off moral messages, about crime and punishment, good and bad, norms and values: didactic functions that trials once shared with other parts of the criminal justice system. Many big trials, frankly, also provide a kind of public entertainment for masses of people. Increasingly, the role of the media has become crucial. The late nineteenth century was the age of "yellow journalism," that is, cheap, mass-market newspapers that specialized in drama and sensational stories. Then, in the twentieth century, came radio and movies, and later on, television. More recently, we have the Internet and all its manifestations. All of these modes of communication would broadcast the facts, the personalities, and the procedures of the headline trials; whether they would change its very function is another story.

3

Political Trials

In the first chapter, we provided a rough typology of headline trials.[1] The division between types is not always sharp; they tend to overlap, and many famous trials fall into several categories. In the next chapters, we will go into more detail about the various types.

The first, and most obvious, type of headline trial is the *political* trial. It is also one of the oldest. Cases fraught with political significance go back quite far in legal and social history, further perhaps than any other type. It is easy to find historical examples. We have mentioned the trial of Socrates. Campaigns against heretics, and attempts to stamp out religious dissent and apostasy have produced notable trials—the trial of Joan of Arc, for example. Anne Boleyn, Henry VIII's second queen, went on trial, and lost both her position and her head.

It has never been difficult to predict the outcome of most of the political trials of history. Anne Boleyn had no chance of winning her case. In the old days, kings put enemies on trial for reasons of malice, lust, revenge, or jealousy—not to serve justice. They used political trials to dispose of a rival to the throne or a subject who had dared to rebel. The king always won. These trials were, in their own way, didactic theater. They sent the message: Defy, anger, or threaten the king (or queen or leader) at your peril.

What makes a trial political? Peter Hoffer lists three criteria: The trial must be "politically motivated"; the "outcome of the trial" must be "affected by political considerations"; and the trial must "have a significant impact on politics."[2] This is a rather severe definition. Its problem is that it leaves out too many trials that, to the naked eye, seem quite political, in the commonsense meaning of the word.[3] The trouble is Hoffer's second criterion. Hoffer does not consider a trial political, for example, if the trial is scrupulously fair and the government plays by the rules of due process. But, of course, as he has to admit, even the outcome of a fair trial can be affected by politics.

I prefer a broader, if less satisfying, definition. For our purposes, a political trial is a trial that has or seems to have political overtones. It is a trial that has political *meaning*. The meaning can vary from trial to trial. Generally speaking, we know it when we see it. A treason trial can quite legitimately be labeled as political. It has political meaning, and a political purpose, even when it is completely fair, and even when the defendant is obviously guilty. Treason and the assassination of political leaders are *political* acts, often done for political motives. Killing a wife's lover is not political in that sense. The trial of O. J. Simpson had, or came to have, political meaning; but it was primarily a murder trial, and the state of California, which prosecuted Simpson, certainly saw it that way.

Political trials are political acts. Like all criminal trials, they are governmental, that is, the plaintiff is the state. The decision to bring an action against, say, an alleged traitor, or a political enemy, is often made at a high level of government; the decision to, say, prosecute a burglar or a drunk driver is made much lower down. Many political trials, especially those of the past, were trials of suppression; defendants were enemies of the regime, not enemies of the people. Today, there unquestionably are genuine enemies both of the people and of the established order: spies, traitors, violent revolutionaries, terrorists. This fact gives powerful public support to political trials against those accused of terrorist acts, or even terrorist leanings. An ounce of prevention is worth a pound of cure, as the saying goes; locking people up *before* they explode their bombs is better than locking them up afterward. And these trials can send important messages: To potential enemies, the message is that you will be punished; to the public at large, that the government is working hard to keep you safe.

This last message is particularly significant in the context of the so-called war on terror. The most notorious attacks have come from abroad, from radical Islamists. The World Trade Center was attacked in 1993 by terrorists; some of the men responsible were arrested, put on trial, convicted, and given stiff sentences.[4] The attack on September 11, 2001, was horrifically successful: the twin towers collapsed, thousands died, and the incident led to a major escalation of the war on terror. One of the prisoners taken in this war was John Walker Lindh, a young convert to Islam, who was captured in Afghanistan, tried as an "enemy combatant," and sentenced in 2002 to a term of twenty years.[5] But many enemy combatants have had no trial of any kind; instead, they were shipped to Guantanamo Bay, the American base on the tip of Cuba, and locked up indefinitely, without trial, and without any limitation of time. The war on terror is used to justify this mode of dealing with the prisoners in Guantanamo. To the public, the message of this nontrial is the same as the trial message: The government is trying to protect you. But when the government chooses to *avoid* trial—as it does in Guantanamo Bay—it is also sending the kind of message the vigilantes sent: Normal process is too feeble in the face of some vast and critical danger.

All governments have made use of political trials, dictatorships and democracies alike. The difference between the two lies in whether the government can actually lose; or, to put it another way, whether the judiciary is truly independent. In totalitarian governments, show trials are particularly sharp examples of didactic theater. The Moscow show trials of the 1930s, under Stalin, were outstanding examples. These Soviet trials were, of course, in many senses a farce; conviction was a dead certainty. Charges were trumped up, and the defendants induced to confess to imaginary crimes and counterrevolutionary action. The trials provided the government with a veneer of legality; at the same time, they delivered a message about the power of the government that was hard to miss.[6] The real point, perhaps (other than Stalin's paranoia), was to strengthen the grip of a regime that ruled through terror.[7]

The Soviet Union no longer exists. But the Russian Republic, its most prominent successor, still seems to have a taste for political trials of a fairly similar type. The trials are often disguised as ordinary criminal affairs. They are, nonetheless, political trials used to suppress dissent or to rob opposition figures of legitimacy. The Russian government has put some of its most prominent oligarchs on trials, especially those that made the mistake of defying the Kremlin. Mikhail Khodorkovsky was once one of the richest, most powerful men in Russia. Unfortunately for him, he ran afoul of Vladimir Putin, the president of the Republic. Khodorkovsky was accused of stealing from his company and laundering its money; he was convicted in 2003 and sent to prison. In 2010, he was tried and convicted again, and he remained in prison until he was suddenly set free in December 2013.

Most people (in the West at least) considered these trials political theater, plain and simple, with Putin and the Russian government pulling the strings. Perhaps the government had no need to pull strings. Perhaps the judge knew what he was supposed to do, and did it, without any explicit orders.[8] In August 2012, a Russian punk band, "Pussy Riot," faced trial for (in effect) offending religious sensibilities.[9] The crackdown on dissent continues. It reached some sort of absurd climax in July 2013, when a court found Sergei Magnitsky guilty of tax evasion. Magnitsky had tried to *expose* government tax fraud. Not only did the charges seem unfair but the defendant was also not even in the courtroom: He had died suspiciously in prison some time before.[10]

The Chinese government, too, uses trials to suppress dissent. Liu Xiaobo, a prominent critic of the government, was convicted of "subversion" in 2009.[11] There have been many other trials of this nature in China. A sodomy trial in Malaysia would not, on the surface, seem to be political, except that the defendant, who claimed the charges were a pack of lies, was a leading figure in the opposition.[12]

Dictatorships can and do dispense with political trials in favor of more direct action. And they can disguise a political trial as something else. They can claim that the defendant embezzled money or evaded taxes, or committed some other conventional crime. But since dictatorships can simply lock people up, they choose to go the trial route for a reason—often the same reason that underlay lynching in the South or vigilante actions in the West.[13] For example, in 1944, a group of military men tried to assassinate Adolph Hitler; the plot misfired, and Hitler survived. The Nazi response was swift and brutal. The regime had no qualms about killing its enemies, but in this case they decided to put them on trial. Hundreds of plotters and suspected plotters were rounded up and tried in the infamous People's Court (*Volksgerichtshof*) in Berlin; the judge, Roland Freisler, was a hard-core and rabid Nazi. Under Freisler, this court sentenced thousands to death. There was never any hope of acquittal.[14] These trials served as an outlet for Hitler's fury against the plotters. But they also sent a strong message to the German people and to the armed forces: If you plot against the regime, this will be your fate.

In all countries, the regime, government, or administration often stages, manages, and closely watches political trials. This is true even in democratic societies. But political trials in democratic countries differ sharply from the Moscow show trials or the trials in Freisler's court. Enemies of the public (or alleged enemies) cannot be locked up simply on the government's say-so. (Guantanamo seems to be, unfortunately, something of a modern exception.) The enemies have to be tried in court. The government can launch these trials and can supervise and strengthen the prosecution. But it cannot guarantee results. Judges, to be sure, are not immune to social pressure; they share the views and prejudices of their fellow citizens, and they prefer to make popular decisions. It takes a brave judge to defy public opinion and ignore subtle political pressure. But it does happen.

When we think of political trials, we usually think of the government side of the case, and the governmental motives that led to prosecution. In political trials, the prosecution will try to paint the defendants as darkly as possible, treating them at times almost as if they were aliens from outer space: foreign devils, enemies of democracy, men who have sworn to bring down the American state. The state is not above the use of outright propaganda. Yet in open societies, so long as the trials are fair, the crimes themselves, which are sometimes horrific, may well be the most "political" aspect of the trial. Political trials, in other words, are often trials of men and women who committed political crimes. The trial of Timothy McVeigh, in 1996, is a good example. McVeigh was a right-wing fanatic who developed an almost lunatic hatred for the U.S. government. He decided to express his views by striking directly at a federal installation. He exploded a powerful bomb outside the Alfred P. Murrah Federal Building, in Oklahoma City, Oklahoma. More than 150 people died, including 19 children in a day-care center on the second floor of the building. McVeigh was captured and put on trial in federal court. He was convicted in June 1997; the jury recommended the death sentence. Four years later, McVeigh was put to death.[15]

Democratic societies approach political trials with caution. They bring these trials strategically, and often according to plan.

During the Cold War, in the 1950s, the U.S. government—and probably most of its citizens—was obsessed with the idea of a global, ideological, and political struggle with the Soviet Union. Communists and so-called fellow travelers were deadly enemies of the American way of life. But there was a sharp divide between the Left and the Right. The Right demanded increasingly sharper measures in the war on communism. The Left, which historically had a certain amount of sympathy with the professed goals of the Soviet Union, reacted in part defensively.

In the midst of this ideological battle, the government put leaders of the Communist Party on trial.[16] These defendants were obvious targets: They were openly members of the hated party. The trial was a kind of declaration of war against those men and women who sided with the Soviet Union. But the Cold War mentality cast a shadow of suspicion over broad sections of society and over many institutions: The Right was sure that Reds and fellow travelers had infiltrated the government itself and that many parts of society—from Hollywood to academia—were riddled with communist sympathizers and even outright spies. The Soviet Union did indeed engage in espionage (most countries do). In the context of the Cold War, this kind of espionage seemed particularly harmful—a knife poised at the heart of the American system.

The Cold War period saw several sensational and flamboyant criminal trials. Most notable was the trial of Julius and Ethel Rosenberg. The Rosenbergs were arrested in 1950. They were accused of betraying their country in the most harmful way: handing over to the Soviet Union secrets of the atom bomb. The Soviets by 1949 had created their own atomic bomb, ending the Western monopoly, an event that shocked the West. The trial of the Rosenbergs was headline news. The two were convicted; the judge, Irving Kaufman, called their crime "worse than murder" and claimed they had to share some of the blame for the Korean War and potentially for the death of millions of "innocent people."[17] This charge was surely grossly exaggerated, but Judge Kaufman sentenced the Rosenbergs to death. Everything about the case was controversial, especially the death sentence, which was unprecedented in peacetime. There was a huge legal and extralegal campaign to spare their lives; but all of these efforts failed, and they went to the electric chair in Sing Sing prison in 1953.[18]

Alger Hiss, accused of spying for the Soviet Union, was put on trial for perjury; his trial was also sensational, drenched with the politics of the Cold War.[19] Hiss was tried twice. The first ended with a hung jury, after a trial of twenty-seven days; the second, however, which lasted forty days, ended with a guilty verdict.[20] This trial also sharply divided the Left and the Right. The Left did not question the bad faith of the Soviet regime, but they decried "witch hunts" and "Red-baiting" and insisted that Hiss was an innocent victim of a smear campaign.

The government won these cases (although Hiss was never convicted of spying, only of lying about the issue). But the government did not always win. And even in cases of convictions, there is always the appeal process; many a political trial comes unstrung at that level. Judith Coplon learned the value of an independent judiciary, and the sometimes-finicky rules of due process. Coplon had, in plain English, betrayed her country.[21] She worked for the Department of Justice and fell in love with one Valentin Gubitchev, a Russian who worked for the United Nations. Under Gubitchev's influence, Coplon agreed to transfer government documents to the Soviets. She was caught, tried for espionage, and (in another trial) for conspiracy. The government presented a strong case, and both juries found her guilty.[22] But Coplon appealed these decisions—successfully. It turned out that the government's case had procedural flaws, at least in the opinion of the appeal court. New trials were ordered. They never took place. The government needed to protect its sources; for this, and other reasons, all charges against Coplon were dropped, in 1967. She married one of her lawyers and "opened a trendy restaurant in New York."[23] She died at the age of eighty-nine in 2011.[24]

Mostly, it is the government, the regime, or the ruling party that brings political cases, and manages them (if it can). The government has a message, and the political trial is the vehicle for broadcasting this message. The Rosenberg trial, for example, spread the message that the United States was locked in a bitter, global struggle with the Soviet Union and that the enemy was recruiting Americans to do its dirty work. A second message was that the government was vigorously defending itself against these treasonous infiltrators.

But two can play at this game. Sometimes, the defendants try to turn the tables on the government: they provoke the government, for political reasons, hoping for a trial at which they can either become martyrs, or, more likely, gain headlines for their cause. In an open system, with an independent judiciary and a tradition of due process, some defendants can turn the tables on the government; they can make the trial into *their* political show. They recognize that big trials are didactic theater, and they want to write the playbook. These trials are public; and the media can be counted on to report whatever is notable, bizarre, or eye-catching.

The "Catonsville Nine," for example, were staunch antiwar Catholics who destroyed draft records in the Baltimore area in protest against the Vietnam War. The "nine" included a Jesuit priest, Father Daniel Berrigan. They went on trial in 1968. The government tried to keep the case simple and factual: did they or did they not burn records. The defendants were eager to use the trial for their own purposes, as a showcase to argue that their acts were moral and that it was the war that was wrong and illegitimate. They were, of course, convicted; but perhaps they had made their point.[25]

The trial of the "Chicago Seven," from 1969 to 1970, was another example of this phenomenon. The defendants were left-wing radicals. They were accused of trying to disrupt the Democratic Convention in 1968. The defendants made every effort to use the courtroom as a stage for their own version of guerrilla theater. They showed utter contempt for the formal system, tried to provoke the judge, and turned the trial into an unruly and disruptive circus. The judge, Julius Hoffman, had very little sympathy for the defendants and (naturally) hated their tactics. At one point, he lost patience entirely: When Bobby Seale, one of the defendants, shouted "accusations and insults" at the judge, Hoffman ordered him gagged and chained to his chair.[26] The defendants were convicted. The judge also cited their lawyers for contempt. All the convictions—and the contempt judgments—were reversed on appeal.[27]

In modern times, in open societies, then, both the state and dissident groups find the political trial a useful vehicle. It is attractive to both sides precisely because it is public and because the trial, if it is sensational enough, will attract the media and help spread the message. In democratic societies, "show trials" can backfire on the government. But the ultimate judge is the public. Whether the Catonsville Nine, or the Chicago Seven, actually aided their cause is a very hard question to answer.

Political trials in democracies, unlike trials in dictatorships, rest on some sort of legal foundation. Treason is one of the most serious crimes, and it is unique in that the U.S. Constitution specifically provides for it. Article III, section 3, states that treason consists only of "levying War" on the United States or "adhering" to enemies of the country, "giving them Aid and Comfort"; it states that no one can be convicted of this crime, except by the testimony of two witnesses to the "same overt Act" or by "Confession in open Court."

Treason trials have not been common in the United States. One of the earliest, and most famous, was the trial of Aaron Burr. Burr was a former vice president of the United States. The charges against him were quite sensational. He was accused, no less, of a plot to detach parts of the American west and set them up as a separate country, under his leadership. This seems rather unlikely, but it is possible that Burr was up to no good. In any event, the administration was eager to see him punished. Ultimately, Burr was acquitted.[28]

The trial of John Brown, in the feverish years before the Civil War, was also deeply political. Brown had, in effect, led a mini-rebellion against the slave power of the South. Brown was charged with murder and with treason (against the state of Virginia). He was convicted and executed. Opinion on Brown was sharply divided along political lines. Many abolitionists considered him a martyr to their cause.[29] People still sing the song about Brown: his body "lies moldering in the grave," but his "truth goes marching on."[30]

Iva Toguri D'Aquino was put on trial at the end of World War II for treason. She was identified (falsely) as "Tokyo Rose," who allegedly betrayed her country by broadcasting Japanese propaganda from Tokyo during the war. Ms. Toguri (she married D'Aquino in 1945), was born in the United States; she was visiting family in Japan in 1941 and found herself trapped there that December, when the Japanese bombed Pearl Harbor and war broke out. Later, she worked as a disk jockey on Radio Tokyo. The military detained her when the war ended. But the Department of Justice decided that her broadcasts were harmless and let her go. Once back in the United States, however, she found herself the subject of a savage campaign against her. This campaign led to a trial; "Tokyo Rose" was convicted of treason and sent to prison. The evidence against Toguri was flimsy, to say the least, and based in part on perjury. She received a presidential pardon in 1977.[31]

More common than treason trials are trials for sedition and related offenses. These are, of course, extremely common in authoritarian societies, which, historically, all societies have been at one time. Democratic governments are supposed to honor freedom of speech, which includes, above all, the right to criticize the government. Still, governments are made up of people; and people are people—you cannot expect them to *like* harsh criticism. Governments therefore often try to punish extreme criticism; at some point they feel they can label this criticism as "sedition." John Adams, the second president of the United States, pushed through the infamous Alien and Sedition Acts in 1798.[32] These laws, among other things, made it a crime to "stir up sedition" in the country or to defame the government. There were some fourteen prosecutions under these laws; the Federalists used them to muzzle the opposition press.[33] Thomas Jefferson, when he became president, promptly (and successfully) moved to have Congress repeal the Alien and Sedition Acts.

The Sedition Act of 1918,[34] passed during World War I, made it a crime to spread "false statements" that might interfere with the war effort; it also made it a crime to encourage disloyalty in the armed forces and to write or print "disloyal . . . or abusive language" about the government or anything that might bring the government "into contempt, scorn, contumely, or disrepute." Arrests and trials under this law produced some of the Supreme Court's earliest and most important cases on freedom of speech—for example, *Abrams v. United States* (1919).[35]

During the so-called Red Scare, after the end of World War I, the federal government and many states launched campaigns against Leftists, Bolsheviks, and other supposed enemies of the republic. California, and other states, passed laws against "criminal syndicalism"; basically, these laws made it a crime to join organizations that were dedicated to the overthrow of the government. Charlotte Anita Whitney, a woman from a prominent family, had joined the Communist Labor Party. After delivering a speech in Oakland, in 1919, she was arrested, tried, and convicted of violating this law. The U.S. Supreme Court upheld the law, and Whitney's conviction, in 1927.[36] Trials like hers were explicitly political, aimed directly at political crimes, for example, sedition. Whatever the label, these laws were designed to punish political opposition that, allegedly, had stepped over the invisible line dividing free speech from criminal advocacy.

In certain trials, which we might call "quasi-political trials," the state charges defendants with ordinary, nonpolitical crimes. But behind these are political motives. An ordinary trial, then, gets converted into a kind of political trial. The classic case here is the trial of Sacco and Vanzetti, one of the most famous in U.S. history. Nicola Sacco and Bartolomeo Vanzetti were "two young Italian immigrants and revolutionary anarchists," one a "heel trimmer" and the other a "fish peddler." They were arrested in 1920 and accused of robbing and murdering a "factory paymaster and security guard" in a suburb of Boston.[37] They insisted they were innocent. The actual crime was serious enough, but suspicion that the arrest was political in nature turned the case into an international cause célèbre. Sacco-Vanzetti polarized opinion in the United States and abroad. Critics claimed that the trial was unfair, that the judge was prejudiced, and that the state was persecuting these men solely for their political beliefs. The two men were convicted and sentenced to death. All appeals, legal and otherwise, were fruitless. Felix Frankfurter wrote a book attacking the trial as unfair.[38] Despite the uproar, Sacco and Vanzetti were executed.

In the Sacco-Vanzetti case, the United States itself was "on trial"; that, at any rate, is the way the subtitle of a recent book puts it.[39] To many people in other countries—in particular, people on the Left—the Sacco-Vanzetti case was a prime example of what was wrong with U.S. justice and U.S. society in general. The trial proved to them that powerful right-wing forces, willing to crush dissent, ran the country. The controversy over the case has never completely died down. Scholars are still arguing over this case. Were Sacco and Vanzetti guilty or innocent? One theory is that Vanzetti at least was completely innocent. The case against Sacco may be a bit stronger.[40] In 1959, the Massachusetts legislature considered a bill asking the governor to pardon the men. It failed to pass. But Governor Dukakis, in 1977, proclaimed the fiftieth anniversary of the executions Sacco and Vanzetti Memorial Day. This caused a stir; the state senate voted "to condemn the governor."[41] The view from overseas is less ambivalent. An Italian movie about the case appeared in 1971. And many Americans might be shocked to find that an avenue, in a Paris suburb, is named after Sacco and Vanzetti or to learn that the largest pencil factory in the Soviet Union carried their name in 1927.[42]

The World Steps In

Political trials are, on the whole, government trials. This remains true. Dissidents, to be sure, can turn political trials into their own form of didactic theater. And in democratic societies those who criticize political trials can and do voice their objections. In the late twentieth century, a new type of political trial evolved: the international trials of political leaders for "crimes against humanity." The Nuremberg trials, in which Nazi leaders were tried, and the other war crimes trials after World War II, were the beginnings of what later became a dramatic, international movement aimed at transcending purely local and national concepts of crime and punishment. In 1945, Germany had been defeated; the armies of four countries occupied a ruined and exhausted country. The victorious powers faced the question: what to do with the captured Nazi leaders, men like Hermann Goering—men who were guilty of incredible crimes. Almost everybody (one hopes) believed that the Nazi leaders richly deserved any punishment they might get. Arguably, though, the Allies had no *legal* basis for inflicting punishment. Nazi Germany was, after all, a rogue state; it allowed and encouraged "crimes against humanity" and aggressive war against peaceful countries. In fact, what the defendants did was simply Nazi policy; it was not a violation of Nazi law. Most people, one imagines, considered this a quibble. Plenty of people (some in high places) felt that the best way to handle mass murderers was to line them up and shoot them, without further ado. In April 1945, Italian partisans caught and killed Benito Mussolini, the fascist leader of Italy; they took his body to Milan and hung it from a meat hook in an Esso station. In many countries that had suffered under Nazi occupation, crowds of people meted out their own brand of justice, dealing harshly with "collaborators," who became "prime targets for attack and assassination."[43]

But the Allies decided on a different tactic. They decided to mount a series of trials, in a court of law, to deal with the Nazi leaders in a fair and rigorous way. The result was the famous Nuremberg trials.[44] The defendants were accused of waging aggressive war and of committing crimes against humanity. For all its faults, the Nuremberg trials have had a lasting, and probably positive, effect. They were—or tried to be—scrupulously fair, although they were not "bound by technical rules of evidence"; rather, any evidence that had "probative value" could be admitted.[45] Indeed, although some defendants received a death sentence, others were given prison sentences; there were even acquittals. The trials were also deliberately framed as an exercise in didactic theater. Visual and oral evidence was presented to drive home some of the horrific facts about the regime, facts that many people initially found hard to believe: the slaughter of millions of Jews, Poles, and others, in the name of a foul ideology of race. The purpose was "establishing incredible events by means of credible evidence."[46] The trials have come to stand for a shining idea and ideal: that there are international norms against aggressive warfare, against genocide, against the mass murder of civilian populations, and that these norms are universal and have a legitimacy that trumps any domestic laws to the contrary.

The Nuremberg trials of the Nazi leaders were part of a series of trials at the end of the World War II. Defendants in the so-called Doctors' Trial, also held at Nuremberg, were medical men who conducted sadistic experiments on human beings—men like Waldemar Hoven, chief doctor at the infamous concentration camp at Buchenwald.[47] In 1947, an American military trial, conducted at Dachau, pronounced a death sentence on forty-nine men accused of war crimes at Mauthausen-Gusen concentration camp.[48] Japanese leaders, accused of various crimes and atrocities, underwent a war crimes trial in Tokyo, more or less parallel to the Nuremberg trials.[49] Many countries under the wartime heel of Germany and Japan conducted their own trials, putting their own private crop of Nazis and Japanese militarists on trial, along with their local satraps.[50] The Norwegians, for example, tried Vidkun Quisling, the local Nazi leader, and sentenced him to death.

To be sure, many Nazis were never punished for their crimes. They were able to escape—with help from various agencies and institutions. Some of them slipped away to Argentina or began a new life under a new name.[51] The start of the Cold War chilled any interest in the process of "denazification," at least on the part of the Allied governments. Still, over the years, relatives and advocates for the victims have never given up; they have searched for, and sometimes found, fugitive Nazis. The most famous example was the capture and trial of Adolf Eichmann. Eichmann was one of the architects of the Holocaust, the deliberate murder of millions of European Jews. Eichmann had been in hiding in Argentina; agents of the Israeli government found him in 1960, seized him, and brought him to Israel to stand trial. He was tried, convicted, and executed.[52] Klaus Barbie, head of the Gestapo in Lyon, France, during the German occupation of France was caught, tried, and sentenced to life imprisonment in 1987.[53] As late as the twenty-first century, there were trials of a few very old men, doddering in court and finally brought to judgment for the awful crimes they had committed in their youth.

The Nuremberg trials did not escape criticism in their day

(and later). The main complaint was that the trials constituted "victor's justice," since the defendants were convicted on the basis of doctrines that were more or less ad hoc and for doing things that were not at the time criminal under the laws of their countries. Most people probably disagreed with this complaint. And the Nuremberg trials were successful in their own terms, in any event, as didactic theater. They were meant to publicize the awful crimes the Nazi government and its allies had committed; and Nuremberg did this, as best it could. It also sent a message about due process of law. The audience was the entire world community, and the messages (perhaps aimed especially at the Germans themselves) were powerful. They were presented in a dramatic form, in headlines and newsreel clips, in country after country.[54]

The Nuremberg trials and their imitators tried to appeal to massive norms of unwritten law, or, to be more accurate, to a feeling that some norms, some fundamental principles, were truly universal and inherent. Crimes that violate these norms are crimes in some absolute sense against the human race. They are crimes, whether or not any written code actually spells them out; they violate rights that are or should be the patrimony of every soul on earth. After all, the Nazi regime—and dictatorships in general—do not consider their atrocities to be "crimes against humanity." Whether the concept of a "crime against humanity" is embodied in any formal text, it is a *social* fact, in this sense: it is something that millions of people in our time have come to believe. Thus, although Nuremberg was something of a novelty, it reflected something stirring in the global soul—a growing human rights culture that has become increasingly important and dynamic over the years.[55] By the end of the twentieth century, the human rights culture had grown strong, powerful, and widespread. It follows logically that if some crimes are crimes against humanity itself, then humanity itself has the right to punish these crimes.[56] At this point, too, these norms were no longer unwritten in the sense they were at the time of the Nuremberg trials. They were now embodied in charters, treaties, and other formal texts, texts like the Universal Declaration of Human Rights (1948), which the United Nations (UN) promulgated. Moreover, basic rights were enshrined in constitutions and bills of rights, which were adopted in country after country.

Hitler and Stalin were not the last monsters in political life. There were horrific mass murders in Rwanda, in Cambodia, and in the former Yugoslavia. But mass murderers, genocidal tyrants and their followers, can no longer operate with the same impunity they once enjoyed. Today they must face a possible trial—at least when the dust settles and the murders stop. A tyrant, if his regime falls from power, often will be threatened with some sort of domestic trial. And today there may also be an international reckoning for despots and mass murderers. The United Nations has been the moving force in setting up international tribunals to bring to justice, and punish, those who are guilty of crimes against humanity—a group that, alas, does not seem in any danger of going extinct.[57] One of these tribunals dealt with the dreadful events in the "former Yugoslavia"; when this country split into pieces, ethnic brotherhood vanished in a volcano of blood. In wars between Serbs, Croats, and Muslims, terrible atrocities were committed. The Security Council of the United Nations set up an ad hoc tribunal in 1993, the International Criminal Tribunal for the former Yugoslavia, with its seat in The Hague; it has conducted some notable trials.[58] In 1994, the UN Security Council established an International Criminal Tribunal for Rwanda, after the horrendous genocide in that African country; the tribunal proceeded to try a number of men for their role in this tragedy—with mixed results.[59] Tribunals have also struggled with the crimes committed in Cambodia and Sierra Leone.

The General Assembly of the United Nations in 1998 held a conference, and later adopted a treaty, setting up an International Criminal Court (ICC). By 2002, enough countries had ratified the treaty for the court to go into operation.[60] This court, too, has its seat in The Hague, and has jurisdiction over four types of crime: genocide, crimes against humanity, war crimes, and aggression. Each of these is elaborately defined in the treaty that gave rise to the court.[61] It remains to be seen whether the court will make a difference in world politics. Not every country has signed on—the United States, very notably, has not. The tribunal has been active; it has prosecuted, for example, two Congolese militia leaders, who, it was said, "sent child soldiers into a village and wiped it out, killing more than 200 men, women and children; some . . . burned alive."[62]

The victors in World War II set up the Nuremberg trials. Democratic and semidemocratic countries have created the international tribunals, including the new International Criminal Court; governments—acting collectively, to be sure—pay for and staff these courts. These trials are different from ordinary political trials. They are grounded in the human rights culture. Most domestic political trials are defensive, and the defendants are private individuals. Defendants before international tribunals are also individuals, but the message is a message of warning *to* governments, rather than *from* governments.

The line of trials and tribunals, from Nuremberg to the present day, testify to the growing power of the human rights culture. The trend toward constitutional government is one of the strongest trends in political history since the 1950s. Dictatorships have fallen like tenpins. Democratic government—constitutional government—was a minority form of government in 1940; some eighty years later, it has become the majority form. Since the days of the Nuremberg trials, Germany, Japan, and Italy have become open, democratic societies. And dozens of other countries in Europe, Latin America, and Asia have made similar journeys.

Many of these countries have faced the question of how to deal with their own dirty history. What should they do with leaders of tyrannical regimes—men like General Pinochet, the former dictator of Chile?[63] Equally important, what about the foot soldiers of autocracy, the ordinary men and women who carried out the commands of the leaders and killed, raped, or tortured innocent people, the alleged enemies of the state? There is never a clean slate. The past does not simply disappear. One can, of course, put the leaders on trial. In Egypt, in 2012, during the so-called Arab Spring, the regime of Hosni Mubarak was overthrown. Mubarak, by then an old man, was put on trial, wheeled into the courtroom in his wheelchair, convicted, and sentenced to spend the rest of his life in prison. In this case, the overthrowing regime was itself overthrown: President Mohamed Morsi, a leader of the Muslim Brotherhood and elected after the fall of Mubarak, was himself deposed by the military and charged with an array of crimes, including the incitement of murder.[64] After the collapse of the Soviet empire, East and West Germany were reunited, and the West put on trial border guards in East Germany, who, in the days of East German rule, shot people for trying to flee to West Germany, which citizens were forbidden to do. Then there is the Nuremberg model: some kind of international trial, as we mentioned earlier.

Trials—national or international—can be politically risky, or undesirable, for all sorts of reasons. This is particularly true when political transition is gradual, rather than sudden and revolutionary. In these situations, the old crew is still around, and perhaps still powerful and still commanding loyalty from a great many people. It might be politically delicate, or even impossible—not to mention undesirable—to indulge in some sort of punitive, wholesale housecleaning.

A number of countries have chosen some form of "transitional justice."[65] In Argentina, after the military government fell from power, the state established a commission to investigate the crimes of the old regime (of which there were plenty) and make a report on what ought to be done. In fact, the country has wobbled back and forth on whether to grant some sort of amnesty to members of the old regime. The legislature and the Supreme Court both weighed in on the issue. But despite legal issues some trials did continue.[66] The Republic of South Africa, under the leadership of Nelson Mandela, chose a somewhat bolder approach. In 1995, the country created a Truth and Reconciliation Commission (TRC). The TRC had the power to conduct hearings more or less on the model of a criminal trial. Victims of human rights abuses could come before the TRC and bear witness to what they had suffered. Those who were responsible for these crimes could also testify; and they could, indeed, ask for amnesty. Clearly, whatever else one could say about the commission, it was meant to make a crucial educational point. The TRC also hoped that its work would bring some sort of closure, that South Africa would be able to come to terms with its sinister, racist past. If enough historical debris, enough anger and hatred, could be cleared away, then perhaps society could declare the past dead and move on. Starting in 1996, the proceedings were televised. This too, then, was an instrument of didactic theater.

It is not clear, to be sure, whether the TRC succeeded in what it had set out to do. Not everybody was willing to forgive and forget. Some crimes were simply too gross. Security forces under the apartheid government had beaten to death Steve Biko, a leader of the antiapartheid movement, in 1977. When apartheid ended, his family wanted to bring the killers to justice. They objected to any notion of amnesty—and indeed, to the whole TRC enterprise. Despite this, the TRC has been a potent model, with a number of imitators. In East Timor, a similar commission "had a close working relationship with the prosecutorial institutions of the country"; the commission had the duty of sharing information with, and referring serious cases to, an "Office of the General Prosecutor." In Sierra Leone, the Truth and Reconciliation

Commission and a special court "operated as two entirely separate entities."[67]

There is an enormous literature on "transitional justice." Of course, there has been criticism, from both ends of the political spectrum. Many victims, like the family of Steve Biko, want punishment, justice, and revenge rather than some sort of cozy reconciliation, or "closure." On the other hand, in some countries there are people who still believe in the goals and tactics of the old authoritarian government—in that harsh but necessary medicine. The group in the middle might worry about the problem of "victor's justice." Many of the "crimes" were not technically crimes when they happened, as was the case with the Nazi leaders.

Each country in transition has its own unique problems and politics. In one regard, Nuremberg had it easy: The Allies had won the war, the old regime was totally overthrown, and the Allies were in firm control of Germany. In Argentina, or Chile, or South Africa, yes, a regime has been overthrown; but representatives of the old regime still had power and influence, including electoral influence. In South Africa, revenge against the white majority, however understandable and morally justified, might have severely damaged the economy, which the white majority controlled. The Truth and Reconciliation Commission, stressing truth, confession, remorse, and amnesty, without sacrificing the right to put some people on trial, was a delicate political balancing act. Each of the commissions has its own issues, its own goals. How these commissions relate to, and coordinate with, the international criminal tribunals, is complex and multifarious.[68]

Political trials are too diverse to be summed up in a simple formula. Their one commonality is that they are always, like headline trials in general, didactic theater. In essence, they are tools government can use to enforce political policies. But, as we noted, some defendants have their own ways to fight back. The rise of the human rights culture has impacted political trials in many ways, including the development of international tribunals. In these trials, too, and in the various truth commissions, the concept of psychological closure plays a prominent role. The dead remain just as dead, but the once-dead past comes to life—and to judgment. A new generation, as if in possession of a time machine, can revisit the past and, perhaps, cleanse society of some of its guilt.

4

Corruption and Fraud

A second category of headline trial takes as its subject *corruption and fraud.* This category is closely related to the first category, and could be considered a subclass of political trials. It includes impeachment trials, trials of government officials accused of taking bribes, and other trials that grow out of corruption in high places.[1]

The impeachment process is a special form of trial reserved for high officeholders. Under the Constitution of the United States, Article II, section 4, the president and other federal officials can be impeached, that is, formally accused of committing treason, bribery, or other "High Crimes and Misdemeanors." Impeachment is the first step in a process: the House of Representatives draws up articles of impeachment, while the actual trial takes place in the Senate. Impeachment proceedings have been brought against two presidents: Andrew Johnson, and Bill Clinton. A third, Richard Nixon, escaped impeachment by resigning his office. Both of the presidents who faced impeachment proceedings navigated the process successfully. Andrew Johnson's real crime was defying Congress, in the turbulent politics of the post–Civil War period. He survived, but barely, when a small group of Republican senators voted against impeachment.[2]

President Clinton was charged with perjury and obstruction of justice, but underneath was a huge scandal: a tawdry tale of sex in the White House. All of this naturally helped to keep the whole country riveted to their television sets; but in the end, the Senate simply refused to convict him.[3]

The one and only attempt to impeach a justice of the United States Supreme Court occurred in 1805; it failed. The justice in question was Samuel Chase, a rabid Federalist. His behavior was almost certainly improper: he had a terrible temper, and his grand-jury charges were bitter political attacks on Jefferson's party. Still, these were hardly crimes, and the impeachment failed; enough members of Congress thought that impeachment was unwarranted or that it was a threat to judicial independence. Chase kept his seat on the Court.[4] There have been a handful of impeachment proceedings against federal judges, all for corruption. The most recent was the impeachment of Judge Alcee Hastings in 1989 for taking a bribe.[5] In a few cases, judges accused of misdeeds resigned (like President Nixon) because the threat of impeachment was hanging over their heads. Judge Mark Delahay, said to be a total drunk both off and on the bench, resigned in 1873. The most notable corrupt federal judge was Martin Manton, of the Second Circuit. He, too, resigned, in 1939, rather than face impeachment; but he was indicted for conspiracy to defraud the government and for obstruction of justice. The trial was headline news; Manton was convicted and sent to prison.[6] In general, the federal judiciary has been remarkably free of corruption. State and municipal judges have been rather less so. During the seedy days of the 1860s and 1870s, scandal after scandal shook the bench of New York City.

Corruption and fraud cases are, in a sense, distinctly modern. The notion of "corruption" could hardly exist in, say, the France of Louis XVI. A public officer or civil servant is "corrupt," when that person violates a duty to the public—by taking a bribe, for example. You cannot apply the term to a system that lacks the modern concept of public service. In seventeenth-century France, for example, the nobility felt they had a God-given right to live off rents paid by their tenants. They built palaces and chateaux for themselves and lived the high life, without paying any rents and taxes themselves. In England, too, the landed gentry lived in grand houses in the country, surrounded by gardens and parks; the rents of their tenant farmers supported their lifestyle. This was considered the natural order of things. In England, the king was the "fountain of honour, of office, and of privileges," to use Blackstone's phrase.[7] The king, in other words, handed out lucrative positions to his favorites and to members of the nobility. Nobody expected these gentlemen to do the actual work these positions required; lowly clerks had that function. Grace and favor permeated the whole system. Much of what we would consider corruption today was the ordinary course of events.

Modern societies espouse a different ethos. Government is supposed to serve the people, the whole people, and nothing but the people. This was, indeed, a theme of the American Revolution: rejecting the regime of grace and favor. Even so, concepts of misconduct, and standards of behavior of public officials, did not change overnight. Members of Congress, in the nineteenth century, acted with regard to business interests and professional lives in ways that today would be considered conflicts of interest. Ethical standards, in short, change over time. The (legal) norm and ideal for public servants is a norm and ideal of complete impartiality. Today, even dictatorships sing a song of public service. They at least pay lip service to honesty and good faith in government.

No country lives up to the ideal of a government free of bias and corruption. But corruption is not evenly distributed among nations. Transparency International is an organization that ranks and scores countries and comes up with a kind of corruption index. For 2013, the cleanest countries were Denmark, New Zealand, and Finland; at the bottom of the list of 175 countries were

Sudan, Afghanistan, North Korea, and Somalia. Many of the countries in the lower depths of the index are so riddled with corruption that they almost amount to "kleptocracy." Favored people (and their relatives) end up wealthy and powerful; the ruler and his kinfolk (or members of his town, clan, or tribe) own businesses, get valuable privileges, drive black Mercedes cars, and open bank accounts in Switzerland or the Cayman Islands. The rest of the country has to pay tribute.

Corruption is a social phenomenon, and like all social phenomena, it has specific social causes. One of its sources is what Edward Banfield has called "amoral familism," a term originally applied to southern Italy.[8] In that society—and many others—there is no strong attachment to the polity as a whole. People with power and influence do not identify with the country; their most powerful commitment is to family, friends, and members of their clan or tribe. Indeed, a cousin of a government minister *expects* to get something from his relative; and would consider it a wrong if he failed to get it. In many countries—China is a good example—corruption is officially described as a major social problem; there are sporadic attempts to deal with it, and these give rise from time to time to big and widely publicized trials meant to convey the message that the bad old ways will not be tolerated. Corruption trials sometimes follow a change in regime, when the old group of looters is thrown out and a new group of looters takes power.

On the whole, in developed countries, corruption is milder, less blatant, and less deeply rooted than in the Third World. Sometimes, in some countries, corruption is almost a kind of necessity: when civil servants get a pittance each month in salary, civil servants find it hard to resist the urge to make something on the side. Even when the salaries are decent, a civil servant can be tempted to sell favors and public goods for money. In some parts of the world, so much money is already in the hands of drug lords and criminal gangs that they can buy judges, police, and other civil servants, or threaten them with death if they refuse to go along.

Fraud and corruption, alas, are hardly strangers to United States history, or, for that matter, the history of other countries. Corruption trials certainly attract attention, though perhaps somewhat less attention than the more prurient murder trials do. The United States has had its share of corruption trials. Municipal government, in the late nineteenth century, was notoriously corrupt. Powerful political machines—Tammany Hall in New York, for example—ran many of the cities; and leading figures in local government lined their pockets. The administration of President Warren Harding, in the 1920s, produced some notable examples of scandalous corruption. The most famous, the Teapot Dome scandal, gave rise to a sensational trial.[9] Albert Fall, who had been secretary of the interior, was found guilty of accepting a bribe of $100,000 from an oil man, Edward L. Doheny, in 1929. In exchange, Fall gave Doheny valuable rights to a naval oil reserve. Fall was the first cabinet member ever to be convicted of corruption. When the verdict was announced, it was "standing room only" in the courtroom, and crowds outside tried vainly to get inside.[10]

In general, hardly a year goes by without one or more important corruption trials. In 2008, the Justice Department brought ethics charges against Ted Stevens, a United States senator from Alaska. The charge had to do with his (alleged) failure to report gifts from a friend who owned a large oil service company in Alaska. The implication was that Stevens had sold influence for money. A jury found Stevens guilty, and he lost his seat in 2008. In this case, Stevens had a kind of happy ending; his conviction was overturned, on the grounds that the prosecution had fatally misbehaved (he was, of course, still an ex-senator; nothing could change that).[11]

One of the more colorful corruption trials of recent years concerned the governor of Illinois, Rod Blagojevich. Senator Barack

Obama had been elected president in 2008, and his Senate seat now fell vacant. The governor was accused of trying to sell the seat to the highest bidder and of extorting campaign funds from state contractors. He was impeached, tried, and sentenced to fourteen years in prison, in 2011.[12] Before he went to jail, he made news with his somewhat bizarre behavior—appearing on talk shows and on reality TV. His wife matched his performance: On another reality program, she "swallowed a tarantula one night and crawled through a muddy pit the next."[13]

In the United States, in the nineteenth and early twentieth centuries, brothels and gambling dens traditionally stayed in business by bribing the police. This was, of course, illegal, and corrupt, but it also reflected the fact that a large part of the public *wanted* brothels and gambling dens, and patronized them. It was once the custom, in Chicago, and probably elsewhere, to keep a $10 or $20 bill next to your auto license. If a police officer stopped you and asked to see your license, the unspoken message was clear: Take the money and leave me alone. These instances tell us a lot about the social meaning of corruption. It tends to flourish where public support for honest behavior is weak. Most people do not think it is a sign of deep immorality to avoid a traffic ticket. A person who, perhaps, thinks "fixing" a ticket is no big deal might be utterly scandalized at the thought of stealing a can of soup from a supermarket. Petty corruption thrives where moral and legal norms seem out of phase. It goes largely unnoticed. Big corruption trials, on the other hand, come out of what one might call grand corruption: corruption in high places or on an enormous scale.

Private corruption and fraud also make news and can produce headline trials: trials of notorious confidence men, fraudsters, or "malefactors of great wealth" (a phrase used by President Franklin D. Roosevelt). Among the examples have been officials of Enron, a huge energy company that collapsed spectacularly;

others include rich Wall Street men (and the rare woman) accused of insider trading, and people who run Ponzi schemes and similar grand scams. In the early twenty-first century, Bernard Madoff, whose Ponzi scheme cheated people out of billions of dollars, made headline news. Before his fall, there were indeed some who tried to warn the authorities that Madoff was a crook and that his investment results were simply too good to be true. They were ignored. Madoff floated on an ocean of money for years. In the end, however, his scheme collapsed. On March 12, 2009, Madoff pleaded guilty and said he was "sorry" he had inflicted so much pain on so many people; Madoff, who was seventy, would surely spend the rest of his life in prison. Because he pleaded guilty, there was no trial; but his guilty plea was front-page news, and "dozens" of his victims "squeezed into the courtroom benches behind him" to see and hear the proceedings.[14]

There can be corruption, too, in the world of sports, entertainment, and even education. The "Black Sox" scandal could be mentioned here: the charge that members of the Chicago baseball team, the White Sox, took bribes and threw away victory in the World Series in 1919. Some of the players were put on trial. They were acquitted, but barred from organized baseball.[15] In 2010, Dr. Celia Chang, dean of the Institute of Asian Studies at St. John's University, in Queens, New York City, was accused of embezzling more than $1 million from the university. It was also claimed that she forced scholarship students, mostly from overseas, to act as her personal servants—cleaning her house, hand-washing her underwear, and bringing her money while she gambled at Foxwoods Casino in Connecticut. In 2012, Dr. Chang put an end to her trial in a gruesome and dramatic way: She committed suicide while the trial was still going on, slitting her wrists and hanging herself with stereo speaker wire.[16]

In all societies, people and institutions make use of "connections" and "clout"; the line between "clout" or "influence," on the one hand, and downright corruption, on the other, is necessarily vague. There is a kind of arms race in modern, bureaucratic, complex societies: Rules to prevent corruption, rules to insure the triumph of "merit," and rules about competitive bidding are matched and often overmatched by influence, the power of lobbies, and all sorts of subtle biases and prejudices.

Cases of economic or regulatory crime—antitrust violations, insider trading, offenses against the Securities and Exchange laws—can be complex, technical, and arcane. Trials for such crimes are more likely to appear in the business section of a newspaper than on the front page; they are unlikely to make a splash on the evening news. There are exceptions: the savings and loan crisis, in which more than 1,000 savings and loan associations failed in the 1990s, made headlines, perhaps because of its sheer magnitude. The chicanery was of heroic proportions, and the cost to the taxpayers was immense.[17] These cases tend to rise and fall with the business cycle. No one complains so long as the money keeps flowing. But during periodic crashes, panics, and depressions, there is an inevitable search for villains. This was certainly true of the stock market crash of 1929, and the Great Depression that followed. Congressional committees investigated Wall Street in a blaze of publicity. The political momentum that resulted helped grease the path to passage of the Securities and Exchange Act.[18]

But in general, corruption trials, though they may be socially of the highest importance, are not likely to provide good theater. When these trials do occur, if they are sensational enough, then they can transmit a warning to others and an important public message. Countries that claim to be serious about corruption may mount huge show trials: the trial of Bo Xilai in 2013, in China, is a prime example. Bo, a former member of the Politburo, a key politician, and the son of a Communist Party leader, was accused of taking massive bribes. He was, of course, convicted and given a life sentence. This was a dramatic trial that "let the public peer into a privileged world of dizzying wealth and . . . excess."[19]

There are perfectly good instrumental reasons to fight corruption, but there is also an ideological reason. In the age of human rights culture, the public tends to embrace an ideal of clean, honest, impartial government (as opposed to "amoral familism"). Human rights culture embraces an ideology of absolute legal equality and rejects "grace and favor." Of course, this not an easy goal to reach, but many governments are either trying, or want to *seem* to be trying. Corruption trials will tend to be most sensational and to grab the most media attention either in countries where corruption is rare, and thus exceptional, or in countries where corruption is in fact an enormously serious problem. China is an example. In countries of this type, corruption is so deeply embedded in the national structure and culture that fighting it requires heroic efforts and dramatic actions.

5

Was Justice Done?

We label another category of headline trial, *Was Justice Done?* These cases are closely linked to political trials; in a way, one can call them a subspecies of political trial. These are cases that become famous, or infamous, because of the way the judge or prosecutor behaved, because the defendants were (or may have been) falsely or unjustly accused, or because they were put through the ordeal of a trial for corrupt or political reasons. The Sacco-Vanzetti case, which we have mentioned before,[1] is a prime example. It generated tremendous publicity, both during the trial and afterward. The evidence against the two men was weak, and many people found the trial itself biased and unfair. As we noted, people still ask about this case: Was justice done?

In France, the notorious Dreyfus case set French society aflame. Alfred Dreyfus was a young officer of Jewish descent in the French Army. He was accused of giving military secrets to the Germans. Dreyfus was convicted in 1894, in an atmosphere of intense anti-Semitism, stripped of his rank, and sent to Devil's Island, where he was confined under appalling conditions. Evidence of an enormous cover-up began to emerge, evidence that strongly suggested that Dreyfus had been framed. In fact, a different French officer was guilty of the crime; Dreyfus was totally innocent. The military tried hard to suppress the evidence that would exonerate Dreyfus. A furious campaign was mounted on his behalf; French society split into Dreyfusards and anti-Dreyfusards, roughly along political lines: progressives were Dreyfusards, reactionaries, anti-Dreyfusards. The scandal shook French society to the core. In the end, justice was (belatedly) done: Dreyfus was freed, and he even rejoined the French army.[2]

These last two examples could also be easily classified as political trials. Other great cases are political only in the sense that the judiciary is a political organ; hence, courts that misbehave, act in a prejudiced way, become a political problem. A prime instance was the famous Scottsboro case.[3] The defendants were nine young black men, arrested in Scottsboro, Alabama, in 1931. They were riding a freight train, between Chattanooga, Tennessee, and Huntsville, Alabama. On the train were some young white men and two girls. A fight ensued between the two groups; the whites were forced off the train, but they sent a "message" ahead, asking that the blacks be removed from the train. The two girls accused the blacks of assaulting them on the train. At Scottsboro, a hostile mob gathered, and the sheriff seized the black men. In a way, the Scottsboro defendants were lucky to escape the mob, which might have lynched them. The trial itself was short and slapdash. It was typical of Southern justice during the Jim Crow period—at least in cases where a black defendant stood accused of committing a crime against a white victim. The defense was brief and inept, hardly worthy of the name. As the Supreme Court later described it, the defendants were "young, ignorant, illiterate, surrounded by hostile sentiment . . . charged with an atrocious crime regarded with special horror in the community"; they were served by a lawyer who had agreed to represent them just minutes before the trial started. There was no time to investigate, and there was in fact no investigation. Eight of the defendants were quickly convicted and sentenced to death.

An investigation would have shown that the Scottsboro

defendants were innocent. Indeed, one of the "victims" recanted later on; she admitted she had lied to protect her own reputation. This seemed to make no difference to white opinion in Scottsboro. But by 1931, the rest of the country had begun to take notice of the case, which quickly became notorious. A move was made to overturn the convictions; an appeal was taken all the way to the United States Supreme Court. The Supreme Court reversed, and ordered a new trial. The original trial had been so unfair, according to the justices, that it violated the defendants' constitutional rights. The failure to give the defendants "reasonable time and opportunity to secure counsel was a clear denial of due process."[4] A new trial, however, before another all-white jury, only led to another flock of death sentences. This verdict, too, was set aside; but each time the case came before a jury, the results were the same. Yet the glare of publicity, national and international, did make a difference in the end. Political and legal agitation paid off; the Scottsboro defendants had to spend long years behind bars; but none of the death sentences was carried out, and in the end, they were released.

The Leo Frank affair was another notorious instance of Southern (in)justice. Frank was Jewish; he was manager of a pencil factory in Georgia. In 1913, somebody brutally murdered young Mary Phagan, a thirteen-year-old girl who worked in the factory. Frank was accused of the crime. The evidence against him was shaky, to say the least, but he was convicted and sentenced to death in an atmosphere poisoned by general hysteria and rabid anti-Semitism. The governor of Georgia, convinced that justice had not been done, commuted Frank's sentence to life imprisonment. But a mob took him from prison and lynched him.[5]

For cases in this category, very often what happens *after* the trial is more significant than the trial itself. The trials tend to be headline trials, but the headlines continue long after the verdict. There may be raging controversy over the conduct of the trial or over the outcome. Sometimes, the punishment seems disproportionate to the crime. This was one of the reasons why the Caryl Chessman case became notorious. Chessman, in California, went on trial in 1948, accused of robbery, sexual assault, and kidnapping. "Kidnapping" could bring a death sentence, but in Chessman's case, the "kidnapping" consisted of moving an alleged victim a short distance; thus the death penalty was based on an extremely technical reading of California law. Chessman was convicted and sentenced to death. He spent twelve years on death row, wrote a book, and became an international celebrity. There were strong efforts made to save him from execution. But they ended in failure. Chessman was put to death in 1960.[6]

The trial of the Rosenbergs, husband and wife, was, of course, a political trial, and one of the most sensational trials in American history. The evidence against Ethel Rosenberg was hardly as strong as the evidence against her husband; moreover, in this case, the sentence was far more controversial than the trial or the verdict. The death sentence, harsh, and fairly unprecedented, since the country was not at war, touched off a national and international campaign to save the couple from the electric chair.[7] But, like the campaigns for Caryl Chessman, and for Sacco and Vanzetti, the agitation brought no results: The Rosenbergs went to the electric chair.[8]

Occasionally, controversy arises because the sentence was too mild rather than too severe or because an acquittal evokes public outrage. We have mentioned the case of Dan White. White, a member of the board of supervisors in San Francisco, resigned his post. He then changed his mind and asked the mayor, George Moscone, to reappoint him. When Moscone refused, White shot him to death; he then killed Harvey Milk, the first openly gay city supervisor. At the end of White's trial, in 1979, the jury convicted White of manslaughter rather than murder. Milk (and to an extent Moscone) had been a hero to the gay community; the verdict seemed like a slap in the face, and riots broke out in San Francisco in protest.[9]

John W. Hinckley, Jr., made an attempt to assassinate President Ronald Reagan on March 30, 1981. Reagan was wounded, but survived. Apparently, Hinckley's act was not political at all; rather, he was infatuated with a movie star, Jodie Foster, and felt that a bold deed of this type would impress her. At the trial, in 1982, a jury found Hinckley not guilty by reason of insanity.[10] This verdict made legal sense (Hinckley certainly seemed unbalanced); nonetheless, the decision was wildly unpopular and evoked a storm of outrage. Largely because of this agitation, the (formal) rules about the insanity plea in the federal penal code were amended. A number of states also changed their laws, and a few even tried to abolish the insanity plea altogether.[11]

The Rodney King affair is another example of a controversial acquittal. In 1991, in Los Angeles, Rodney King, an African American, led the police on a high-speed chase. When the police finally caught him, some of the them beat him mercilessly. The beating was caught on videotape, and the incident led to widespread protests in the African American community. Four members of the police force were put on trial, but in April 1992, a jury found them not guilty. After the verdict was announced, "angry demonstrators torched buildings, looted stores and assaulted passersby."[12]

Race was a confounding issue, too, in the famous Massie-Fortescue trials, in Hawaii, in the 1930s. Thalia Massie, the white wife of a naval officer, was found late one night in September 1931 walking along Ala Moana Road; her mouth was swollen, her cheeks red, her jaw broken. She was picked up by a passing driver and taken home. She claimed that a gang of native Hawaiian men had attacked her; later, she added that they had raped her. Five men—none of them white—who were picked up for a minor traffic infraction around the same time were arrested and charged with the crime against Thalia Massie.[13] Almost certainly, Massie had been telling lies. No one really knows what happened to her that night. A physical examination showed no signs of rape, and there was, in any event, nothing to connect her to the five men who were arrested. The trial was headline news in Hawaii. The local jury failed to reach a verdict, and the five men were discharged. Lieutenant Massie and his mother-in-law, Grace Fortescue, refused to accept this result. They connived to kidnap one of the defendants, Joe Kahahawai. The plan, apparently, was to get him to confess. But things went tragically awry, and Kahahawai was shot to death.

Now there was another trial: this time, the defendants were Lt. Massie and Grace Fortescue, along with their confederates. A mixed-race jury, after long wrangling, found the defendants guilty of manslaughter (not murder) and recommended "leniency." Even so, the verdict was wildly unpopular—with white people. Indeed, race and racial politics had permeated the atmosphere of both trials. A letter to the prosecutor called him "a disgrace to American manhood" and a "reproach to the entire WHITE race."[14] Pressure was put on the authorities to do something on behalf of the defendants. The court had sentenced them to ten years in prison; but the governor reduced their sentences to one hour, and they simply walked out free (and left the islands).

Race also played a key role in the trial of George Zimmerman in 2013. Zimmerman, a neighborhood-watch volunteer, was accused of second-degree murder in the death of a young black man, Trayvon Martin, in Florida. Zimmerman, who carried a gun, had followed Martin one night, perhaps because he thought Martin was up to no good; what happened afterward is obscured by a fog of factual uncertainty. Zimmerman claimed he fired his gun in self-defense, after the teenager "instigated" a fight. Many people found this claim hard to believe; they thought that Zimmerman had singled out a young black man wearing a hood because of Zimmerman's racist assumptions and then killed the young man without any justification. Martin had been unarmed, and he ended up dead. Zimmerman went to trial; the trial made headlines all over the country. After weeks of testimony, the jury in July 2013 found Zimmerman not guilty, both of second-degree murder and of manslaughter. There was "anger over the verdict" from members of the black community.[15]

Some of these cases were political to begin with; all of them ended up politically potent. Headline trials are public. They are spectacles, and by definition, they are of enormous public interest, which, in modern times, the media fan. These cases often split along national fault lines, racial or political. Trials, of course, always have winners and losers. By definition, a big trial reverberates outside the courtroom; and the verdict on the streets is not necessarily the same as the verdict inside. The trials, as always, are didactic theater, but sometimes the audience finds the message so repellent or unfair that they take to the streets. It is usually easy to see where the fault lines lie.

Headline trials are theater, and, like theater on Broadway, they unfold in a specific, enclosed space and follow a script (or scripts). The audience may have a subtle influence on what goes on in the courtroom—especially when the normative atmosphere inside and outside of the courtroom is the same. Americans in general surely thought that the Rosenbergs were guilty and that Sacco and Vanzetti were guilty. The protests came from a minority outside the courtroom. Where, on the other hand, we are in the presence of a strong dividing line—race is a prime example—then there is likely to be more of a feeling, among the losers, that justice has not been done. The result can range from grumbling to outright violence in the streets.

There Ought to Be a Law

Most crimes have one or two or a few victims. When the alleged crime is the murder or destruction of a large number of people, there is a much more powerful demand for action. People feel that *something* should be done, something *must* be done. This feeling often emerges after some unusually tragic occurrence, a huge natural or man-made disaster. If somebody is blamed and goes on trial, these trials acquire an edgy, political thrust. They may give rise to a political movement or to general demands for changes in the law.

The Triangle Shirtwaist fire occurred in March 1911.[16] Fire broke out high above the street, in a shirtwaist factory in New York City. The workers were young women, many of them immigrants, who worked long hours for small pay. More than one hundred women, and about twenty men, died a tragic death. At least one door through which they could have escaped was apparently locked. Some women died when they plunged down an elevator shaft. Others, desperate to escape an agonizing death in the flames, chose a quicker death: They jumped from the windows and crashed onto the pavement as crowds of horrified New Yorkers watched helpless in the streets. Fire-fighting equipment could not reach the upper floors of the building. After this horrific tragedy, the grand jury indicted the owners of the factory, Max Blanck and Isaac Harris, for second-degree manslaughter.[17] At the trial, the men denied knowing that the fatal door had been locked. In December 1911, the jury brought in a verdict of not guilty after deliberating for all of an hour and forty-five minutes. This was hardly a popular verdict: Blanck and Harris were taken by a "squad of policemen through a maze of courtrooms" and then out of the building, surrounded by a "guard of policemen and detectives, amid the hissing and reviling of relatives of victims of the fire."[18] In civil suits, the victims and their families received piddling amounts, but the incident reverberated in the legislative halls and put pressure on the state to do something about the factory conditions that led to this awful incident.

Catastrophes have political resonance. In 1942, more than five hundred people died when a nightclub, the Coconut Grove, went up in flames. The nightclub had violated city safety rules.

The owner was not at the club that night, but he was arrested and put on trial. He was found guilty of involuntary manslaughter.[19] A significant trial also emerged out of the Exxon Valdez catastrophe—a disastrous oil spill in the waters off Alaska.[20] In these cases, as in the Triangle Shirtwaist case, trials were politically and emotionally necessary, if only to fix blame and to satisfy the cry for justice or, in some cases, for scapegoats. Putting owners and managers on trial was also a way of excusing the state, regime, or society at large for the failings—regulatory and legislative—that led to the catastrophe. Some of these criminal trials ended with convictions, some (as in the Triangle Shirtwaist case) with acquittals. In most of these incidents, there were also civil cases for damages, but until recently, victims and their families collected little or nothing.

These trials were, of course, meant to serve a purpose. They were, as always, theatrical. In open societies, catastrophes and scandals are often the catalysts for changes in the law. They attract attention to new or slumbering issues. Their political consequences can be huge. Trials that also raise, for whatever reason, some important issue of policy or principle are also political, at least in the broad sense of the word. And the political issue is most acute when public opinion outside the courtroom is sharply divided: the trials of draft dodgers during the war in Vietnam, for example.

Religious disputes have been the basis of a few notable headline trials. The Mormon polygamy trials of the nineteenth century are a good example.[21] Christian Scientist parents have been tried for child abuse or neglect when they refused to use orthodox medicine for sick children, and the children died.[22] The most famous religious—or quasi-religious—trial was the Scopes trial, otherwise known as the famous "monkey" trial, in Dayton, Tennessee, in 1925.[23] Scopes, the defendant, was a high-school science teacher. His "crime" was teaching Darwinian evolution. The laws of Tennessee strictly forbade this and made it an offense to instruct students in what was considered dangerous doctrine. In one way, relatively little was at stake in this trial. If Scopes were found guilty, he would simply have to pay a small fine. But the case exploded into a dramatic confrontation between science and religion. Huge numbers of reporters and sightseers swarmed into Dayton. The trial itself was an utter sensation. Two famous lawyers, William Jennings Bryan and Clarence Darrow, battled it out in the courtroom: Bryan for the strict, fundamentalist account of creation, Darrow for science and skepticism. Scopes, the actual defendant, seemed to be little more than a bystander. The trial was (rather inaccurately) turned into a play in 1955 and a classic film, *Inherit the Wind*, in 1960. Bryan died soon after the trial; supposedly, science won the battle. But the struggle over the teaching of evolution has never really gone away.

6

Tabloid Trials

On Wednesday, January 23, 1907, in New York City, Harry K. Thaw went on trial for murder. Thaw was a member of a rich and prominent family. No expense was spared in his defense; no less than five lawyers formed his team. His crime can only be described as spectacular. The victim was Stanford White, probably the leading architect in the United States, the man who designed some of New York's most dramatic new buildings, including Madison Square Garden. And it was on the rooftop of that building, in 1906, that Thaw shot White to death, at 11:05 p.m., "just as the first performance of the musical comedy 'Mamzelle Champagne' was drawing to a close."[1] Thaw had a long history of erratic behavior. If he was one of the stars in the drama, the other star, who in many ways overshadowed him, was his wife, Evelyn Nesbit Thaw. She was young and achingly beautiful; as a teenager, she had been one of the "Floradora" girls on Broadway. The story she told her husband was that Stanford White had raped her, when she was just sixteen. White, as Evelyn told the tale, had taken her to a small bedroom in his apartment, which was furnished with "exquisite taste." He gave her champagne that was "bitter and funny-tasting"; after she drank the champagne, "everything went black." When she woke up, she was in bed, naked. There were "blotches of blood on the sheets." White brought her a kimono and said, "It's all over."[2] Afterward, he begged her to be quiet, to tell nobody what had happened.

Evelyn later met Harry K. Thaw. He asked her to marry him. She said it was impossible. When he wanted to know why, she told him about Stanford White. Thaw, according to Evelyn's account, burst into tears. She did marry Thaw—one of the worst decisions of her life. Thaw was a man of dubious character, probably mentally ill; at some point, he decided to put an end to the life of Stanford White, the man who had "ruined" Evelyn Nesbit Thaw.

The Thaw trial, when it occurred, was the most notorious, the most scandalous, the most flamboyant of its day. It was, in the words of one commentator, so "spectacular" that it "sucked dry the descriptive reservoirs of the American press."[3] More than a thousand spectators "gathered each morning to catch a glimpse of" Evelyn Thaw. Extra seats were provided for the mob of reporters. A telegraph office, in the main hall of the Criminal Courts Building, was set up, the better to spread the word to the waiting world. The jury was sequestered in a hotel for about two and a half months. The climax was Evelyn Thaw's appearance on the stand. She was "infinitely appealing," with the "slim, quick grace of a fawn, a head that sat on her faultless throat as a lily on its stem [and] . . . a mouth made of rumpled rose petals."[4] In shocking detail, she told about her relationships with White and with Shaw, how she had visited White's studio and "played in his red velvet swing," and tearfully, how he had debauched her.[5] In part, the case hinged on Thaw's mental condition: was he or was he not insane? In the end, the jury deadlocked, and the whole thing had to be done again. In a second trial, the jury found Thaw not guilty by reason of insanity.

This was a case that had everything: sex, show business, drama. Incredibly famous in its day, the story still reverberates in popular culture. "The Girl in the Red Velvet Swing," a 1955 movie, was based on the trial and the dramatic story of Stanford White, Harry K. Thaw—and Evelyn Nesbit Thaw.

Political trials, and those closely allied to political trials, may be the headline trials that mean the most to society. They are prime examples of didactic theater, but their messages would be useless unless they held the public's attention, unless they were also gripping news.

Big trials are therefore also *entertainment.* And this function has become increasingly salient as the mass media have come to play more of a role in public life. Witness the drama of the trial of Harry K. Thaw—the flocks of reporters, the telegraphed news. Trials like Thaw's are not overtly political. Their entertainment function, if you can call it that, is far more significant. This trial, and others like it, was political only in the sense that anything that creates a stir, makes headlines, and captures the eyes and ears of the public is to some degree political. If we imagine a continuum of big trials, the overtly political would stand at one end; at the other would be trials that have no (obvious or clear) social meaning and that the public loves for the sheer thrill or scandal they present—in essence, for their entertainment value. Often enough, as we will see, these trials *do* have a deeper, if only symbolic, meaning. And we have to ask: Why are these trials so fascinating? What do they tell us about the larger society?

The Thaw trial is a prime example of what we might call "*tabloid* trials" (it also fits into two categories we will discuss later: celebrity trials and soap opera trials). Tabloid trials titillate the public and cause an enormous ruckus because of the nature of the crime itself. The defendant is accused of sensational, lurid, or disgusting acts; the odor of sex and scandal hangs over them. Some of these tawdry affairs seem to plumb the lowest depths of human pathology. Indeed, the trial itself may come as an anticlimax; it is the crimes themselves, when they occurred, that made the biggest headlines. And if the crimes remain unsolved—think of Jack the Ripper, the famous serial killer of late-nineteenth-century London—there is no trial at all.[6]

In many cases, everybody knows (or thinks they know) who committed the crimes, and the trials serve as a kind of public horror show. Jeffrey Dahmer, of Milwaukee, Wisconsin, killed and mutilated more than a dozen young men. He had sex with most of them, either before or after they were dead; he dismembered many of them, and even practiced cannibalism. He was arrested in 1991. He pleaded guilty to the crimes. The main issue was whether or not he was insane. He was found mentally competent (though one wonders) and sentenced to life in prison (there is no death penalty in Wisconsin); a few years later, when Dahmer was thirty-four, another prisoner beat him to death.[7]

William Heirens was convicted of three bloody and horrifying murders in Chicago in 1946. He was called the "lipstick killer" because at one of the crime scenes, Heirens left a message scrawled in lipstick on the wall: "For Heaven's sake, catch me before I kill again." Heirens confessed to these crimes, although he later recanted. He then claimed that he was innocent and that the police had forced him to confess. He spent sixty-five years in prison before dying in 2012, at the age of eighty-three. There were many discrepancies in his case, in terms of both evidence and procedures. Heirens, until the end, claimed he had been falsely accused; and there are those who believe him.[8]

As lurid as the case of Jeffrey Dahmer was the case of Armin Meiwes, the German cannibal. Meiwes had a strange desire: he wanted to kill and eat someone, preferably a young man. He searched for his victim on the Internet. There were many false leads; some men who responded assumed, not unreasonably, that Meiwes had in mind some kind of neurotic role-playing. But then Meiwes found the sacrificial lamb he was looking for. This was Bernd Brandes, an engineer from Berlin. The two men agreed to go ahead with the plan and to videotape the proceedings. In March 2001, Meiwes began the grisly work. He and

Brandes both tried to eat bits of Brandes' flesh (his sex organ, to be exact). Then Meiwes stabbed Brandes to death and butchered the body. Meiwes had recorded the ritual on videotape, apparently for his private entertainment. When Meiwes began to look on the Internet for a second victim, somebody got suspicious, went to the police, and Meiwes' secret was revealed to the authorities. He was arrested, tried, convicted, and sent to prison. As one can imagine, the tabloids of Germany (and elsewhere) had a field day with Armin Meiwes.[9]

Crimes that hover at, or cross, the border of insanity seem to fascinate the public, especially when sexual pathology plays a role. Crime literature feeds on such crimes and the trials that follow them. Sexual innuendos were staples of cheap broadsides and brochures in the nineteenth century; the *National Police Gazette*, which flourished in that period, specialized in crimes of this type. The murder of a prostitute, Helen Jewett, in 1836, led to a sensational trial and also produced a flock of pamphlets, brochures, and the like for sale to the mass public.[10] A similar case was the murder of another prostitute, Maria Bickford, in Boston, in 1845; it was covered extensively in the newspapers and featured in the *National Police Gazette.*[11]

In the twentieth century, people seemed to find serial killers endlessly fascinating.[12] Serial killers are (for the most part) men who commit crime after crime, sometimes without any obvious motive and often against random victims. Serial killers are rare creatures in real life. But they loom large in books, movies, and television. They both frighten and attract the public, perhaps because their crimes seem so arbitrary, and their thought processes so mysterious. Dr. Hannibal Lecter, the central figure in *The Silence of the Lambs* (1991), a wildly successful movie, was a cannibal and a serial killer. Another figure who inspired horror was Charles Manson, a kind of cult leader, who gathered about him a group of disturbed women and embarked on a murder spree in 1968; among the victims was Sharon Tate, a movie actress, who happened to be pregnant. The press had a field day with Manson.[13]

Of course, "news" is whatever is strange and unusual; and tabloid crime fits the bill. Serial killers, cannibals, men who kidnap and enslave girls, and a slew of other "monsters" are reminders of the sheer complexity and randomness of modern life. They are also a sign of the mystery of identity: the impossibility of knowing *who* people are and understanding what makes them tick. The idea that the quiet man next door, the man we said hello to every day, had corpses in his basement and body parts in his freezer reminds us of the endless mystery of identity in modern life. We will return to this theme in a later chapter.

What we might call the "*soap-opera* trial" is a variant of the tabloid trial. Soap-opera trials feature love triangles, romantic entanglements, disappointments in love, abandoned or scorned lovers, and similar situations. In many of the more sensational trials love, or at least sex, plays a major role.[14] Most of the defendants in these trials are men, but occasionally a woman sits in the dock. In Oakland, California, the trial of Clara Fallmer was headline news in the 1890s. Clara was a young girl, seduced and abandoned—or so she said—by young Charlie La Due. Clara, fifteen or sixteen years old and pregnant, shot Charlie on the streets of Oakland in 1897. He died of his wounds.[15] She went on trial for murder, and the newspapers covered every aspect of the trial in breathless detail: the pale young girl, so cruelly treated by a cad (at least as the defense presented it), sitting in court, clutching a bouquet of violets. A sympathetic jury acquitted her. Another woman defendant was Laura D. Fair, who shot her lover, Alexander D. Crittenden, a San Francisco lawyer, in 1870, on board a ferryboat in San Francisco Bay in front of his wife and children. Her lover, she claimed, had gone back on his promise to divorce his wife and marry her. The trial generated enormous excitement. Her defense was (temporary) insanity, brought on by delayed menstruation.[16] The jury, however, was not persuaded and, after less than an hour of discussion, they found Laura Fair guilty. The Supreme Court of California reversed and remanded the case for a second trial. This jury found Laura not guilty "by reason of insanity."

Love, hate, jealousy, and lust are timeless elements of the human condition and have been with us since human beings evolved out of some primordial soup. Nonetheless, the precise form that the soap-opera trial takes is, like everything else, socially conditioned. In particular, gender roles and gender stereotypes mold the form, and determine the outcome, of these cases. Success for the defense depends on telling the jury an appealing story; success for the prosecution depends on rebutting that story—and, in many cases, admonishing the jury to follow the formal law instead of gut instincts.

The trial of Dan Sickles, in 1859, was a sensation for any number of reasons. Sickles was a congressman from New York, living in Washington, D.C., with his young wife, Teresa. Sickles received an anonymous note warning him that Teresa was unfaithful; she was meeting secretly with Philip Barton Key (son of the man who wrote "The Star-Spangled Banner"). Sickles confronted his wife, who burst into tears and admitted everything. The next day, Sickles went out, found Key, and shot him to death on the streets of the capital. Sickles was arrested and charged with murder.

As one can imagine, a congressman in the dock, charged with murder, makes headlines. At the trial, the basic facts were not in dispute. Sickles had killed Key in broad daylight and in public. The defense dragged in a fairly dubious claim: temporary insanity. The idea was this: The shocking news about Teresa had at least temporarily unhinged Sickles' mind. But the real defense was not this flimsy argument; the real defense, the one that almost certainly moved the jury, was the so-called unwritten law. A man had a right to do what Sickles had done. Key was an adulterer, a home wrecker; the Bible condemns such people to death; Key deserved what he got. Sickles was only defending his honor. The defense hammered away at this theme.[17]

This was one of the earliest examples of the so-called unwritten law in the United States. The phrase has been attached to a number of situations, but the classic unwritten law is the law that let Sickles go free. A man is entitled to kill his wife's lover. Of course, no such rule appeared in the criminal code of the District of Columbia or, for that matter, in any criminal code in the nation. But the unwritten law was a powerful doctrine, regardless of what the penal codes said. It saved Sickles from prison or the gallows; and it did the same for other men (and a few women) who invoked the "unwritten law" in the late nineteenth and early twentieth centuries. In the typical cases, juries simply would not convict.[18]

The famous photographer Edward Muybridge, for example, invoked the unwritten law in the 1870s. Muybridge later became a protégé of Leland Stanford; he produced a notable series of photos of men, women, and animals in motion—proving, among other things, that a running horse could have all four of its feet in the air at the same time. Muybridge's wife, Flora, took up with a man named Harry Larkyns. When Muybridge found this out, he became enraged (it was said), his eyes turned glassy, and he gasped for breath. He traveled to Calistoga, California, found Larkyns at the Yellow Jacket Mine, and shot him to death. At the trial, the defense was "justifiable homicide" (legally flimsy to say the least) and (temporary) insanity. His lawyer argued that the situation "drove him to mania"; from the moment Muybridge learned about his wife's adultery, "he was not himself" but was "[s]trung up to the pitch of insanity." The jury acquitted him. When Muybridge left the courthouse, "a large crowd in front of the courtroom erupted in cheers and applause, and he was mobbed."[19]

This was the usual result: quick acquittal. In 1908, Dr. E. W. Dakan, of Oklahoma, slit the throat of his wife's lover. The jury deliberated all of ten minutes before announcing that Dakan was not guilty.[20] A jury in Richmond, Virginia, beat this record: in 1900, the jury needed only seven minutes to acquit William J. Rhodes, who "shot down Frank Burnett for having destroyed his home," that is, by sleeping with his wife.[21] In Texas, in 1897, Colonel John Hallum went on trial after shooting Reverend W. A. Forbes five times in a railroad station at Texarkana, Texas (amazingly, the reverend survived). The colonel insisted that "seducers" deserved to die; a true man would defend his home life "in defiance of all the puny mandates of man" (the formal criminal code was, apparently, one of these "puny mandates"). The jury found him not guilty of assault with intent to kill but fined him (as he suggested) $50 for a misdemeanor offense. Hallum's friends had paid the fine in full before he even left the courtroom.[22]

In a Virginia case that made headlines, two brothers, James and Philip Strother, were put on trial in 1907 for killing William Bywaters, the husband of their sister, Viola. Actually, he was her husband for only a few short hours. It was a shotgun marriage. The two brothers had forced it on Bywaters, who had gotten their sister pregnant. She had had an abortion in Washington, D.C.; it left her ill and in pain. The brothers, when they heard her story, angrily confronted Bywaters. They insisted that he marry Viola and make her an honest woman. The wedding took place, but the bridegroom made it clear that he wanted no part of this domestic arrangement. First he tried to escape down a back stairway; then he climbed out through a window. It was at that point that the brothers killed him.[23]

The high point of the trial was Viola's testimony. Her sister wheeled her into court "in an invalid's chair." "Pale and wan, her face showing traces of illness and suffering," she told her tale of woe.[24] The judge, in his charge, did not specifically mention the unwritten law, but everybody knew that this was an honor killing, justified by that doctrine. The judge did tell the jury about "emotional insanity," which was the main *legal* defense. It had been (in various forms) the figleaf defense for Sickles, Muybridge, and many others.[25] The outcome of the Virginia case was probably never much in doubt. The jury brought in a verdict of not guilty. Cheers broke out in the courtroom. Indeed, the judge told the jurors that they had done the right thing: In Virginia, "no man tried for defending the sanctity of his home should be found guilty."[26]

The Strothers case was about family honor; it reeked of stereotypes about (respectable, middle-class) women who were vulnerable, innocent, easily victimized by designing men. Of course, Viola *was* in many ways a victim—a sick, pathetic figure. Yet no one seriously suggested that Bywaters had raped her. That she was in any way complicit, that she had in any sense consented to sex, or even enjoyed it, was out of the question—at least in the drama that unfolded in the courtroom. The characters in these dramas were stock figures, and the lawyers painted them in terms that conformed to social stereotypes, especially the Victorian image of (respectable) womanhood.

The unwritten law also figured in cases of love triangles, but perhaps "triangle" is not the right word. The three angles of a triangle are all equally significant, but curiously perhaps, in cases of the classic unwritten law, the woman seemed hardly to matter. The unwritten law almost implied a husband's *duty* to defend family honor; killing the wretch who "destroyed his home" was the macho thing to do; any real man would behave the way Sickles or Colonel Hallum had behaved. So, in 1909, local officials and businessmen signed a petition, asking for mercy on behalf of John H. Cradlebaugh, of Wallace, Idaho, who killed his rival, Fred Walton, on the streets of Denver. Cradlebaugh had done only what "any other man would have done under the circumstances."[27] And Muybridge's lawyer insisted to the jury that a man "who would not shoot the seducer of his wife . . . is a coward and a cur"; such a man would be nothing more than a "wretched . . . cuckold."[28]

The woman in the case, on the other hand, was never really blamed. She was, almost by definition, a helpless victim who had fallen prey to an immoral seducer. She was, as a woman, considered a "domesticated and passionless being"[29]—passionless, and innocent.[30] In some regards, the Thaw-White trial was the peak, the climax, of the career of the unwritten law. It was also a soap-opera trial, par excellence. No blame was ever attached to the beautiful young woman at the heart of the case. The case was deviant only by virtue of the flawed, unbalanced character of the defendant, Thaw himself.

The notion of the woman as inherently pure (and passionless) coexisted with an earlier notion: that some women were lustful and evil, perhaps more evil than the most evil of men. And, indeed, in many trials, while one side harped on the purity of the woman in question, whether victim or defendant, the other bangs the drum of evil incarnate. When Lucretia Chapman went on trial for poisoning her husband with arsenic (a neighbor's ducks and chickens, who had been feeding in her yard, also died), both sides hammered away at stereotypes: to the defense, Chapman was an innocent victim of circumstance; to the prosecution, she was a sex-mad, greedy devil in the shape of a woman. Thus the trial was a "case study in the cultural contest over the nature of womanhood that shaped Anglo-American gender ideology" in the nineteenth century.[31] Which one was more powerful? In this case, the answer was clear: Lucretia Chapman was acquitted.

The rhetoric of the nineteenth century, and the early years of the twentieth century, seemed to assume that women—that is, respectable, white, middle-class women—were weak, trusting creatures, naïve, easy marks for any beguiling and loathsome man who used her body to satisfy his lust, a lust that she, of course, did not share.[32] In these cases of unwritten law, if one follows the newspaper accounts, there never seems to be the slightest hint that possibly, just possibly, the wife could have been if not the aggressor then at least an eager participant.[33]

There was a female variant of the unwritten law: the woman's right to kill an abusive husband or a man who had dishonored her. Thus, in 1908, a jury took a scant eighteen minutes to acquit Angelina Anselone. She had killed Philip Ferreo, who, allegedly, had "pursued her with his intentions" after he had "succeeded in turning her husband against her."[34] One study showed that, in Chicago between 1870 and 1930, 265 women had killed a husband or lover; only 24 of these women were convicted, and even fewer went to prison.[35] One exasperated prosecutor remarked in 1906 that if every woman "who is attacked or is beaten by her husband," had the right to shoot him, "there [wouldn't] be many husbands left in Chicago six months from now."[36]

One question comes to mind immediately: If these norms were so powerful and so deeply embedded in society, why did they stay unwritten? Why did they not come out of the shadows and become official policy? Part of the answer lies in the nature of that ancient common law institution, the jury. A jury is never asked to explain its decisions. It discusses and argues in secret. It has great power; indeed, it may hold life and death in its hands, but its deliberations are shrouded in mystery and it expresses its conclusions in the tersest manner possible: one or two words. Hence a jury can, if it wishes, change the (living) law, dispense with a rule, elide technicalities, but in a quiet, subtle, and subterranean way. Patterns of jury decisions can move the law in one direction or another. Legal systems need flexibility; and this is one way the common law gets it.

But that does not tell us why *this* kind of flexibility developed. The cheapest, and easiest, answer is the floodgates argument. A slight crack in the levee and whole oceans can pour in. The argument may be logically and empirically weak, but as a social norm, an intuition, or a commonsense notion, it can be very strong. Yes, there are people who deserve to die—people like Philip Barton Key or men who beat their wives to a pulp. And their private executioners do not deserve to be punished. But if we make this norm into a *rule*, too many people, or the wrong people, might make use of it. Where will it end? Will women kill all the husbands in Chicago? Will every adulterer be shot down on the streets? Better to let juries do justice, case by case.

The legal system is, in fact, riddled with unwritten laws. Love triangles are not the only morality plays that produce them. Another unwritten law comes out of a very different situation: mercy killings, killings performed out of love. An old man whose wife, his life companion, is lying in bed terminally ill, tormented with pain may respond to her desperate pleas for relief by helping her into another world. Technically, this, too, is murder. But the old man is very unlikely to go to jail. A kind of unwritten law is at work. Similarly, when a caring, merciful doctor does the dirty work. In a headline case in 1950, Dr. Herman Sander, in New Hampshire, was put on trial for murder. He was accused of killing his patient, Abbie Borroto, by injecting air into her veins. She was bedridden, in agony, and dying of cancer. Dr. Sander admitted he had administered the injection; but he claimed Borroto was already dead when he did so. This claim, to be sure, was hard to swallow: If she was dead, why bother? The prosecution insisted: this was murder. But Dr. Sander came across as a kindly, empathetic man. The jury acquitted him after less than an hour of discussion. The Borroto family was happy with the result; and women in the courtroom "gasped and cried out in joy." Dr. Sander lost his license to practice, but it was later restored. As far as the public was concerned, justice had been done.[37]

Trials that invoke the unwritten law are very much didactic theater. They are morality plays, but their messages are complex and ambiguous. The prosecution talks about law and order. It tells the jury the law must be followed. People should not take the law into their own hands. But the actual outcomes often undercut this message. They send a different message—about mercy or justifiable revenge.

Mercy killings are still with us; they represent a real, contemporary problem. Modern medicine saves and prolongs lives—sometimes beyond the point of rationality. The dilemma these cases pose is one many families will face. The classic unwritten law—which rested, as we saw, on Victorian notions of gender role—is another matter. Men still kill other men out of jealousy, but they cannot invoke the classic unwritten law. That law died out by around 1950, along with the stereotypes that gave it its power.[38] Women are no longer assumed to be naïve, innocent, sexless creatures. They can still be victims, and often are, but they now have "agency": they can make choices, about sex as well as many other things. Law and society draw a line between seduction and actual violence. Meanwhile, adultery may be—who knows?—more common than ever. It can still give rise to powerful emotions. It may at times lead to bloodshed. It can become the backdrop of a criminal trial. But the lawyers will have to use a different playbook for their drama.

7

Celebrity Trials

At the very beginning of this book, we mentioned the trial of O. J. Simpson. Simpson was a football hero, a member of the Pro Football Hall of Fame, a superstar, a familiar figure in movies and on television. He was charged with the double murder of his wife and a friend of hers. Roscoe Arbuckle ("Fatty"), a silent-movie star and film director, one of the most famous Americans in show business, went on trial in 1921, accused of raping a starlet, Virginia Rappe, who later died. In the trial of Harry K. Thaw, it was the victim who was famous: Stanford White, the great architect. The victim in the trial of Charles Guiteau, in 1881, was even more famous: James Garfield, president of the United States.[1] Bruno Hauptmann went on trial in 1935 for kidnapping and murdering the infant son of Charles Lindbergh, the first man to fly solo across the Atlantic and a tremendous national hero.[2]

These are all examples of what we might call "*celebrity* trials." These trials make headlines, not so much because of the crime itself but because either the victim or the defendant, or both, are famous or public figures, or, in our times, because they were celebrities. Technically, the older trials were not "celebrity" trials, even when the victim or killer was extremely famous, because they took place before the age of the true celebrity. Abraham

Lincoln was famous, but he was not, strictly speaking, a celebrity. Today, however, a trial with a famous defendant or victim *would* be a celebrity trial. This is because we live in a celebrity society. The public is endlessly curious, fascinated, and attracted by the affairs of celebrities, their habits, and their trials and tribulations.

But what exactly *is* a celebrity? A celebrity is not simply a famous person; rather, a celebrity is a famous and *familiar* person. Familiar because of the media, especially television, which gives us the illusion that we actually know these people, or, at any rate, that we somehow have access to their everyday lives. The king or queen of England or France, the Pope, the president of the United States, or the emperor of Japan: In the past, these were all enormously famous people, but it would be incorrect to think of them as celebrities. To the French peasant, the English tenant farmer, the humble priest or nun, or the American farmer, men like Louis XIV, or Henry VIII, or Pope Innocent III, or George Washington, were distant and remote. Only a member of the royal court, and a narrow circle around the court, actually knew Queen Victoria as a person rather than as an image, an exemplar, a face on coins and postage stamps, and perhaps, a small dumpy figure riding by in a gilded carriage. To most of her subjects, jingling coins and pasting stamps on envelopes was as close to the queen as they would ever get. For much of the late nineteenth century, the queen was a far-off figure, and after her husband, Prince Albert, died, the "Widow of Windsor" was even more isolated from her subjects. The pope was the head of the Catholic Church but remained a remote and obscure figure to millions of ordinary Catholics. Until the second half of the twentieth century, popes rarely left the Vatican. The Dalai Lama, or the emperor of Japan, were if anything even more distant from their people. Indeed, they were *supposed* to be awesome, remote, and unknowable.

All of this has changed, and quite dramatically. Today, the pope is a celebrity; he travels widely, visits many countries, and millions of people see him on television. The Dalai Lama gives talks at universities to thunderous crowds. The queen of England is a celebrity; she has become a very familiar figure. Her subjects see her on television, almost daily. She appears in public; she has garden parties, she christens boats, she presides at the opening of institutions. People know exactly what she looks like. They know about her clothing, her hats and coats; they know about her dogs. Cameras roam up and down the halls of her palaces. People recognize the sound of her voice. They know a great deal about her family as well: the children, grandchildren, and now, the great grandchildren. The baby born to Prince William, her grandson, and his wife was an instant celebrity from the day of his birth.

What is true of the queen is true of the president of the United States, and indeed, of all major celebrities. A huge public audience sees them frequently, almost on a daily basis. We know how they look and how they sound; we know details of their everyday life. Even the emperor of Japan has emerged from his palace in Tokyo (and is no longer a god). The president of the United States is perhaps the celebrity of celebrities, the most exposed of them all. His face, his voice, what he eats, his basketball games, his wife and children: these are familiar to millions of people in the United States and abroad. People know about his blood pressure and why at one point he was wearing a Band-Aid on his finger.

The celebrity culture did not appear overnight. Whatever its causes, the mass media played a major role in the process. Newspapers and personal appearances were the first carriers of a primitive form of celebrity culture. Gail Collins argues that the "celebrity class" emerged in the late nineteenth century. She mentions John L. Sullivan, "the world's bare-knuckle boxing champion," who was, she feels, an early and important example of celebrity. In the late 1880s, Sullivan was enormously famous and popular. His "picture was everywhere—in magazine ads, on . . . cigarette cards . . . [and] behind the mirrors of . . . saloons." He toured widely, giving exhibition fights, and he made a fortune.[3] She also mentions a "new class of heroines" consisting of "professional beauties"; Lillie Langtry was an example. These women were "famous just for being photogenic," and their "pale brown portraits" were pasted in albums all over the country.[4] Stage actors and actresses also approached celebrity status. Women like Sarah Bernhardt and men like Edwin Booth were on their way to becoming celebrities in the modern sense. They were not only famous but were seen and heard by thousands of people. Opera singers, too, were at least proto-celebrities.

The same was true of concert artists. They no longer only played for small, aristocratic audiences; they played for masses of people. Virtuosos like Paganini and Clara Schumann toured and gave concerts in many countries. The magician Houdini became spectacularly famous; he performed his incredible feats before huge audiences—escaping from impossible situations, shackled, tied, upside down or right side up, handcuffed, and apparently helpless.[5] Actors and actresses, magicians, and vaudeville performers were becoming more than famous; they were becoming familiar as they moved about from city to city, to be seen by crowds. "Wide audiences," however, were not yet audiences in the millions. Audiences of this scale were the work of the media.

Without the media, celebrities in the modern sense could hardly exist. The mass public in the past had no real access to the rich and famous, the powerful and consequential; there was no window into their lives. The rich and famous could *afford* to be remote; this remoteness was one of the things power and money could buy. Celebrity culture began to be possible with the rise of cheap, mass-circulation newspapers. But newspapers, even those with reporters (including the women reporters called "sob sisters") and with pictures, could not make celebrities in as powerful a way as the mass media in the twentieth and twenty-first centuries can. Nor could touring companies and road shows.

Movies created a whole new class of celebrity: the glamorous men and women of the silver screen. This medium began its amazing career around 1900. Movie houses sprouted everywhere, like mushrooms after rain. They were cheap, and they appealed to a mass audience. As early as 1909, movies had progressed to the point where the audience "experienced strong feelings of intimacy with actors." Audiences "were able to identify and sympathize" with the stars on the screen. Acting, too, had shifted "from an exaggerated pantomime to a more natural, subtle style"; the fans "began to feel as if they knew, quite personally, the characters in films and the actors who played them."[6] The stars were idolized. Fan magazines gushed over them. These magazines, like *Photoplay* and *Modern Screen*, thrived because they claimed to tell the adoring public everything they wanted to know about the stars.[7] The studios themselves made huge use of the dark arts of public relations. Much of what the public read about the stars, in fan magazines and elsewhere, was pure hokum, but that hardly mattered. The "news" at least *purported* to tell people what Jean Harlow or Gloria Swanson or Clark Gable were really like offscreen; to give people an insight (often fake) into their private lives: how and where they lived, their love lives, their personal habits and tastes.

The invention of radio spawned another group of stars—great comedians, for example, like Jack Benny and Fred Allen. Radio allowed all of us to listen to the voices of celebrities. This was particularly significant for political actors. With radio, the whole country could hear the smooth, dulcet tones of President Franklin Delano Roosevelt. Roosevelt was a master of radio communication; his "fireside chats" were justly famous.[8] Newsreels, too, were shown regularly in movie theaters. In the newsreels, we could *see* the president, as well as hear him. We could watch him in motion.

Each advance in technology fed the celebrity culture. With television, celebrity culture took a quantum leap forward. Television is vivid and luminously alive. It breaks down the "*apparent* barrier between elites and the mass audience."[9] Television became a household standard, a virtual necessity, in the 1950s and

1960s. Today, almost every family in the developed world has a television set, and often more than one. Big screens replaced small screens; and now, in many homes, giant screens have replaced the merely big ones. The old black and white images gave way to vibrant, thrilling color. Now, day in and day out, millions of people see images of the rich, the famous, the important: presidents, prime ministers, the pope, the Dalai Lama, basketball stars, movie stars, television stars, even an occasional big businessman like Warren Buffett or Bill Gates. Television *creates* celebrities. The people mentioned, to be sure, almost always have some reason to be famous; it is easy for famous people to make the leap from fame to celebrity. They "typically perform some deed, however modest, to attract initial attention." True enough. But by the 1980s and 1990s, "literally worthless individuals" could and did become celebrities, men and women who "commanded interest for nothing in particular."[10] Simply showing themselves, or being shown, on television made them into instant celebrities.

Television, then, made celebrities familiar—more familiar perhaps than the next-door neighbor or the family down the street. So familiar in fact, that it is easy to forget that television is a one-way mirror; we see and hear the celebrities, but they do not see or hear us. As the culture made the very familiarity of celebrities familiar, it was easy for people to jump to the conclusion that they somehow they had a *right* to familiarity, that the life of celebrities should be visible, open to the public, transparent. This generates powerful pressure on the law of privacy, for example. And, as it happens, presidents—and celebrities in general—have lost a good deal of their privacy rights.[11] Not all of it, of course; perhaps not even most of it. Certainly, cameras never peep into the president's bedroom or record his sessions with the head of the CIA. But much of the president's public life has become an open book, or at least what *appears* to be an open book. The same is true of the queen of England. Indeed, the public *expects* to see her and hear her.

The celebrity trial is, thus, an extension of celebrity culture; for those celebrities on trial (and even for the victims), it is another window into celebrity life. Even before the true celebrity age, headline trials were proto-celebrity events, insofar as they explored the personalities, lives, and actions of the major characters in these legal dramas. A headline trial is no doubt an unwelcome intrusion into the lives of these actors—who wants to be on trial?—but the intrusion occurs nonetheless. In the past, big trials made the defendant, and others, into proto-celebrities; today, big trials make a celebrity victim or defendant even more of a celebrity.

O. J. Simpson is the most famous celebrity defendant of recent years. His trial, from 1994 to 1995, was an incredible media event, beamed into millions of homes on television and indeed watched all over the world. The trial was long and sensational—more than a year elapsed between jury selection and verdict. Everyone associated with this trial became a celebrity; by the end of this long affair, the judge, the lawyers, and even witnesses were famous in ways they perhaps never expected to be.[12] Thus headline trials also *create* celebrities; this has happened in case after case.

One of the most notable celebrity trials was the Los Angeles trials of "Fatty" Arbuckle.[13] Arbuckle was one of the most famous and successful men of Hollywood, a genuine star. The events that led to his trial took place in 1921. Arbuckle had arranged a party in his suite in the St. Francis hotel in San Francisco. Among the guests was a young actress, Virginia Rappe. Exactly what happened that night in Room 1219 of the St. Francis is not clear. The newspapers talked about an orgy, but that is surely an exaggeration. There was drinking, to be sure (it was during the days of Prohibition; but that hardly mattered). Fatty was wearing pajamas and a purple robe. Virginia Rappe wore a jade skirt and blouse.

That night, something happened that somehow damaged Rappe. Perhaps she and Arbuckle were kissing and hugging, perhaps he pressed his body on top of hers. She lost consciousness.

Arbuckle tried to revive her. When she woke up, she was in pain. She died a few days later. One of her friends claimed Arbuckle had raped her; Rappe herself, before she died, apparently said something to the effect that Arbuckle had hurt her. Arbuckle was arrested; the prosecution wanted him tried for murder, but the magistrate, at the preliminary hearing, decided on a charge of manslaughter. This was serious enough. There were three trials in all. The first trial ended in a hung jury—apparently almost all of the jurors wanted to acquit Arbuckle, but at least one holdout, a woman, insisted on his guilt. He would have to be tried again.[14]

The second trial also ended in a hung jury—but of the opposite type. This time ten jurors wanted to convict for manslaughter, while two holdouts insisted the actor was innocent. The scandalous overtones of sex and depravity in Hollywood, drunkenness, so-called orgies, and the like—all vastly exaggerated—made these trials particularly titillating. The third jury took a very different tack from those of the first two. It deliberated all of six minutes, and then acquitted Arbuckle. Indeed, the jury did more than that: It issued a statement exonerating Arbuckle completely, saying, "a great injustice has been done him" and deeming him "entirely innocent and free from all blame." In short, the state had needlessly persecuted Arbuckle; he had suffered through a long and pointless ordeal.[15]

It is not clear whether Arbuckle was quite as innocent as the third jury insisted he was. Yet if "reasonable doubt" means anything, it was right to acquit him. In any event, even though "Fatty" went free, the trials had ruined his career, blackened his reputation beyond redemption, and probably shortened his life. He died in his sleep at the age of forty-six. No doubt millions who read newspapers were convinced that he was guilty, or, if innocent of *that* crime, guilty of some other offense, or at a minimum, guilty of vice and debauchery.

In 1991, William Kennedy Smith, a young medical student, was put on trial for rape, in Palm Beach County, Florida.

Reporters flocked to the trial like moths to a flame. Smith had met a young woman at a bar. They went out together, and then they had sex. She claimed he raped her on the beach. He said the sex was completely consensual. Dozens of rape cases each year take roughly this shape: she claims he used force; he claims she gave her consent. But this case was different; it "exploded on the American consciousness." The defendant was a Kennedy, the nephew of John, Robert, and Teddy Kennedy.[16] Everything about the case made headlines and provoked massive television coverage. Graphic and explicit testimony was lovingly reported to an eager public. What actually happened on the beach, like the mystery of Room 1219 of the St. Francis hotel, will never be known. Here, too, the celebrity defendant was acquitted; basically, it was his word against hers, and the jury must have thought there was reasonable doubt.[17]

Celebrity and tabloid trials often overlap, for obvious reasons. There was a strong element of sexual misconduct in the Smith trial and in the trials of "Fatty" Arbuckle. Celebrity trials may overlap with other categories as well. The attempt to impeach President William Jefferson Clinton was certainly political, but it was also about misconduct in office (perjury), and behind the charge of perjury was a sordid tale of lust and sex in the White House between the president and Monica Lewinsky, an intern. In general, celebrity trials make the biggest splash when they are lurid and sensational, but the sheer power of a celebrity name almost guarantees public hunger for news. The trial of Charles Manson in 1970 was a celebrity trial; Manson was accused of murdering (among others) the well-known actress Sharon Tate. Manson did not commit the crimes himself; rather, he was the guru and leader of a strange, cult-like group that carried out this murder and others.[18] Manson's trial combined celebrity elements with other, more sinister tabloid elements; it was the most sensational trial of its year.

Celebrity trials make headlines for a number of reasons, including one that is fairly mundane. The rich and famous can afford to hire the best, most flamboyant, most newsworthy lawyers. This was certainly true of O. J. Simpson and "Fatty" Arbuckle. In Simpson's case, it was definitely money well spent. The rich and famous can buy other things as well: private investigators, forensic evidence, expert witnesses, and so on. They can stretch out the proceedings, if they wish. All of this helps turn their trials into media events. Some poor wretch, accused, say, of killing another poor wretch in a barroom brawl, can never aspire to this kind of fame and misfortune; and he cannot afford to buy a headline trial.

Four American presidents have been assassinated. In all four cases, the act led to highly sensational trials. John Wilkes Booth was killed before he could go on trial for killing Abraham Lincoln, but his accomplices, or alleged accomplices, were put on trial in 1865 before a military tribunal. The trial lasted 50 days, more than 350 witnesses testified, and at the end, 8 defendants were found guilty and 4 were sentenced to be hanged.[19] Charles Guiteau shot President Garfield, in broad daylight, in the Baltimore and Potomac Station, in Washington, D.C., in 1881. Garfield died of his injuries some weeks later. Guiteau's trial was the perfect example of a trial that made headlines because of the victim's identity. Guiteau readily admitted that he pulled the trigger, which was obvious in any event. The trial turned, then, on his only defense: insanity. Guiteau's behavior was certainly bizarre enough, and his behavior turned the trial into a weird kind of circus.[20] It was also a battle between warring schools of psychiatry. To anyone today who looks back on the proceedings, it seems obvious that Guiteau was clinically, if not legally, insane. A medical degree is not needed for this diagnosis.[21] The jury felt otherwise. Guiteau, after all, had killed the American president. He was convicted, sentenced to death, and hanged in 1882. Leon Czolgosz, the anarchist who killed President McKinley, was also tried and executed in rapid order in 1901; he had refused to cooperate with his defense lawyers and went to his death in the electric chair at Auburn, New York, with, apparently, no regrets.[22]

Lee Harvey Oswald was the most recent presidential assassin; he shot President John F. Kennedy in 1963, as the president was visiting Dallas, Texas. Oswald was quickly captured, but he never went on trial; Jack Ruby shot him to death while he was in custody. Ruby's trial, which followed, was in a sense a celebrity trial at one remove.[23] Unsuccessful attempts to kill presidents have also led to significant trials. Giuseppe Zangara tried to kill President Franklin Roosevelt; he was unsuccessful, but the shots he fired wounded Mayor Anton Cermak of Chicago, who died of his wounds. Zangara went on trial and was sentenced to death in March 1933.[24] The trial of John W. Hinckley, Jr., in 1982, was also a sensation; Hinckley shot and wounded President Ronald Reagan, as the president was leaving the Hilton Hotel in Washington, D.C. A jury found Hinckley not guilty by reason of insanity—a most unpopular result, as we have seen.[25]

One paradox of celebrity trials is illustrated most graphically by the Simpson and Arbuckle cases. Before the development of celebrity society, "celebrity trials" (if we can call them that) were trials of famous men and women or trials about famous victims. But they were not "true" celebrity trials, because we had not yet become a celebrity society; they were at most, proto-celebrity events, as we said. Today, there are true celebrity trials—Simpson and Arbuckle were huge celebrities—but because of television and the mass media, in headline trials *everybody* becomes a celebrity. By the end of the Simpson trial, Judge Ito was better known, and more familiar, than any of the nine Supreme Court justices, and poor Virginia Rappe, who lost her life in San Francisco, was as famous in death as Arbuckle was in life. Hence, in contemporary society, all the characters in a headline trial are celebrities, and the line between a celebrity trial and other headline trials blurs to the point of irrelevance.

8

Mystery and Identity

Claus von Bulow was a handsome and well-connected man with ties to European nobility. In 1966, he married a rich American heiress, Margaret Crawford, whose nickname was Sunny. She had been married before, to an Austrian prince; she had two children from this marriage. She and von Bulow had a daughter, Cosima. The von Bulow marriage was not a happy one, and Sunny apparently had a history of drug abuse. In 1980 Sunny went into a coma from which she never emerged. Claus' two stepchildren became convinced that this was no accident; they believed that Claus, their stepfather, was responsible. They claimed he had injected Sunny with insulin in an attempt to get rid of her. One of Sunny's faithful maids agreed. The stepchildren launched an investigation. They gathered what seemed to be damning evidence. Had Claus really injected his wife with insulin? A sensational trial followed. Sunny was still alive at the time of the trial, but "curled in the fetal position . . . a tube implanted in her throat and a feeding tube in her mouth."[1] Tons of newsprint, and enormous amounts of television time, were devoted to this case. Medical testimony was crucial. The jury deliberated for six days and then found von Bulow guilty as charged.

But was Claus really responsible for his wife's condition? He launched an appeal, which Professor Alan Dershowitz of the Harvard Law School handled. The conviction was reversed on evidentiary grounds. A second trial took place. This was even more of a medical battle than the first trial. The defense argued that Sunny had brought on her coma herself, that she had an alcohol problem, and that the drugs she swallowed led to her condition. They deployed a whole corps of medical experts. This jury found Claus innocent, and he went free. Sunny remained in a coma for twenty-eight years before she died.

Dershowitz wrote a notable book about the case.[2] The book hints that Claus might have been, in fact, innocent, as the second jury had decided. The crucial medical evidence is disputed by the experts. An air of mystery hangs over the case. Even Dershowitz admits that, as in "so many other legal mysteries, the law will never resolve all of the doubts"; many will "still wonder 'Who done it?' or whether anything criminal was done at all."[3]

This case had strong elements of a tabloid trial. All the principal figures were members of high society, with connections to European aristocracy. The two stepchildren had noble titles. Claus was not exactly a model husband. He had a mistress and had behaved quite callously toward Sunny. Sunny herself was a weak, addictive personality; many details of the case, and of the lives of the principal characters, were tawdry in the extreme. All of this, together with the doubts, the mystery, and the tantalizing questions, only added to its notoriety. Dershowitz's book was made into a movie, *Reversal of Fortune*, in 1990. Jeremy Irons, who played von Bulow, won an Academy Award.

The von Bulow trial is in a category I call a *whodunit*, to use a slang term. These trials gain their special tingle of excitement from the air of mystery and doubt that surrounds them. Mystery and doubt are, of course, quite common in trials. The two sides, after all, present different stories, paint different pictures, flash different images on the screen. But in some trials, the mystery is darker and deeper, the doubts more profound. These doubts—about what actually happened, about who did what, and why—may be a major factor in making the trial sensational and putting it on the front page of the papers. These trials are the antithesis of such trials as Guiteau's or Hinckley's or Dan Sickles'. These killers did what they did in plain view.

Erle Stanley Gardner, beginning in the 1930s, wrote about eighty mystery novels. They featured a (fictional) criminal lawyer, Perry Mason. He is hired in these novels to represent a man or woman put on trial for murder. Mason's clients, unlike clients in real life, are always innocent, but they always *seem* guilty, to the police and the prosecutor at any rate. The climax is usually a dramatic courtroom scene where Mason destroys the prosecution's case. Through masterful deduction, cross-examination, or new evidence, he unmasks the real killer and saves his client's neck.

The real world, of course, is quite different—and, at times, more tantalizing. In some of the most famous American trials, the uncertainty still hangs in the air, and the intriguing question of who did it may linger for centuries. This was true of the Lizzie Borden trial, in the 1890s, which remains one of the most famous murder trials in American history. Did Lizzie Borden murder her father and stepmother? The case attracted scores of reporters and generated miles of newsprint. In the end, Lizzie went free. But what twelve men thought is not necessarily what other people, then and later, thought. A whole library of books deals with this celebrated case. Many of them try to present some new, ingenious, but logical "solution" to the mystery.[4] We will say more about the Lizzie Borden case, and what it meant, in the next chapter.

Elements of mystery and uncertainty dominated the notorious case of Dr. Sam Sheppard. Dr. Sheppard, an osteopath, was accused in 1954 of murdering his pregnant wife, Marilyn. The Sheppards lived in the Cleveland area; they were well-to-do, typical suburbanites. Dr. Sheppard hardly fit the image of a killer.

He insisted all along that he was innocent. A bushy-haired intruder had broken into his home, he said; this stranger had killed Sheppard's wife. Sheppard claimed he fought with the man and suffered injury himself. Sheppard had a strong argument: he *was* in fact injured, and there was no blood on him, which should have been the case, if he had killed his wife. But somehow many people—and the police—became convinced that Sheppard was guilty. The Cleveland newspapers screamed for prosecution. The *Cleveland Press* ran this headline: "Why Isn't Sam Sheppard in Jail?"[5] Sheppard was formally charged with murder. The trial that followed was raucous and sensational. The prosecution hammered away at Sheppard's story; they sneered at "the phantom burglar, the phantom killer" and insisted that Sheppard had killed his wife and then jumped off a platform, to injure himself and deflect suspicion onto somebody else. The jury found Sheppard guilty of second-degree murder, and he was sentenced to life in prison.[6]

Ten years later, the United States Supreme Court ordered a new trial. Eight justices felt that the trial had been grossly unfair. Local publicity had been so poisonous, and the trial so tainted with hysteria, that Dr. Sheppard had been deprived of his constitutional rights. In the Court's opinion, "bedlam" had "reigned at the courthouse," a "carnival atmosphere" had pervaded the trial, fatally poisoning the results.[7] In the new trial, a jury of seven men and five women deliberated for twelve hours and then announced their verdict: not guilty.[8] It seems quite likely that Dr. Sheppard was telling the truth all along: that he was innocent of the crime and that the story of a mysterious intruder was correct. An element of mystery still hangs over the case, but on balance, the case for innocence seems stronger than the case for guilt.[9]

In 1902, Albert T. Patrick, an attorney, went on trial, accused of murdering William Marsh Rice, a very wealthy man (the founder of Rice University), and Patrick's client.[10] Rice died alone in his apartment in 1900. Charles Jones, Rice's valet, had almost certainly killed him with chloroform. The prosecution argued, however, that Patrick had masterminded the plot to kill Rice. Patrick was tried, found guilty, and sentenced to death. Patrick was certainly up to no good. He almost surely forged Rice's (alleged) last will, which unaccountably left a fortune to Patrick, but whether he planned the murder is not so clear. Ultimately, the sentence was commuted to life imprisonment, and in 1912, the governor of New York pardoned Patrick. "There has always been," the governor said, "an air of mystery in this important case."[11]

In my own town, Stanford, California, the case of David Lamson provided a notable local *whodunit*.[12] Lamson, who lived on the Stanford campus and worked for Stanford University Press, was accused of murdering his wife in 1933. One summer morning, Mrs. Lamson was found dead in her bathroom with a wound on the back of her neck; there was blood splattered everywhere around the room. The police jumped to the conclusion that Lamson had deliberately killed his wife. Lamson insisted he was innocent. He blamed his wife's death on some freakish accident in the bathroom. Lamson had no obvious motive for killing his wife: the couple seemed to be happily married, and Lamson had nothing much to gain financially. The case was front-page news all through the summer of 1933. Newspapers "hired motorcycle couriers to speed the copy and photos back from the courthouse and police headquarters." At the trial, Lamson was convicted and sentenced to death, but his conviction was reversed on appeal. The California Supreme Court ordered a new trial, calling the evidence "mere suspicion," too weak to justify the verdict of guilty.[13] A second trial resulted in a hung jury. A third trial was "aborted due to jury list irregularities." The fourth trial resulted in another hung jury, and the prosecution basically gave up at this point. Lamson went free. To this day, the case remains a mystery: did he or did he not kill his wife?

Four trials and this much jury vacillation are rare. Trials normally end in a blunt and definitive way: guilty or not guilty.

Often, trials lay doubts to rest (for the public, at least). But this is not always true. O. J. Simpson is an outstanding example; millions of people—especially whites—are convinced that he was guilty, never mind what the jury decided. There are those who insist that Bruno Hauptman did not kidnap and kill the Lindbergh baby; Hauptman, they feel, was framed.[14] There are some who think that William Heirens, the "lipstick killer," was also framed. Sometimes these doubts arise during the trial; sometimes they come later, even much later. Sometimes these doubts can never be removed. Scholars are still arguing, as we have noted, over whether Sacco and Vanzetti were actually guilty.

Doubt is, like everything else, a social phenomenon. What we feel sure about and what we doubt are social facts, and they vary across time and place and from individual to individual. Conservatives absolutely *knew* that Sacco and Vanzetti were guilty; liberals were just as sure that they were innocent. People in the middle, perhaps, were just puzzled. In some political cases, those who mistrust the government are more likely to imagine some kind of frame-up than are government loyalists. Trials, moreover, unfold inside a tangled web of rules. Trials have two sides, two versions, which only adds to the distortion and uncertainty. It is no surprise, then, that trials often leave us feeling unsure of what actually happened.

Yet, if we probe a bit deeper, we can ascribe many of these doubts to one specific cause: the mystery of personal identity. The decay of traditional society and the rise of the urban, industrial order brought about a situation that made *identity* more problematic than it had been in other periods of human history. The rise of the mass media heightened this problem. This fundamental uncertainty helped produce the *whodunit* type of headline trial. In the next chapter, we will deal in greater detail with the identity crisis, how it impacted society, and how it helped create specific types of big trial.

9

The Worm in the Bud

In the morning of August 4, 1892, in an atmosphere of stifling heat in Fall River, Massachusetts, a brutal and vicious crime was committed.[1] Andrew Borden, a well-to-do man and leading citizen of the town, and his second wife, Abby Borden, were savagely murdered. Abby died first, struck down in an upstairs bedroom with nineteen blows of an axe, around 9:30 in the morning. Andrew, who had been out, came home at 10:45 a.m., went upstairs to his bedroom, and met a similar fate.

Andrew had two daughters, Lizzie and Emma, from his first marriage. Both were in their thirties; neither was married. Emma was away at the time of the murders. The investigation cast suspicion on Lizzie; she was arrested, indicted by a grand jury, and put on trial for the murders. Her trial attracted hordes of reporters from all over the country. Probably, they would have paid less attention to an equally brutal crime if the victims had been nobodies, killed in the slums of some big city. But the Bordens were pillars of society, leading members of the community. And the defendant was a churchgoing spinster, the very picture of bourgeois respectability, and secretary-treasurer of the local Christian Endeavor Society. In her photographs, she looks out at us, primly, neatly, and conventionally dressed. How could such a woman have committed so terrible a crime?

How indeed. Yet there was evidence that pointed the finger of guilt at Lizzie Borden. She was one of only two people in the house at the time of the crime. The other was Bridget, an Irish maid. Lizzie was known to resent her stepmother, her father was stingy, and the house might have felt stifling, narrow, imprisoning. Her behavior after the murders—burning one of her dresses, for example, despite the oppressive heat—and other bits of circumstantial evidence built up something of a case against her. She never took the stand, and the defense attacked weaknesses in the prosecution's case. But above all, the defense insisted that a woman like Lizzie—"a daughter . . . associating with the best people and devoted to the service of God and man"—could not be a murderess. To feel otherwise "would be a condition of things so contrary to all that our human life has taught us that our hearts and feelings revolt at the conception."[2] The prosecution suggested mental instability. The jury, at the end of the trial, brought in its verdict: not guilty.

The minds of the jurors are inscrutable, but they must have taken the defense arguments to heart. The jury found it impossible—unthinkable—that a woman of her type and class could have committed this fiendish crime. No, a Lizzie Borden would never bash in her father's head with an axe. To find her guilty would have been, in a sense, to indict everything she stood for in bourgeois society. Not literally, of course, and yet, to a degree, bourgeois society *was* on trial. Putting Lizzie Borden in the dock, accusing her of two savage crimes, was like turning over a big, smooth stone and watching the vermin crawl out. And it is this basic incongruity—between what Lizzie Borden seemed to be on the surface, a prim and devout spinster, and the image of Lizzie Borden the axe-murderess—that made the case so notorious in its day and accounts, perhaps, for its endless fascination.

This is Cara Robertson's point in her perceptive article about the case: To convict Lizzie Borden was to convict the world in which she lived. A guilty verdict would call into question the most basic assumptions of American society in the late Victorian period. Convicting Lizzie would cast doubt on "the entire basis for social order and hierarchy." This "subversion" was "buried at the heart of the case." To the jury—and no doubt to others—it seemed better, then, "to let one woman get away with murder than to suggest that a dutiful middle-class daughter like Miss Lizzie might be capable of it."[3] The trial is famous, then, precisely because it asked a basic question about bourgeois society in the late nineteenth century—and asked it by asking who Lizzie Borden really was, what really made her tick.

The Borden trial is a prime example of a group of trials to which I apply the phrase "the worm in the bud."[4] These trials catch the public fancy because they expose, or threaten to expose, the sleazy underside of prominent or respectable society. They call into question bourgeois reality or threaten to reveal secrets that might undermine important institutions.

The Lizzie Borden case is the archetype: A mask of respectability protected the daily life of the Bordens, pillars of society. But behind the mask (if indeed Lizzie was guilty) there was a hidden pathology, an inner dry rot, that (arguably) had corroded those pillars. Earlier in the century, in 1832, a young woman named Sarah Cornell was found hanging from the rafters in a haystack, near Fall River, Massachusetts. Cornell was pregnant; the father of her child was a Methodist minister named Ephraim K. Avery. Avery was tried in Rhode Island. The defense tried to smear Cornell's character: How could a man of the cloth, a man of unsullied reputation, be guilty of such a crime? The jury, like the Borden jury, acquitted him.[5] In the trial of Lucretia Chapman, also in 1832, who was accused of poisoning her husband (with arsenic), the defense painted Chapman—a woman from a respectable family, a churchgoer—as "a helpless and largely passive, female victim."[6] Arsenic also figured in a later case, in New Haven, Connecticut. Young Mary Stannard died of arsenic poisoning. The finger of blame pointed toward her lover, a married minister, Herbert Hayden (who was almost certainly guilty). He, too, was acquitted. The reason, most likely, was that "no one wanted to believe that a family man, a preacher of God's holy word, could have done what he was accused of doing."[7]

These were instances where the jury refused to believe that the bud was infested with worms. Other cases that exposed hidden worlds ended differently. The Thaw-White case was sensational, at least in part, because it seemed to reveal a naked reality behind the lifestyles of the rich and famous—the seamy habits and sex lives of members of Broadway and high society. It was a "rare glimpse at the private life" of the elites; it "swept aside the curtain of privacy that had previously kept hidden from view what it meant to lead a life of wealth and privilege in the upper crust of New York society."[8] The Fatty Arbuckle case did the same for Hollywood in the 1920s.

The notion of the "worm in the bud" was a prominent feature of the Loeb-Leopold case, another (of many) that has been called the "crime of the century" (the century in question was of course the twentieth). Two young, rich, and intelligent men, brilliant students from good families, Nathan Leopold and Richard Loeb, murdered a fourteen-year-old boy, Bobby Franks, in 1924, apparently just for the thrill of it and to show that they could commit the perfect crime. Their crime turned out to be far from perfect. Loeb and Leopold were caught fairly soon; Leopold had dropped a pair of eyeglasses near the scene of the crime, and they were easily traced to him. The two men quickly confessed to the crime.[9] What followed, then, was not strictly speaking a trial at all; it made headlines, but guilt or innocence was not the issue. The issue was the punishment: Would they die for their crime? The Loeb and Leopold families hired Clarence Darrow, perhaps the most famous lawyer in the country. They paid him an enormous fee hoping that he would save Loeb and Leopold from execution. In the event, the judge did spare their lives; they were sentenced to life terms in prison. Many people saw something sinister and disturbing in this whole affair: a collapse of traditional values, a kind of moral decay that affected rich, spoiled kids.

This perhaps was true of the so-called preppy murder: the murder of Jennifer Levin, strangled in Central Park, New York City, by Robert E. Chambers, Jr., in 1986. Chambers hardly fit the preppy image, but the media soon pinned this label on the case. The crime did have troubling overtones. It gave off an aura of dissolute, hedonistic, sex-mad youth—young people with "too much money to spend, too much time to fill and too little guidance by parents."[10] Chambers and Levin had been having sex just before she died. He claimed she was "pushy" and had "squeezed" his testicles. There were tabloid elements in the case, but generally, it was described as a crime that grew out of the "fast-paced world of sex and underage drinking."[11]

A subcategory of the worm-in-the-bud trial might be called *who would have thought?* Jack the Ripper and most serial killers seem like monsters: deranged, abnormal, and not quite human, as if they had come from another planet. A different kind of shock results when the horror hits home, as it were, when it happens in places that are supposed to be innocuous, and the monster is a neighbor or a friend, someone who seemed harmless or even beneficial. Lizzie Borden fits this mold. And who, for example, would have imagined that Harvey A. Crippen, a mild-mannered, bespectacled English doctor, could have murdered his wife and stashed her body in his cellar?[12] Or, more recently, who would have imagined that Scott Peterson, a fertilizer salesman with no criminal record, could have murdered his pregnant wife in 2002, in Modesto, California? Or that the people who ran a day-care center in Los Angeles could have grossly abused the children in their care and indulged in all sorts of satanic practices? This was the (wild and fantastic) claim in the infamous McMartin case in Los Angeles, on which more below.

The Parkman-Webster case of 1850 produced one of the most famous trials of the nineteenth century. The defendant was John Webster, a professor in the Harvard Medical School. Who would have thought that a man of his type could have killed Dr. George Parkman, chopped up his body, and secreted the pieces in the basement of the school? Medical school professors are not exactly celebrities, but they are prominent people in their community. To accuse one professor of murdering another, at Harvard no less, is a shocking event. Parkman, moreover, was a member of an old, rich, and very prominent Boston family. A good deal of circumstantial evidence pointed the finger of guilt in Webster's direction. Webster was heavily in debt to Parkman; and Parkman wanted his money. Webster thus had an obvious motive for killing his colleague. Judge Lemuel Shaw, the most famous Massachusetts justice of the day (and father-in-law of Herman Melville), presided over Webster's long and memorable trial. Parts of a body—almost surely Parkman's—turned up in the basement of the medical school. The jury found Webster guilty. Appeals and calls for clemency were unsuccessful, and Webster went to the gallows. He was, in all likelihood, guilty of killing Dr. Parkman, but there are still open questions about the how and the why.[13]

In these cases, it is the shock of discovery, the unveiling of a dreadful secret—that a neighbor, perhaps, or a friend, or a relative, has been committing some hideous crime. This shock lies at the heart of many tabloid crimes: Meiwes, the cannibal; or Dahmer, the meek and unobtrusive man in Milwaukee, who had been systematically killing and dismembering young men. When the shock is collective when it goes beyond particular individuals, we call it "moral panic." The term, as applied here, refers to a kind of mass hysteria, an irrational fear that grips the community and spreads like an infectious disease. The (American) granddaddy of all moral panics was the one that took hold of Salem in the seventeenth century and led to the famous witch trials. These trials, of course, took place long before the age of headlines, but in the small, ingrown New England communities, these trials created an enormous stir. They fed on popular beliefs about witches, about the power of Satan and his plots to entice the godly into choosing a life of wickedness and sin.[14] Some of the "witches" did confess and were put to death; and for a time, the accusations piled up. More and more people were labeled as instruments of supernatural evil. The community was engulfed with fear and panic.

Few today believe in witches—at least not literally. These colonial trials, however, gave us the phrase "witch hunt." The phrase is bandied about during episodes of moral panic, for example, the political trials and general atmosphere during the McCarthy period in the 1950s. A grim, cold fear had seized much of the public, fear of a huge, secret Communist underground, boring from within. This conspiracy was undermining and perverting American institutions, which had become riddled with traitors and spies. "Spies," by the very nature of their business, hide themselves from the rest of us. They pretend to be loyal citizens. They wrap themselves in a cloak of lies; this makes them all the more dangerous and difficult to detect.

In the classic movie *Invasion of the Body-Snatchers* (1956), aliens from outer space come to earth and take over the bodies of ordinary people. The movie is set in what looks like a plain, average town in America. The body-snatchers plan to dominate our planet. They are not the usual green, squiggly monsters of science fiction; whatever their original form, they insert themselves into and inhabit the bodies of ordinary citizens. As a result, they look exactly like us, like our friends and neighbors, or what seem to be our friends and neighbors. After the "invasion," it is impossible to tell who is human and who is not. It would be hard to imagine a more terrifying situation. A man goes to sleep, and when he wakes up, his wife is no longer his wife; she has become a strange alien creature. But she still looks exactly like his wife; it is his wife's face, her body, her voice. The movie can be interpreted as a metaphor for the threat of Communist subversion. Subversives look like ordinary people, but in fact they are body-snatchers—an alien force, whose goal is the destruction of the American way of life.[15]

In any event, the espionage trials of the Cold War did evoke a kind of identity crisis. They fed on the same paranoia that the movie so brilliantly evoked. There was, of course, a backlash against the national Red Scare, and in the end, McCarthy fell from power. The spy trials of the 1950s were also deeply political, in ways that went beyond the Cold War duel between the superpowers. They tended to pit Right against Left. Progressives flocked to the defense of Alger Hiss, who, they insisted, was no spy but the victim of a witch hunt. The American right wing, on the other hand, tried to portray the Left as unpatriotic, even un-American. Some of the more cynical cold warriors probably saw a chance to discredit the whole New Deal and drive progressives out of power.

The infamous McMartin day-care trial in southern California, in the 1980s, came from, or stimulated, a moral panic that was probably as far from cold reality as the Salem witch trials.[16] The McMartin trial was the longest and most expensive in American history. It began when Judy Johnson, a mother, accused workers in her child's day-care center of sexually abusing children. Johnson was a paranoid schizophrenic and a chronic alcoholic who died of liver disease a few years later; no one should have taken her accusations seriously. But people did. The accusations caught on and snowballed. Dozens of parents came to believe wild and incredible stories about what went on at the day-care center—not just sexual abuse but horrendous and devilish rituals. A lot of the charges were based on extremely dubious evidence—tales told by small children, after coaxing and prompting by psychologists, who used extremely shaky tactics. In hindsight, the charges seem utterly absurd. But the trial went on and on. Moreover, the moral panic spawned satellite trials in many other cities, as if there was an epidemic of satanic day-care centers all over the United States. In the end, the defendants in the McMartin case were acquitted. Not all of the defendants in the satellite trials were so fortunate.

The Salem episode strikes us today as a kind of mass delusion. The Cold War trials probably deserve the label "witch hunt" that many people pinned on them; McCarthy's motives, and the motives of other leaders of the Red Scare, were, as we said, politically suspect.[17] Reckless charges were leveled against innocent people. But, of course, there *was* a Soviet Union, and it did have actual spies, doing actual espionage. Moral panics do not come from nowhere; in each case, the social context helps explain what touched off the particular panic. There is, for example, a big literature that tries to explain what ignited the Salem witch trials.[18] Similarly, there are ways to explain the panic over Reds during the Cold War.

But what lay behind the McMartin trial and its moral panic? Our times place severe strain on family life; one may even speak about a crisis. Millions of women, of all social classes, now work outside the home. They have to make arrangements for child care. Day care is one solution, but it leaves many parents feeling anxious and guilty—they have, after all, turned their children over to the care of strangers. The McMartin allegations tapped into our most profound fears as parents, our most savage nightmares; guilt hovered in the atmosphere, like a bad smell, poisoning the air in the trials.

Similar anxieties about child rearing were in the background of the "Boston nanny" case, probably the most sensational trial of 1997. The defendant was Louise Woodward, a nineteen-year-old au pair. She was accused of causing the death of an eight-month-old baby, Matthew Eappen. The prosecution claimed that Woodward shook the baby violently and that this shaking caused his death.[19] The trial was televised. As it proceeded, it turned into a battle of medical experts. The trial commanded the biggest television audience since the O. J. Simpson trial. According to one expert, it touched on a "deep sense of unease about the welfare of American children, now that most mothers work outside the home."[20] Here, too, parents had turned their child over to a stranger, a young woman from abroad. How much can we trust these nannies, governesses, au pairs, and others? Are the children really safe? A British company produced a documentary, "Nannies from Hell," that was widely distributed and tapped into this anxiety.[21] In 2012, a nanny on the Upper West Side of New York City, where "nannies are often an integral part of children's lives, pushing strollers or walking their charges by the dozens," killed two children in her care, fatally stabbing them in a bathtub. This could only increase the fears and anxieties of parents who depended on these women.[22]

10

The Reason Why

In the preceding chapters, I have given reasons why each type of trial tended to make headlines, and I have tried to put them into social context. All headline trials are, in some sense, didactic theater. But their messages differ from period to period, and from category to category.

Political trials, in all senses of the word, provide us with many of our biggest trials. But there are many others, some of them among the most sensational, that fall into a category that Fox and Van Sickel call "tabloid justice."[1] Some of these cases were international sensations (for example, the Sacco and Vanzetti trial and the O. J. Simpson trial); most were at least national or regional sensations. Others were of interest mostly to a particular city or area. In Emporia, Kansas, in 1885, Minnie Walkup went on trial for poisoning her husband. She was sixteen years old and beautiful; she had been married for only a month to the mayor of Emporia, James Walkup, who was more than old enough to be her father (he was forty-nine). The trial was a sensation in Emporia and the surrounding region. The courtroom was jammed with spectators. Seven hundred people showed up for the first day of the trial. By early afternoon, the courtroom had grown so crowded that the sheriff had to close the courthouse doors.[2]

Whether locally, nationally, or internationally famous, these trials launch a thousand conversations and produce acres of film, print, and comment. They are the tabloid trials, the celebrity trials, the whodunit trials, the worm-in-the-bud trials. We have discussed, in part, why they cast such a spell. Each category has some meaning, some value for the study of social history. Each tells us something about society. In this chapter we want to go a bit further.

To begin with, many cases attracted attention because they were part of a larger American drama or touched on a sensitive policy issue. Race relations were at the heart of the Massie-Fortescue trials in Hawaii, an American territory with a mixed-race population. The trials of O. J. Simpson and of George Zimmerman also featured race in a crucial role. Like race, ethnicity features in a number of trials, for example, the so-called Chicago trunk murder case, in the 1880s. Three Sicilians were convicted of murdering Filippo Caruso; they shoved his body into a trunk and sent it on to Pittsburgh. In this case, the victim and the defendants were from Italy, and the prosecution stirred the boiling pot of popular prejudice against Italian immigrants.[3] Defendants in the famous "Sleepy Lagoon" murder case, in Los Angeles, in the 1940s, were Mexican-Americans; that trial turned into a kind of public drama about relations between Anglos and Mexicans in that city.[4] Gender and sexuality played a significant part in the notoriety of the Dan White case; White had murdered Harvey Milk, a hero and role model for the gay community.

Some of these cases do more than simply reflect or dramatize a social problem. They may have an impact on the problem as well. The Scottsboro case was something of a turning point. For decades, nothing had stood in the way of Southern injustice. But the Scottsboro defendants were neither hanged nor lynched; indeed, in the end they won their freedom. Their case in the Supreme Court became an important precedent.[5] And Scottsboro was a sign that American race relations were slowly changing. Also, in the twentieth century, the national media began to shine a brighter light on Southern practices, and what the rest of the country saw was not to its liking. In the civil rights era of the 1950s and 1960s, the northern media played an even more critical role.

The O. J. Simpson affair began as a simple case of murder but morphed into a trial about race; at any rate, this is how many people saw it. Significantly, this may have been how the jury saw it. The defendant's lawyers injected race into the case, and this turned out to be a winning strategy. Whites, generally speaking, were convinced that Simpson was guilty. African Americans were more skeptical. The local black newspaper in Los Angeles consistently slanted the news in Simpson's favor and heaped praise on Johnnie L. Cochran, Jr., Simpson's lead lawyer.[6] But race in the Simpson case and race in the Scottsboro case were very different beasts. In the Scottsboro case, the judge, the court personnel, and all the jurors were white; the defendants were poor Southern blacks. The Simpson jury was racially mixed. And Simpson was rich and famous. He was black; his ex-wife and the second victim were white. That fact alone would have guaranteed conviction, or a lynch mob, in the South before the civil rights era.

In many cases the trial or the crime somehow touches a raw nerve in American society. Race relations is a prime example, but big trials also touch on issues of family, marriage, sex, and reproduction, the problems of the young, and the problems of an aging society. Behind the McMartin case and the trial of the Boston nanny, as we have pointed out, were raw, naked fears and anxieties about family life in a period in which there are millions of working mothers. In 2011, the trial of Casey Anthony mesmerized the country. Anthony was accused of killing her daughter, Caylee, who was two years old. She had certainly buried the body, which was suspicious enough, but had she actually killed her child? The defense insisted Caylee had drowned.

The evidence for murder was hardly overwhelming. The jury no doubt took seriously the concept of reasonable doubt; they acquitted Casey Anthony of murder and convicted her only for telling lies to the police (which she most certainly had done). Nancy Grace (once a prosecutor in Georgia, then a co-host on Court TV) gave the trial vast coverage and expressed outrage at the verdict. This made for good television, if nothing else.[7] Most people outside the courtroom felt Casey Anthony was guilty of murder.[8]

The Anthony case had clearly struck a nerve: How could a mother kill her own child? In fact, in the nineteenth century, infanticide was not an unknown crime. Unmarried women, facing scandal and perhaps economic disaster, sometimes hid their pregnancy and killed the baby as soon as it was born.[9] But this was 2011; unwed motherhood was no longer so shameful. And Caylee Anthony was two years old. The prosecutors had a different, and damning, argument: Casey was lazy, she hated the burden of a child; she wanted to be free, to have fun, to enjoy life. Small children are hard work. Parents have to cope with soiled diapers and sleepless nights; children rob their parents of the freedom to come and go as they please. They are also, of course, objects of intense love and devotion. The result, at times, is a deep ambivalence. It is human to resent children sometimes, and human, too, for this resentment to evoke shame and guilt. The trial of Casey Anthony brought these ambivalences to the surface. It evoked fears about a loss of responsibility, about a rotting, hedonistic society and all the family pathologies that feed these fears.

Still other cases reflect anxieties about flaming youth and the alleged decay of morality and responsibility among the young. These anxieties were a factor in the "preppy" murder case; and in the public reaction to the Loeb-Leopold case. The trial of the Menendez brothers very much fit this pattern. Lyle and Erik Menendez were two rich, young brothers who murdered their parents in 1989. After the murders, they watched a movie, *License to Kill.* In the next six months, they lived high on the hog, going on shopping sprees, traveling, and spending vast amounts of their parents' money. Their trial was televised. To most onlookers, and to the jury, they seemed like the ultimate in rotten, spoiled, hedonistic, selfish youth, the embodiment of thoughtless evil.[10]

Another form of family anxiety came to the surface in the trial of Anthony Marshall. Brooke Astor, Marshall's mother, was a very rich woman. She was widely admired in New York society, a patron of the arts, well known for her philanthropy. She lived to a ripe old age—too ripe perhaps. Before she died, at the age of 105, she was frail, sick, and confused, a pale shadow of her former self. Anthony Marshall's son—Brooke Astor's grandson—accused his father (himself an old man) of mistreating Brooke Astor, cheating her and her estate, and abusing her when she was old and demented. The trial sparked a tabloid war; New York City newspapers vied with each other for the best coverage and "assigned reporters, columnists, editorial cartoonists, and courtroom sketch artists to record the antics."[11] At the end of the trial, Anthony Marshall was convicted of grand larceny; he faced the prospect, at eighty-nine, of ending his years in prison. In the end, though, after just eight weeks in prison, he was "so sick and frail" with Parkinson's disease and congestive heart failure that he was granted medical parole in August 2013.[12]

The case was hotly contested, and the facts were in total dispute. Brooke Astor was a famous woman, which is part of the reason why the case created such a stir. But underlying the case was an important social issue. In contemporary society, some people seem to live far too long. Elder abuse is in the news. Elderly people themselves dread dependence, especially the dependence that comes with dementia. How the old, sick, and feeble are treated was at the heart of the Astor case and of countless small dramas in American homes. The case, then, touched on a grave family issue, one that evokes anxiety in the elderly and in their families. The long, sensational trial pointed to a sad modern truth: not even wealth and fame can guarantee protection from the ravages of time, or from the greed, incompetence, or malice of one's next of kin.

The social factors mentioned in this chapter help explain what make headline trials so fascinating. But beyond these is another factor that weighs in on perhaps almost all of them. This is the question of identity: Who are we, really? Or, to be more exact: These men or women, on trial in the glaring light of publicity, who are they, really? We turn next to this question.

II

Who Are We?

Identity and the Headline Trial

Our fascination with mysteries, great murder trials, and the like is so widespread and seems so natural that we rarely stop to ask the fundamental question: What is the source of our fascination? Yet big nonpolitical trials, celebrity trials, tabloid trials, soap-opera trials, and the like do not go back very far in human history. You can rummage around in ancient China or medieval France and perhaps find something analogous, but as a social phenomenon, these trials are no more than two hundred years old. They are, in many ways, a creature of the mass media; but the media, for all their power, do not make social phenomena out of whole cloth. These trials come in many shapes and sizes; they touch on many issues. But there is, in a way, a common theme. They are all about *identity*, usually the identity of the defendant, but sometimes of the victim as well.

Identity has become problematic, questionable, even mysterious, only recently, in our modern world. This is especially so in big trials. Open and shut cases rarely yield dramatic trials.[1] On the contrary, dramatic trials are those that contain some mystery: Did he or she actually commit the crime? And if so, then how and why? These questions became salient in the last two centuries or so, a period of enormous social change, a period that produced the mystery novel, the confidence man, and the blackmailer. This is an age in which simulated identity became, for the first time, a social problem. It is out of this soil that the modern headline trial would grow.

In the first half of the nineteenth century, social relationships in Europe, North America, and elsewhere became much more fluid than in the past. This was a period of high mobility in every sense: geographical, but also social. Old traditions and customs tottered on their thrones. It was possible to climb up and down the social ladder. It was possible to go from rags to riches, and back to rags. There were no fixed stations in society, no hereditary nobility. Even in England, the class structure showed signs of change. A new middle class was emerging. Factories were replacing farms.

The nineteenth century was also a period of restlessness; it was an age of movement, of immigration and emigration. The United States was, most obviously, a society of immigrants. It was also a society of rolling stones. Millions of people flooded in, mostly from Europe. But millions of native citizens were also on the move, too. There was a relentless drive to settle the West—to farm on the frontier or pan for gold in California. The old countries of Europe were also, in an important sense, immigration countries. Huge numbers left for the United States (and Australia, Canada, and Argentina), but there was also massive internal migration. People left their villages and farms and poured into the slums and the back alleys of big cities.

In a traditional village, everybody knows everybody else. In the big city—London or Paris or New York—people are surrounded by strangers, on the streets, in the teeming slums, in the business districts, and even in middle-class neighborhoods. A person can get lost in the maze and anonymity of city life. And the cities expanded enormously in the nineteenth century. Big cities became bigger. Small towns turned into small cities. In America, waves of people flowed west, creating whole towns out of nothing. In these new towns, everyone was a migrant or a newcomer. Even in older towns, new people were constantly coming and going. The towns grew dense with strangers, with secrets and secret lives, people with hidden pasts, many with worms in the bud. From the nineteenth century on, sheer *identity* became an issue, something not to be taken for granted, something obscure, something more difficult to parse and to read.

Take, for example, the phenomenon of "passing." In the American racial code, even a small amount of African ancestry made a person legally and socially black. White society, especially in the South, imposed the same harsh rules on someone who was one-eighth black as it imposed on a full-blooded African American. Indeed, in the twentieth century, some states adopted the so-called one-drop rule. This meant that a person with *any* African ancestry, no matter how remote, was a "Negro." This was a distinctly American peculiarity; other countries did not follow such a rule.[2]

During slavery, white slave owners had total power over slaves—including sexual power. Men on plantations often used that power. As a result—after generations of sex across racial lines—thousands of American "blacks" could pass for white. In the course of time, many of these men and women did this in fact, that is, moved into white society and kept their family background a secret.[3] In Mark Twain's famous novel *Pudd'nhead Wilson* (1894), a slave woman switches her newborn child with the master's child, so that the slave child grows up as a master, and the master's child as a slave; the number of so-called blacks who looked white made this a plausible literary device.[4] Sometimes, after generations, a family lost all memory of their mixed-race background; descendants, checking the family tree, are amazed to find a black ancestor, a slave perhaps, hidden in the family's background.[5]

Of course, slaves themselves had no power to change venue or pass into white society. But when Thomas Jefferson freed the children of his slave Sally Hemmings—who were almost certainly his children, too—some of them promptly went north and passed as white.[6] The children of Michael Healy, an Irish Catholic, and the slave woman he loved, moved north and passed for white. Some of them had successful careers in the white world. Indeed, one of Healy's sons, a priest, became president of Georgetown University in 1873; another Healy served as the Catholic bishop of Portland, Maine. Still another son served as a captain in the Coast Guard. In no case was the white world aware of their secret past. And in no case could they have followed these careers, and climbed those social ladders, if they had been exposed to American society as black.[7]

In one celebrated case in 1925, Leonard Rhinelander, a member of a wealthy and prominent New York family, married Alice Jones, a woman from a much more modest background. His family bitterly opposed the marriage. Leonard ultimately came around to their point of view. He filed a lawsuit to annul the marriage. Rhinelander claimed his wife had committed marital fraud, which was grounds for annulment in New York. Jones, Rhinelander claimed, was passing for white but was really a woman of color. At one point in the trial, Mrs. Rhinelander was forced to strip in front of the jury so that they could see for themselves whether she at least *looked* nonwhite.[8] Leonard lost his case. The annulment was never granted. The jury probably thought Alice was, in fact, a woman of mixed blood. But they also probably thought this was something Rhinelander knew when he married her. She remained Mrs. Rhinelander for the rest of her life, but the two never lived together again.

"Identity" or "true" identity was the key issue in a number of big trials from the nineteenth century on. The Tichborne case, in England, is one of the best known of these cases.[9] Roger Tichborne member of an upper-class English family, was lost at sea in 1854 and pronounced dead the following year. His mother refused to believe he was dead. She clung to the hope that he had somehow survived. She offered a reward for information about his fate. A man appeared in 1865, out of Wagga Wagga, New South Wales, Australia, claiming that he was the lost Roger Tichborne. This would make him heir to a title of nobility and a fortune as well. Roger's mother was eager to believe him, even though his story was in many ways improbable. "Roger" was in fact an Australian, Arthur Orton: in short, a shameless impostor. In the end, Orton was convicted of perjury and sent to prison. After prison, he became a saloonkeeper in New York; he died in poverty.

The Tichborne case was a sensation in its day: the dramatic story of a missing heir, a peerage, and a mysterious stranger from Australia. Literature and folklore are full of long-lost children: princes turned into frogs, orphans who end up as missing heirs. These are appealing stories. Even after Orton was convicted of perjury, "the same old multitudes," as Mark Twain put it, "still believed in him." Even when he confessed, in writing, and on his deathbed, that he was nobody other than "Arthur Orton . . . able seaman and butcher," some people still kept the faith.[10] A twentieth-century parallel was "Anastasia," another intriguing impostor who claimed to be the daughter of the Czar of Russia. During the Russian Revolution, the Bolsheviks seized the royal family and held them captive; in 1918, on orders from the government, the Czar and his whole family were murdered. The story of "Anastasia"—that one of the Czar's daughters had somehow, miraculously, survived the slaughter and, after many adventures, emerged to claim her rightful place in society—was mysterious and romantic.[11] Unfortunately, Anastasia was as bogus as Arthur Orton.

In general, in the nineteenth century, tales of mistaken or lost identity were exceedingly popular. People relished "the performance of illegitimate identities"; it was a kind of a "leitmotif of popular culture" in Victorian England.[12] Identities lost and found were a staple of Victorian literature; it was a well-known trope of Victorian novels, for example, that an orphan turned out to be someone's long-lost heir.[13] In Charles Dickens' *Nicholas Nickleby*, the sad and pathetic orphan, Smike, is revealed at the end as the child of the wealthy miser, Ralph Nickleby. Did things like this happen in real life? One "Amelia Radcliffe," for example, popped up in northern England in 1868, claiming to be heiress to James Radcliffe, the Earl of Derwentwater, who had been executed in 1716. She was, most probably, a fake; but her real identity remains obscure to this day.[14]

Identity in the literal sense was the issue, too, in the late-twentieth-century trials of John Demjanjuk, which took place in three different countries. Was Demjanjuk a sadistic Nazi, "Ivan the Terrible," responsible for the death of thousands of Jews in death camps, or was this (as he insisted) a case of mistaken identity? Everything about the case was controversial, including the way the courts handled the evidence. In 1993, the Israeli high court reversed Demjanjuk's conviction, partly on the grounds that there was still confusion about his actual identity.[15] Eventually, the United States deported Demjanjuk, who had been living in the United States; he then faced trial in Germany. A German court convicted him, but by this time he was an old, sick man of ninety-one. The German court allowed him to go free while his lawyer planned an appeal.[16] Demjanjuk died before a final resolution could be reached.

These are cases of identity in the literal sense. But in a broader sense, identity is at issue in most headline trials. These trials ask: who is this person, *really*, this person sitting in the courtroom, whose fate is in the hands of the jury? Is he or she a respectable citizen, falsely accused, or a heartless killer? Has the defendant lied to us and lied to society? Has he or she falsely pretended to be innocent, or is professed innocence the truth? What did the defendant do, and why did he or she do it? Was it self-defense? Justifiable homicide? Is the defendant an innocent, trapped in a web of appearances, or a cold-blooded murderer, with an evil, cheating heart?

The worm-in-the-bud cases grapple with identity in this sense, Lizzie Borden is in a way the classic example. Of course, all families have secrets. There are skeletons in thousands of closets. But it was important—certainly in the nineteenth century—to keep these matters private, to hide them behind a curtain of secrecy.[17] It was particularly important to protect the elite from scandal; otherwise, how could privilege be justified in a democratic, egalitarian society? The leaders of society, the rich and the powerful, had to deserve their high positions. Headline trials sometimes ripped off the masks; they opened doors into secret rooms the public was not meant to see. This was one source of their drama, flair, and fatal attraction. Bourgeois society or Hollywood or the government or the rich and famous were on trial. In the trial of Henry Ward Beecher in 1875, one of the country's most respected religious leaders came under the microscope. Theodore Tilton brought a lawsuit, claiming that Beecher had committed adultery with Tilton's wife, Elizabeth.[18] A trial that posed questions about such fundamentals was in itself quite dangerous. It could (in a small way) threaten society's balance and harmony. Yet so long as the jury reached the right decision, some of the damage could be avoided or repaired.

I have argued this thesis—about the protection of elite reputation—in more detail elsewhere.[19] Certain ins and outs of nineteenth-century law suggest a tendency, unconscious or at least implicit, to protect the reputations of elites through one legal device or another, even when the elites did not deserve that protection. Nineteenth-century society, like all societies, rested on pillars of legitimacy. The top layers of society needed to command respect. It was important for people to think that authority was rightful and proper and had earned its place in society. Faith in the honesty and virtue of those at the top was essential.[20] To undermine this faith was to undermine society itself.[21]

In worm-in-the-bud trials, there was always, underneath the surface, at least a faint odor of social critique. This critique came, mostly, from the prosecution. Lizzie Borden's key defense was a defense not only of her but also of bourgeois society in general. Of course, the prosecution never *explicitly* attacked these values. The critique was implicit: Lizzie Borden, churchgoer, daughter of a leading citizen, might be a violent criminal. Another subversive suggestion was explicitly made in this trial: Lizzie, according to the prosecution, "violated the nineteenth-century standard of femininity."[22] Women of her class were by definition honest, respectable, and *innocent* (in all senses of the word). Hence, they had to argue that she somehow deviated from the norm, that she was an exception to the general rule, a kind of jezebel.

The period of the Lizzie Borden case—the late nineteenth century—was one of great insecurity. The old order was changing. A rural, Protestant society was morphing into an urban, industrial, and polyglot society. Millions of Catholics and Jews, immigrants from southern and eastern Europe, swarmed into the country. Of course, every historical period has its insecurities, its points of transition. But each period, like Tolstoy's famous line about unhappy families, is insecure and in transition in its own peculiar way.

The worm in the nineteenth-century bud was the vice or rot that lay beneath the surface of people who *seemed* to be normal, healthy, respectable, law-abiding but were, in effect, living double lives. In Robert Louis Stevenson's famous novel *The Strange Case of Dr. Jekyll and Mr. Hyde* (1886), the double personality is explicit: Dr. Jekyll and the evil Mr. Hyde are one and the same.[23] We think we know who people are and what they are like by reading their outward signs: the way they talk, dress, or behave. But how can we know, for sure, that we read the signs correctly? We think we can, if we actually *know* the people, in the way village people know their neighbors. But in the big city, the mobile society, where people come and go, they can more easily invent, and pass off, a counterfeit self.

Modern mobile societies also breed a distinctive form of

individualism that has been called "expressive individualism."[24] This has increasingly become the common type of personality. The expressive individual has a strong sense of his or her unique self and the urge to develop that self in its uniqueness. This sense implies, among other things, the ability to change, to transform oneself, at least to a degree. More than in the past, a man (less so a woman) could adopt new habits, move to a new place, and start a new life. It is also possible to start a new life without moving, perhaps shedding the old self like a reptile molting its skin.

Identity as problematic, people living double lives, worms in the bud: these ideas were at the base of a new literary form that suddenly burst forth in the first half of the nineteenth century: the mystery or detective novel.[25] Whether Edgar Allan Poe, or someone else, was the first in the field hardly matters. The chronology is significant. Poe's story "The Murders in the Rue Morgue" appeared in 1841. Shortly afterward, he wrote "The Mystery of Marie Roget." This story was based on a real incident, the sensational case of Mary Rogers, a young woman strangled to death in 1841, in Hoboken, New Jersey. The "circulation-crazed press," a relatively new mass institution, hungrily glommed onto the case and, in the opinion of Raymond Paul, who wrote a book about the case, "firmly established the gentle practices of the yellow press."[26] But this was hardly the first example of "yellow journalism." The murder of Helen Jewett in 1836 was a slightly earlier instance. Jewett, a prostitute, had been killed in a brothel. A young man, Richard Robinson, was accused of the crime. Two newspapers, the *New York Herald* and the *New York Sun*, competed with each other to cover the case in as sensational a manner as possible.[27] Later on, William Randolph Hearst and other newspaper barons raised "yellow journalism" to an even higher (or, if you will, lower) form of journalism.

Despite the efforts of the police, the press, and Edgar Allan Poe, the death of Mary Rogers remains something of a mystery.[28] But the art form that Poe pioneered was on the threshold of an amazing career. In 1865, Charles Warren Adams published *The Notting Hill Mystery*, which many regard as the first full-length mystery novel.[29] The Frenchman, Emile Gaboriau, wrote a number of mysteries from 1866 on; he was an important influence on later writers. Charles Dickens' friend, Wilkie Collins, published *The Moonstone* in 1868. This marvelous book, a literary masterpiece, has all the features of the classic mystery novel. A crime is committed—in this case, the theft of a fabulous gem. We, the readers, have no idea who committed this crime; the secret comes out only at the very end of the book. Moreover, the man who solves the mystery is an actual detective, Sergeant Cuff.

From then on, there was no stopping this dark literary art. In the United States, Anna Katherine Green was an early practitioner; *The Leavenworth Case: A Lawyer's Story* appeared in 1878 and was a runaway success. Arthur Conan Doyle created Sherlock Holmes, probably the most famous detective of them all, in the 1880s, when he published *A Study in Scarlet.* Holmes had a fabulous gift for deduction and detection. Doyle's books have never been out of print. There are millions of fans, and Sherlock Holmes has been the protagonist of countless movies and television shows.

What these early writers of the mystery began turned into an ocean of print. Fans of the genre have had their pick of thousands of novels and short stories. The most popular writers, like Agatha Christie, Erle Stanley Gardner, and Dorothy L. Sayers, have sold millions, perhaps billions, of books. England, France, and the United States have long since lost their monopoly on the genre. Mysteries appear in dozens of languages; currently, gritty, wintry novels from Scandinavian authors are in vogue. Mystery novels have made use of every possible setting; the "detective" has been anything from an actual detective, to priests, rabbis, stockbrokers, English lords, lawyers, doctors, members of Indian tribes, village old maids—in short, people of any age, shape, or form.

In the classic mystery, a crime is committed—usually, but not always, murder—and nobody (especially the reader) has any idea who might be responsible. One of the author's jobs is to keep the reader guessing. At the end of the book, the truth comes out; we learn the identity of the criminal. In a successful mystery, this unmasking comes as a big surprise. If the author has played fair, she has strewn subtle clues along the way, but this is not necessary, strictly speaking. The typical reader, in any event, probably wants to be fooled. The "twist" at the end is most effective when it is startling and unexpected: the obvious suspects turn out to be innocent; someone else, someone we never suspected, turns out to be guilty.

Crime is largely an urban phenomenon, but not exclusively. Studies of small towns in the nineteenth century in the United States show an astonishing amount of crime, pathology, and social disorganization.[30] The rural world was no paradise. No community was immune to dark forces in an age of turmoil, mobility, and social change. New events and situations had unsettled old expectations and arrangements and shuffled the deck of peoples' lives. Agatha Christie, perhaps the most successful mystery writer aside from Arthur Conan Doyle, often set her novels in small, quiet English towns. A village spinster, Miss Marple, figures in many of these books. The first Miss Marple book, published in 1930, bears the significant title, "Murder at the Vicarage." Miss Marple seemed, on the surface, nothing more than a harmless and naïve old maid. But Miss Marple had keen insight into human nature. She knew all there was to know about village life—and what she knew, as it turns out, was not all tea and crumpets. There were worms in many, many of these village rosebuds.

There have been, as we said, thousands upon thousands of mystery and detective novels and short stories. They continue to pour out of the presses.[31] Despite their kaleidoscopic variety, they have this in common: they are stories about simulated identity. They depend on their ability to fool the reader; their subtext is that people are not always what they seem. The person unmasked in the last chapter, the villain, the cold-blooded killer who dispatched the victim in chapter 1, is someone who seemed both innocent and unlikely. But he or she had some hidden aspect. He or she, in a sense, was leading a double life.

Why did this literary form appear at this particular point in time, and why did it flourish? What was it about nineteenth-century structure and culture that served as a catalyst? Clearly, the mystery story, like any literary form, has to be understood in context. And that context was social and geographic mobility and the problem of identity. The genre, then, grows directly out of the conditions of life in industrial society: the mobility, the uncertainty, the dissolution of village life, the development of a society of strangers. Even the settings of Agatha Christie's novels—the vicarage, the quiet country village—had been transformed; strangers moved in and the rhythm of life became unsettled. People were no longer always what they seemed to be.

The genius of the (fictional) detective has always been the ability to strip away the masks to find the true (and hidden) identity of the man or woman who committed the crime. The genius of the great Sherlock Holmes was his ability to decipher codes. He could read the book of identity from tiny outward signs—a cigar ash, a piece of wood. In *The Hound of the Baskervilles* (1902), a man comes by when Holmes is out. He leaves behind his walking stick. Holmes returns before his potential client; Holmes has already deduced a tremendous amount from the "data" he read in the walking stick.

The period that gave rise to the detective story also gave rise to the so-called confidence man. A confidence man is a scam artist; he pretends to be something or somebody else in order to squeeze money out of his victims. New York in the 1870s, according to one writer, was full of these impostors: "The immense size of the city, the heterogeneous character of the population, and the great variety . . . of the people, are all so many advantages to the cheat and the swindler."[32] The earliest mention of the term "confidence man," according to the *Oxford English Dictionary*, dates to 1849.[33] The confidence man himself appeared earlier than this, but he was, no question, a figure of the nineteenth century. Social and geographic mobility had opened the door to the confidence man and his tricks in a new and dramatic way. In a world full of strangers, a fake accent and fraudulent manners were harder to detect. Confidence men were clever cheats. The game called for skill; its practitioners tended to be "men of education, glib talkers with no end of assurance, gifted with a good knowledge of human nature" who liked to help themselves to "other people's money."[34] They battened on the gullible, passing themselves off as lawyers, doctors, members of the nobility, priests, or simply wealthy men. In 1831, in Andalusia, Pennsylvania, a "young stranger" appeared; he claimed to be "Lino Amalia Espos y Mina," a fabulously wealthy Mexican and son of a governor of California. He duped his hostess, Lucretia Chapman, into sharing her money and her body (and possibly into murdering her husband). "Mina" was in fact an impostor, who, when he appeared on Lucretia Chapman's doorstep, had just been freed from the penitentiary.[35] In 1880, a "well-dressed, gentlemanly young fellow" cheated a prominent New York jeweler out of $600 worth of "diamond sleeve-buttons." He claimed to be the son of the ex-president of the Board of Aldermen. He paid for the jewelry with a check that turned out to be forged.[36] There are countless other such examples.

Just as the confidence man benefitted from the new world of ambiguous identity, so, too, did the spy or secret agent. Spying has a long history, but it took on a particularly dramatic form in the late nineteenth century. The technology of warfare made spying a more important game than before. Armies had always been eager to know the enemy's strategy. Now, new technologies increased the value of spies, who, for example, could steal blueprints of new weapons. The British Official Secrets Act dates from 1889.[37] And just as social conditions gave rise to the detective novel, a new genre, the spy novel, was born in the late nineteenth century; it, too, became extremely popular.[38]

It is in the first half of the nineteenth century, too, that blackmail first became a crime in the criminal codes.[39] Blackmail was and is a curious, even puzzling, crime. A blackmailer forces his victim to pay money in exchange for silence. He threatens to tell the police, or friends, or the community, about something the victim has done. But notice the paradox: it is the "victim," not the "perpetrator," who has a guilty secret; the victim has been hiding the fact that he did something wrong, shameful, or illegal. Yet, instead of punishing the so-called victim, we punish the blackmailer. The blackmailer—and this is crucial—is almost always less rich or powerful or respected than his victim. Blackmail, then, is a crime against elites, a crime that threatens their reputation. It is no defense that the blackmailer, unlike the victim, is telling the truth. The victim often insists that the blackmailer's story is a lie. More likely, it is the victim who is lying. Not that it makes any legal difference. Blackmail is blackmail, whether or not the claims are true. The point of making blackmail a crime is to deter the blackmailer and to protect the victims and their secrets.

Newspapers in the nineteenth century and later told horror stories about blackmail. Some blackmailers were lone wolves, preying on gullible or indiscreet victims. There were also gangs of blackmailers, who extorted money from wealthy men using all sorts of dirty tricks. Their techniques were, to say the least, disreputable. But the so-called victims were hardly blameless. In 1916, we read that federal agents had arrested one William Butler, "a gambler and wire tapper," and accused him of a scheme to "blackmail rich violators of the Mann white slave law." Butler demanded (it was said) $8,000 from a "society woman of Philadelphia to protect the name of her son." At the same time, in New York, a blackmailer was arrested who had "attempted to extort money from several New York physicians" by threatening to expose them for "performing illegal operations."[40] The woman's son, one imagines, probably did violate the Mann Act (the White Slave Traffic Act), and the New York physicians could well have been abortionists at a time when abortion was illegal. Some blackmail schemes perhaps were frame-ups. Others surely were not. And one rarely hears about *successful* blackmail—blackmail, that is, that never came to light because the victims simply paid and paid.

The detective was the mortal enemy of the blackmailer and of the confidence man in general. The office, the role, and the word "detective" itself (with this particular meaning) date from the first half of the nineteenth century. The "con man" did his dirty work through tricks, artifices, disguises, and outright lies about his identity and motives. The detective, in a way, did the same, but from the other side. He was an expert at discovering the hidden, devious criminal. The regular police dealt with urban mobs and brawlers; they monitored public behavior in bars, restaurants, public squares, and other open spaces. The police officer wore a uniform and a badge to advertise who he was and to act as a visible deterrent.[41] The detective, on the other hand, wore ordinary clothes. In a way, he fought con men and other secret criminals with the tools of their own game. In the words of a nineteenth-century detective, his job, of necessity, was to be "dishonest, crafty, unscrupulous." But the "trickeries" and lies of the detective were in the interests of justice; his work was part of the battle against social corruption and crime.[42]

The "detectives" in mystery novels are often amateurs, but like real-life detectives, their goal is to ferret out secret, hidden crime. The classic mystery novel follows a formula. It poses a question—Who is guilty of this crime?—and, in the end, it gives a complete and definitive answer. The last chapter is crucial. Puzzles are solved, knots are untied; the whole truth, the absolute truth, comes out. Miss Marple is never wrong, never even baffled. Sherlock Holmes, too, always has the answer; Perry Mason never loses a case. The criminal *trial* has a different structure, but it, too, has a narrative design: a story with two sides. The lines of narrative may be messy and in conflict, and the evidence may come out in ragged and piecemeal fashion; nonetheless, each side tries to tell a coherent story. And the trial, like the novel, provides at least some kind of answer. In a few cases, the jury hangs; but mostly the jury emerges from its locked room and brings in a verdict. The verdict is, in its own way, definitive. In the justice system of the United States, there is no appeal from an acquittal. If the jury says, "not guilty," the defendant can stand up and walk right out of the courtroom. The law cannot touch him again—at least not for that particular crime.

Yet, as we saw, there is often a nagging doubt, intriguing questions of fact that may never be quite resolved. The verdict ends the case, but it may or may not be correct. Purely factual doubts are a symptom of a deeper and more insidious doubt: who *is* this person? Is he innocent, as he says; or is he like Hyde to Dr. Jekyll, the worm inside the bud. And even when guilt is clear and the facts are obvious, we may still wonder who this person is. Thomas Neill Cream was tried and executed in 1892; there was overwhelming evidence that Cream was a serial killer. He poisoned at least four women in England, along with others in the United States. Cream was a doctor who lured women into his web and gave them pills laced with a deadly amount of strychnine.[43] He hid his pathology behind a veneer of charm and professionalism. The jury, at his trial, found him guilty in short order—it took only ten minutes, in fact. He was guilty beyond a reasonable doubt—a Jack the Ripper brought to justice. But the question remains: Why did he do what he did? Was he insane? Again, who *was* he? We can never know.

There are important parallels, then, between the headline trial and the mystery novel. They both involve the puzzle of identity. They both grow out of the world of nineteenth-century mobility.

They both attract an audience to the question of innocence or guilt. But the jury lacks the God-like power of an author. Agatha Christie controls her world; the jury does not. The trial still leaves us guessing. *Was* Lizzie Borden an axe-murderess? Did Claus von Bulow inject insulin into Sunny von Bulow's veins? What about O. J. Simpson? Many African Americans, as we have mentioned, were sure he was innocent. One African American, for example, felt Simpson knew "who did it" but kept silent to protect his kids from the Mafia.[44] The case was fertile soil for conspiracy theories.[45] Most white people, on the other hand, simply thought Simpson was guilty.

As we have mentioned, the Simpson trial, which began as an ordinary case of murder (if murder is ever ordinary) was transformed—by Simpson's lawyers—into a trial about race. They tried to persuade the jury, successfully as it happens, that the prosecution was racist and not to be believed. The mountain of evidence against Simpson got shoved to one side; instead, the issue became whether Lt. Fuhrman, a key witness, had lied when he said he never used the n-word. Simpson's *racial* identity moved to center stage. In other words, one question of identity (was he really a murderer?) was absorbed by another question of identity: How black was he, and how white was Lt. Fuhrman?

In headline trials, particular issues of identity sometimes merge with more general forms of identity. Was Fatty Arbuckle a man who preyed on helpless women? Had he raped or otherwise damaged Virginia Rappe? This was the immediate question. But here, too, a larger question of identity took over: the nature of Hollywood, the morals and immorals of the entertainment world and of the stars and directors who inhabited that world. The Thaw-White case asked a similar question about show business and high society in New York City. In many of the famous trials, the mystery of the defendant's particular identity merged with a larger question of identity: racial, social, ethnic, or the like.

Juries are supposed to convict only when guilt is proven

"beyond a reasonable doubt." What this means is never exactly clear. As we said, verdicts cannot clear away all doubts, reasonable or otherwise.[46] Twelve jurors thought there was reasonable doubt about the guilt of O. J. Simpson. The same facts led a civil jury, later on, to award damages against him for killing two victims.[47] Identity in big trials, in this world at least, sometimes cannot be resolved beyond reasonable doubt.

12

Enter the Media

Since the late nineteenth century, the story of headline trials has also been the story of the mass media, in particular, of the way the media deal with crime and punishment. The why and wherefore of headline trials must take into account the why and wherefore of headlines. More and more, the study of these trials is not so much a study of law, legal process, and the justice system as it is a study of the mass media and their role in society. The media propagate these trials. In some sense today, they create them. Headline trials, in the hands of the media, constitute a form of public entertainment. They are didactic theater, yes, but with the emphasis on *theater*, that is, on entertainment.

Headline trials, as we have pointed out, could hardly exist in the literal sense before there were headlines. Broadsides, pamphlets, and books about crime and criminals date back to the eighteenth century, if not earlier. But the true headline trial came into its own only in the nineteenth century. Political trials have a long pedigree, but the other forms of big trial were rooted in the dramatic social changes—increased social and geographic mobility and a complicating sense of identity—that overtook society roughly around the time of the Industrial Revolution. The headline trial and the mass media evolved together, like flowers and the bees that pollinate them. This connection only sharpens as we progress (if that is the word) from newspapers to radio to movies to television, and now to the Internet.

As early as the 1830s, the "penny press"—mass-market newspapers and magazines—gave a lot of play to crime and punishment. The murder of Helen Jewett in 1836, and the trial of Richard Robinson, who was accused of killing her, was, as we saw, reported in lip-smacking detail in the New York newspapers;[1] cases like this were the bread and butter of the penny press.[2] In the course of the nineteenth century, newspapers became cheaper, more popular, and competed fiercely with each other. Each paper used vivid and sensational coverage to win the circulation war. Flashy trials were an important weapon in the war. Periodicals like the *National Police Gazette*, along with cheap pamphlets and broadsides, also zestfully recounted (and embellished) tales of crime and punishment, feeding a vigorous public appetite.[3] Before movies and television, few people could actually *see* a sensational trial or hear what the witnesses said; the size of the courtroom was a crucial limiting factor. For notorious trials, there was money to be made by printing transcripts of the court proceedings. This was the case, for example, in the Parkman-Webster trial.[4] Then came the great age of "yellow journalism,"[5] with screaming headlines, investigative reporters, and "sob sisters" (women reporters who emphasized the "human interest" aspects of trials"[6]). The media could provide a vicarious thrill; they could make people feel almost as if they had a peephole into the courtroom, an experience much cheaper, and perhaps more exciting, than actually going to the trial.

Reporters flocked to big trials in great numbers. Even such dignified newspapers as the *New York Times* found it impossible to avoid the frenzy; they felt compelled to compete with the down-market press.[7] The papers fed their readers gory and extensive details of trials such as Lizzie Borden's or Harry K.

Thaw's, with their irresistible cast of characters and their undercurrents of sex and scandal.

The way the press covered the trial of Martin Thorn in 1897 is a good example of late-nineteenth-century styles and techniques of the mass media. Thorn was accused of killing a man named William Guldensuppe. Guldensuppe, a rubber in a bathhouse, had once been the lover of Augusta Nack; Thorn, a barber, replaced him as Nack's lover. The media uproar began when parts of a body, wrapped in oilcloth, turned up in the East River, in New York. Later, other body parts were found. The head was never recovered, but the body was identified as Guldensuppe's. The crime, and the trial, touched off a circulation war between two leading purveyors of yellow journalism, the *World* and the *Herald*. They competed frantically with each other and even conducted their own investigations, almost shoving to one side the work of the regular police. They carried on their war with scandals, accusations, fat and breathless headlines, and all sorts of dirty tricks.[8] Nack and Thorn were both convicted; Nack got fifteen years in prison. Thorn went to his death in the electric chair on August 1, 1898. The *New York Times*, not to be outdone by its rivals, reported his death in detail—how he spent the night talking, how he dreaded the walk to the execution chamber, how he calmly carried a crucifix, with a priest beside him, how a current of 1,950 volts went through his body for five seconds, the current then reduced to 400 volts.[9]

Newspapers were *the* mass medium of the nineteenth century. With the twentieth century came radio, then the movies, and then television. From the very beginning, crime and punishment were staples of the movies.[10] Many movies have featured criminal trials: *The Red Kimono* (1927), a silent movie, took up the murder trial of Gabrielle Darley, who shot and killed her lover and pimp,[11] later classics include *12 Angry Men*[12] and *Anatomy of a Murder*.[13] Television, when it burst into most peoples' homes, was more vivid than radio and more immediate than movies; it could broadcast news about sensational trials, along with actual footage, to an audience of millions. In a few cases, the trial itself was televised. Television has always had an insatiable appetite for material; it needs a constant flow of dramas and news to fill all the channels and all the hours. Cop shows, law and order shows, lawyer shows, and mystery dramas remain exceptionally popular.

In our society, it would be hard to exaggerate the influence of the media. We live in a time of mediatization. This ugly word refers to "the process whereby society to an increasing degree is submitted to, or becomes dependent on, the media and their logic."[14] It is as if the media, like the body-snatchers in *Invasion of the Body-Snatchers*, have come from outer space to take over the world. Politics in the age of the media, we are told, "has lost its autonomy, has become dependent . . . on mass media, and is continuously shaped by interactions with mass media."[15] The media also shape the modern headline trial.

"Mediatization" has both pluses and minuses. The media can educate; they can expose weaknesses and flaws in government; they can make it more difficult to lie and cheat in office. They also miseducate. In the media society, lies spread with the speed of light and are harder to expose and to refute. Politics is reduced to sound bites. The media's impact on criminal justice seems on the whole to be negative; the media magnify the crime problem and disseminate the demand for more and more toughness. On the other hand, the media—today at least—seem to foster tolerance for diversity; they show racial, sexual, and ethnic minorities in a positive light, and with increasing frequency, in programs and commercials. And the public has never seemed so hungry for big trials, in all their bizarre, frightening, and disturbing aspects. Every night on television, before audiences of millions, real and fictional crime shows enact, parse, and (usually) solve a multitude of murders, rapes, and other violent crimes. This is the age of what Fox and Van Sickel have called "tabloid justice," the focus on "the sensationalistic, personal, lurid, and tawdry details of unusual and high-profile trials."[16] Fox and Van Sickel claim that tabloid justice reached some sort of climax in the 1990s, when trials like O. J. Simpson's offered audiences "almost total cultural immersion" to such a degree as to constitute, in their view, "a new phenomenon."[17] More recently Internet sites like YouTube and other forms of instant communication (texts and tweets, for example) have been added to the mix.

Many of these trials, as we said, grip the public because they touch a nerve or evoke latent fears and dreads. The media, however, exaggerate and exacerbate the fears and the trials that invoke them. Putting a case in the headlines automatically makes it a headline case. Dr. Sam Sheppard's case was a classic example. The crime—the brutal murder of Sheppard's wife, a wealthy and pregnant suburbanite—was certain to get a fair amount of coverage. But the Cleveland newspapers had a field day with the case. They decided, early on, that Dr. Sheppard was the killer. They demanded action. They were partly responsible, too, for the atmosphere in the courtroom: the excitement, the turmoil, the crowds of reporters. The scene was shrill and exaggerated—hardly the place for a calm, impartial search for truth. The Supreme Court, as we saw, found the trial so unbalanced that the Court called it a gross violation of Sheppard's rights. Indeed, at the second, more neutral, trial, Dr. Sheppard was acquitted.[18] Newspapers also helped create the hysteria that led to the lynching of Leo Frank. In the Fatty Arbuckle case, the newspapers screamed about an "orgy" and a "wild party" in the star's hotel room and helped create the carnival atmosphere that surrounded this case.[19]

In some instances, the media seize on one aspect of a trial—accurately or not—and blow it up out of all proportion.[20] The media had a grand time with the notorious "Twinkie defense" in the trial of Dan White. White, who killed the mayor of San Francisco and supervisor Harvey Milk, was on trial for murder. The defense was diminished capacity—something between legal insanity and complete normality. White had gobbled down a great deal of junk food; there was a hint—just a hint—in the testimony that this might have had some kind of impact on his mind and body. The main defense was White's crushing depression, which had many causes and many symptoms. But the newspapers and TV reports magnified the idea that junk food had somehow clouded his judgment, to the point where you might imagine that the whole defense rested on this junk food high—the notorious "Twinkie defense." This defense in fact never existed; it was a myth, based on the slimmest of evidence, a few scraps of testimony in an ocean of words. It was almost purely a creation of reporters and pundits.[21] In fact, the word "Twinkie," and any reference to this food product, never appeared in the testimony.

Trial by Television

Big trials are open, highly public events. People jam into every corner of the courtroom. Reporters and curiosity seekers push and shove for space. The reporters carry the news to a wider audience. Today, the press has been supplemented—perhaps supplanted—by radio, TV, and the Internet. But only the most sensational trials get even a sliver of time on the evening news. And a handful of trials, bigger and noisier yet, reach a higher stage, beyond the evening news: They are televised in full.

The Nuremberg trials took place before the television era, but there were cameras in the courtroom and the trial was filmed. Newsreel and other footage were also shown during the trial as part of the prosecution's case.[22] Today, of course, it is possible to televise a trial and show it to an audience, live. Whether this live broadcast is consistent with fairness is a matter of debate. Blatant notoriety makes some jurists, and judges, uncomfortable. The Supreme Court, as we saw, reversed Dr. Sheppard's conviction on the grounds that the trial was a media circus. Rules of the American Bar Association (ABA) call for "fitting dignity and decorum" in criminal trials and other proceedings. Photographers buzzing about in the courtroom do not seem to fit the image of "dignity and decorum." In 1952, the ABA recommended a total ban on TV cameras in the courtroom.[23] This was just a suggestion; it had no binding effect. Some courts went ahead and gave the green light to TV cameras.

Was this acceptable? In *Estes v. Texas* (1965),[24] a bare majority of the Supreme Court said it was not. Billie Sol Estes, the defendant, was a fabulous wheeler-dealer who hobnobbed with presidents and also happened to be a tremendous swindler responsible for: "Nonexistent fertilizer tanks. Faked Mortgages, Bogus cotton-acreage allotments. Farmers in four states bamboozled."[25] Estes was exposed in 1962, arrested, charged with fraud, convicted, and sentenced to a term in prison. The trial was televised. Later, the Supreme Court reversed his conviction. The press can be a "mighty catalyst in awakening public interest in governmental affairs," but televising trials was another matter entirely. When a trial is televised in all its "morbid" details, the Court said, it "becomes a *cause célèbre*." People become "self-conscious and uneasy when being televised." Television could demoralize and frighten some witnesses; others could become "cocky and given to overstatement." For the defendant, television could be "a form of mental—if not physical—harassment, resembling a police line-up or the third degree." In the *Estes* case, the courtroom was a "mass of wires, television cameras, microphones and photographers." This, the Supreme Court decided, made a fair trial impossible. The Chief Justice, Earl Warren, in a concurring opinion, issued a stern warning about televised trials: the public might "equate the trial process with the forms of entertainment regularly seen on television." Indeed, trial tapes of the Estes affair had run at night, punctuated by commercials for "soft drinks, soups, eyedrops and seatcovers." Television, Warren felt, was simply incompatible with the idea of a fair trial.[26]

But in 1981, in *Chandler v. Florida*, the Court changed its mind.[27] Florida had embarked on a pilot program, allowing some court proceedings to be televised. The state also surveyed jurors in four Florida murder trials, along with spectators and others who had been involved. Most of these people saw nothing wrong with cameras in the courtroom, including TV cameras. Most—though hardly an overwhelming majority—did not think the cameras became a distraction or that television was unfair to defendants.[28] In *Chandler*, the defendants were accused of "conspiracy to commit burglary, grand larceny, and possession of burglary tools" and of "breaking and entering a well-known Miami Beach restaurant." The defendants wanted the cameras out of the courtroom, but the judge refused. The defendants were convicted, and they appealed. The Florida Supreme Court decided to leave the issue to trial courts; the judge could decide whether or not to allow cameras. On the whole, said the Florida court, more was to be gained than lost when proceedings were televised. The Supreme Court of the United States agreed, distinguishing the *Estes* case. In the Court's judgment, nothing in the constitution prevented states from "experimenting" with courtroom television.

The Court, as it turned out, was swimming with the tide. Television was on the march. Until the 1960s most states had flat-out forbidden cameras in the courtroom. *Estes* reflected this point of view, as did *Sheppard v. Maxwell* in 1966, which reversed a conviction because of the "carnival" atmosphere in the courtroom.[29] By the time of *Chandler*, however, the tide had turned. By the 1990s, most states were comfortable with cameras in the courtroom. At the beginning of the twenty-first century, forty-two states gave judges the authority to broadcast criminal trials, as long as certain procedures were satisfied. Only eight states and the District of Columbia had an outright ban on television in the courtroom.[30] By 2013, the number of states that allow cameras had increased to forty-four, and the rest permitted appellate arguments to be televised; only the District of Columbia maintained an absolute ban.[31] Interestingly, the United States Supreme Court still holds out against television; federal courts cannot be televised, and there is no televising of oral arguments before the United States Supreme Court.[32] The rest of the world, however, has given in—the Supreme Courts of Canada, Brazil, and the United Kingdom all allow television at their hearings.[33]

A special television channel, Court TV, made its debut in 1991. It aimed to broadcast live coverage of trials. It covered the trial of the Menendez brothers, and the O. J. Simpson trial; these two sensational trials beamed something of a spotlight on this channel. Court TV never actually restricted itself to broadcasting trials. But its success proved (if proof was needed) that big trials fascinated people; opposition to television in the courtroom had essentially collapsed. To be sure, the ratings on Court TV did not hold up. Court TV abandoned its focus on trials and adopted a different business model; it rebranded itself in 2007 as truTV and now emphasizes reality TV, featuring shows like "Hardcore Pawn," about the owners of a Detroit pawnshop, and "Killer Karaoke," in which contestants sing their favorite songs while performing dangerous or disgusting acts.

Not that this change proves that people are less interested in big trials. In fact, televised criminal trials were rare and exceptional. The trial of Claus von Bulow in 1982 was among these few; CNN provided live coverage. For this trial, which had the qualities of a "dark soap opera," the courtroom was packed every day. Other networks showed the juicier bits in their news broadcasts. In London, Thames Television let British audiences in on the trial and regularly devoted a half-hour special to the case. When the verdict came, television cameras "zoomed in for a close-up of von Bulow's face and hands in an attempt to capture his emotional state."[34] The O. J. Simpson case was perhaps was the high point of television in the courtroom (or low point, if you prefer). It was, in a way, the ultimate in reality TV. Millions of people watched the case, gavel to gavel, on television. Indeed, the home audience saw more than the jury did. Members of the audience also had access to endless television commentary from various talking heads. Some people in England stayed awake long hours to see these proceedings live. Few cases, of course, have had the emotional zing of this trial or the trial of Claus von Bulow. But when these trials occur, they command enormous attention.[35]

The question remains: *Does* the camera in the courtroom have an impact on judge, jury, witnesses, lawyers, and defendants? Nobody can answer this question definitively. There is, after all, no obvious control group. The "invisible, but palpable, presence" of the television audience might make participants act more responsibly or it might make them nervous and unreliable.[36] One witness might be cowed, another made to feel humiliated; some might wallow in the world's attention.

Perhaps the impact is different for each televised case. It is hard to know. One trial that was televised was the sensational trial of Joel Steinberg in 1987. Steinberg lived in New York City with his partner, Hedda Nusbaum, and two children they had adopted (though in an irregular way). Steinberg abused his partner, and one of the children, a six-year-old; the child died from the abuse. Steinberg was put on trial and convicted of first-degree manslaughter. Did it matter that the case was televised? The judge thought not. There was "intense public interest in the case" and the cameras, in his opinion, did not "meaningfully add to that." Steinberg felt otherwise. The media, he thought, "selectively chose images and information" that were "biased and slanted"; "emotionally charged visuals," constantly repeated, "reinforced the notion that he was guilty."[37] These responses were what one would expect from a convicted defendant; but whether his or the opposite opinion is correct is unknown. The impact of TV in the courtroom remains a mystery.

The triumph of television in the courtroom was, of course, not predetermined. Courts might have stuck to their guns and outlawed cameras. But the pressures from the other side, in a society obsessed with celebrity and entertainment, are massive. Some judges probably love the idea of showing their stuff before an audience of millions and gaining their own fifteen minutes of fame.[38] And the triumph of television shows that headline trials still fascinate the public. The media are, after all, in the business of making money; and they make money when they give the public what it wants or thinks it wants. The public seems willing, even eager, to immerse itself in the trials of O. J. Simpson, or the Menendez brothers, or Casey Anthony.

Some cases, as we said, touch a nerve—on race relations or the problems of the modern family, for example. But even these trials succeed in part because they are superb entertainment. And entertainment is crucial to contemporary society. To be sure, entertainment, in the form of festivals, rituals, games, dances, cockfighting, bear-baiting, Mardi Gras, and celebrations of holidays, is a feature of all social groups. All societies have ceremonies, holidays, and other ways to relieve the boredom, pain, and struggle of ordinary life.

But today, in middle-class societies, entertainment is more central than ever. Middle-class life in particular is orderly and (relatively) comfortable. It is, for many people, both humdrum and stressful. Life may feel like a scramble, a challenge, a treadmill; a dreary trip in the slow lane. People may need two jobs to make ends meet; family and kids soak up enormous amounts of time and effort. And yet, ordinary people, in Japan, Finland, Australia, have more resources than their ancestors did, more room, and more leisure time; they have evenings, weekends, national holidays, paid vacations. They also have discretionary income jingling in their pockets. Their appetite for entertainment is almost insatiable. Very likely, in most countries in Europe or North America, no industry is as large as the entertainment industry, if you add together amateur and professional sports, movies and television, video games, bridge and other card games, and hundreds of hobbies, from gardening to origami, collecting old bottles to playing the guitar or collecting stamps. For most families, a television set is not a luxury; it is as essential as their refrigerator or indoor plumbing. Without some way to beam entertainment into the house, life would be unthinkable. And video games, smart phones, and the Internet have only added to the rich mix of entertainment sources.

Entertainment as big business gained enormous importance in the nineteenth and twentieth centuries.[39] Today, television stands at the center of the entertainment world, at least so far. Social networking and the Internet may be on the verge of pushing it off its throne. Television is, of course, above all about entertainment. As Neil Postman has pointed out, television has "made entertainment itself the natural format for the representation of all experience."[40] Even "news" has to qualify as entertainment. A news program with low ratings is doomed. Reporters and anchormen become stars; drama, novelty, and human-interest stories shape the news programs.[41] Entertainment also has transformed political life. Politicians sink or swim in terms of image, personality, likeability, and something vague called "charisma." Like soccer matches or rock concerts, political speeches *must* entertain; campaigns fall dead if they bore or confuse their audience. A stutter or a high-pitched voice could kill a career. These things mattered much less in the time of Thomas Jefferson or Abraham Lincoln.

Through television, a politician or celebrity can reach a huge audience; space and time hardly matter. It is not the same as standing for Parliament in a rotten English borough in the nineteenth century or trying to win the votes of Illinois farmers in the 1850s. In 2011, people in Patagonia, Helsinki, and Seoul could all watch the marriage of Prince William, grandson of Queen Elizabeth II; this pompous and gaudy ceremony was televised live from Westminster Abbey. Or, if the time zones were wrong, they could record this great event and watch it later or wait until some local station broadcast highlights of the wedding. Two years later, they could gorge themselves on news about the birth of the royal baby.

Television is the key to modern politics. It is the only way to reach masses of voters. Television ads are short—and expensive. Ads must be enjoyable, forceful; in a word, they must entertain. The worlds of entertainment and politics are hopelessly entwined, so much so that one author has called the president the "entertainer-in-chief."[42] The president, after all, is on television virtually every day. The United States may be an extreme case, but modern politics in all developed countries suffers from the same disease. The British prime minister, the heads of European governments, leaders in Japan and Australia: They all need to connect with the masses of voters. And the future of, say, the monarchy in the Netherlands or in the United Kingdom, and perhaps even of the papacy, depends at least in part on the personality of the monarch or pope.

Why is entertainment so popular and powerful? There surely is no single, simple answer. It might be some sort of primal urge except that today people can afford it more often and in greater quantities. Moreover, we live in the age of the *individual.* The individual—and not the group, the clan, the family, the tribe, or the community—is at the core of personal life. Modern individualism is *expressive* individualism.[43] It is the notion that each of us is uniquely human, uniquely ourselves, with unique desires, goals, and wishes. Of course, we still belong to families and groups, but we each have, and ought to have, a unique path to self-realization. And that path, whatever else it may include, has room for the pursuit of pleasure, fun—entertainment, in a word. Self-realization is not just about finding the right career; it also means finding the right partner and the right road to happiness.

And today entertainment is one of the basic pillars of the pursuit of happiness—for masses of people, not just the rich and highborn.

Crime and punishment help feed this hunger for diversion and excitement. Millions of people are enthralled with what goes on above them, in the world of celebrities, and below, in the seedy, vice-ridden realm of the underworld. They are fascinated, too, by the secrets within their own ranks: scandals that occasionally erupt out of middle-class society, events that explode the walls and windows of other people's houses, crimes that drag into daylight things that happen mostly in darkness, behind bolted shutters and closed doors. Big trials work on all three of these levels: the trial of O. J. Simpson or Fatty Arbuckle on the level of celebrity life; the trial in 2013 of Whitey Bulger, a murderer and member of an organized crime group on the level of the underground (movies like *The Godfather* and television programs like *The Sopranos* testify to the same urge);[44] and the trials of Scott Peterson or Sam Sheppard grow out of the seamy side of middle-class life.

Stories of crime and punishment may appeal to hidden longings, secret wishes, and suppressed desires. Things that are radically different from the treadmill of everyday life have their own fascination. Headline trials can serve as a kind of emotional and psychological tourism, like a visit to a foreign country. And these trials are all the more intriguing in that they claim to be a slice of life. They are at the same time alien and familiar. The crimes that lead to headline trials—certainly to the tabloid trials—bubble up out of familiar emotions and sources: jealousy, lust, anger, or greed. For most people these emotions are private and constrained. Murder is not part of everyday life.

Nicole Rafter, writing about crime films, tried to sum up why people find these movies so appealing. They provide, she says, "escape from daily life, opportunities to solve mysteries, chances to identify with powerful and competent heroes, and discussions of morality that are comfortingly unambiguous." They also offer "access to places most of us never get to in person"—prison cells, police stations, and the like. They open a "window on exotica," we can become "voyeurs, secret observers of the personal and even intimate lives" of other people, people whose lives are quite unlike the lives of the audience. These films also "offer . . . the pleasurable opportunity to pursue justice"; they also "provide a cultural space for the expression of resistance to authority."[45] There are, in short, many reasons for our fascination with crime and punishment. The reference to "voyeurs," however, has a particular resonance. In the celebrity society, all of us are voyeurs (or think of ourselves that way), as we peep into the lives of the president, the queen of England, rock stars, movie heroes, talk show hosts, and all the other figures we see on TV.

Certainly, all societies have had stories, legends, and myths; rituals and mysteries; tales about ghosts, spirits, and the supernatural. Modern societies have by and large abandoned ghost stories. Many people, of course, still love to hear about spirits, phantoms, and miracles, tidings from beyond the grave, not to mention visitors from other worlds. But mystery and mysteries, and tales of crime and punishment, have an even bigger place in popular culture. Jack Katz has suggested that crime both horrifies and attracts the public, because it tends to undermine faith in social institutions. He gives as an example "reports of torture or sexual abuse occurring at child care centres," no doubt with the McMartin case in mind.[46] Trials that follow these horror stories add another layer of interest; they dramatize the story. Personalities come alive on the witness stand during cross-examination in a way that a cold narrative cannot achieve.

Trials may indeed raise questions about social institutions. A trial like Lizzie Borden's, we have argued, was in a sense deeply subversive, though probably the crowds at the trial, and the ones who gobbled up newspaper accounts, did not think of it that way. Whether contemporary trials "undermine" anything is an open question. Trials are still didactic theater, even in an age in which other forms of "theater" compete with trials. Trials do open doors into unfamiliar worlds. The trial of Lizzie Borden put the Bordens, a local elite, under the microscope. The trial of Frank Walworth in the 1870s became a sensation; Walworth was accused of killing his own father.[47] The Walworths were an extremely distinguished New York family; Reuben Hyde Walworth had been chancellor of the New York court system. Frank Walworth's father was the black sheep of the family; he was separated from his wife, seemed somewhat deranged, and had a tendency toward violence. The trial ripped open the private world of the Walworths "for mass consumption." Reporters, who usually went "trawling among the lives of saloon keepers and . . . Tammany toughs" were now allowed to "rifle—with the license only a violent crime could give—through the hidden past of . . . a distinguished family."[48]

The same thrill of exposure attended the trial of Fatty Arbuckle. It stripped away the glamorous veneer of Hollywood, the hype spread by fan magazines, and exposed to the public what appeared to be a sick, debauched way of life. The newspapers called the party in Arbuckle's hotel suite an "orgy." The party certainly violated Prohibition laws, but this was hardly unusual. The newspaper accounts hinted darkly at much more sinister goings-on. Arbuckle and another man "were garbed in pajamas, bathrobes and slippers," and one woman "danced about the room in pajamas," all of which was suspicious and had sexual overtones.[49] Women in jazz-age Chicago who killed their lovers were very much the stuff of front-page news—tough, sexually active women who took the law into their own hands. Juries tended to acquit them.[50] The trials of Belva Gaertner and Beulah Annan in the 1920s intrigued the public and made a mockery of the old image of women as chaste, demure, and asexual—an image that had become obsolete in the age of the flapper.

Rich or poor, defendants in headline trials became public figures almost by definition. A kind of circular process was at work.

The media helped *create* the sensational trial. Once the public was hooked, the media claimed a right, indeed, a duty, to cover the trial in all its gory details. The defendants lost much of their privacy, just like the president, movie stars, and celebrities in general. Their lives became, in a sense, part of some giant soap opera. They became "public figures." Anything about them was fair game for the press.

Real-life trials—especially the headline trial—are, in a way, cousins of reality TV. In the last decade or so, reality TV—programs with or about real people—has grown exponentially. Of course, "real people" have been on television for many years—on quiz programs, for example, as contestants; or on programs like *Queen for a Day*, which gave gifts and money to women who spilled their guts to the masses, telling their tales of woe, or on *Candid Camera*, which played humorous tricks on unsuspecting people, or the *Amateur Hour*, where ordinary people could sing and dance and show off their real or imagined talents.[51] But the genre has exploded in recent years. For one thing, it is cheap to produce. For participants, it is their chance at fifteen minutes of fame. But the audience can also share in the drama, can take part in the game of fame. The people on reality shows are familiar, partly because they are *not* rich and famous. Instead they are people from all walks of life: men looking for women to marry, women looking for men, young people living in a house and gossiping about each other, people marooned on islands who must do strange things to stay on television, people who want to lose weight, people who want to wear better clothes, people who are looking for houses, for love, for help with their personal problems, and so on. Reality TV, like TV in general (and now, also, the social networks) both complement and compete with headline trials; they provide alternative routes to the thrills these trials had produced, and sometimes still produce. Indeed, the headline trial, in a sense, was the forerunner of reality TV; it paved the way.

The appeal of headline cases, then, arises in part out of celebrity culture and in part out of our thirst for entertainment and our curiosity about the strange, the lurid, the exciting. Certainly, most headline trials do not, on the surface, present us with deep questions, big social issues, or political dilemmas; most never did. Whether Mary Alice Livingston, in 1895, sent a pail of clam chowder laced with arsenic to her mother, Evelina Bliss,[52] was a question that enthralled the public, but it did not touch off debates in Congress, or anywhere else. Nor, more than a century later, did anything much seem to turn on whether Scott Peterson was or was not guilty of killing his pregnant wife (and her unborn baby, Connor) and dumping her body in San Francisco Bay.

Crime, of course, is a serious social problem, a threat to personal security. Crime waves can unsettle society. Crime, especially violent crime, was the talk of the town in the 1950s. People were frightened and crime control became an issue in local, state, and national elections. In 1987, Willie Horton, a convicted murderer in Massachusetts, slipped off from a weekend furlough program and raped a woman in Maryland. In 1998, George Bush, running for president, made devastating use of Willie Horton (who was black) in ads against his Democratic opponent, Michael Dukakis. Dukakis was governor of Massachusetts when Willie Horton escaped and was thus, in a sense, responsible for the furlough program.[53] Crime has, in the twenty-first century, receded somewhat as a political issue, partly because of a real decline in violent crime.[54] High crime rates put pressure on the political system; but on the whole, crime in developed countries is not a threat to the very foundations of society.[55] More burglaries, or auto thefts, or even murders, unless catastrophically many, are not about to touch off a revolution.

In any event, the crimes that figure in headline trials are not typically what worry people. People are afraid of muggers, rapists, armed robbers, and burglars who might break into their homes. Claus von Bulow or Fatty Arbuckle do not give them nightmares. Nor does Lizzie Borden. These cases were, to be sure, more unsettling in a way than cases that come out of barroom brawls, or gang fights, or a holdup in a convenience store that kills a clerk. Political trials *can* be unsettling and stir up fear of anarchists, Reds, and Soviet spies, or, today, jihadists and suicide bombers. The fears that underlay the McMartin trial or the trial of the Boston nanny may also cut deep. But a lurid murder trial, most of the time, is no more frightening than a trial on a TV cop show or in a movie. Indeed, their very remoteness is part of the attraction.

Headline trials are, and have always been, didactic theater. But messages change, and theater evolves. A modern jury could certainly still acquit Lizzie Borden, but not because she was a virgin (if she was), a churchgoer, or a member of the upper middle class. Identity is still problematic, but in subtly different ways. People have learned, from the movies, from television, and from crime writers—whose books have gotten increasingly darker—about the secret horrors that can lie beneath the surface. Agatha Christie wrote about foul and desperate crimes that happened in sweet country villages; she gave us corpses in the vicarage. In today's society, nothing is unthinkable. No horror is censored; nothing is taboo and no one is immune. Television and the movies present instance after instance of the grossest, most extreme pathology: sex criminals of every conceivable kind, cannibals, serial killers who prey on the innocent, terrorists who blow themselves up in shopping malls. Nothing is off limits, not even evil aliens from outer space. No form of violence, no kind of sick behavior, is too extreme to occur in society, even next door. Headline trials have lost their capacity to shock, though not their ability to fascinate and entertain.

But even if people are less easily shocked, they are all the more willing to believe in the reality of nameless evil. The McMartin case is a prime illustration. An older generation lived through the Holocaust; a later generation lived through the slaughter of countless innocents in Cambodia, Bosnia, Rwanda, Darfur, and South Sudan; and this kind of horror persists, in Syria and elsewhere. Big trials are dramas about evil on a small scale, when they are about evil at all. They are also, at times, about innocence falsely accused. This, too, in the age of DNA and scandals about guiltless men on death row, is something readily believed.

The Vexed Question of Influence

We have mentioned television in the courtroom. A critical question was raised: Does television have an impact on the trial itself? There is also the broader question: What impact do the media have on trials and on criminal justice in general?

The media cater to public taste, but they also help form it. Collectively, they constitute a giant system that both feeds on and helps form mass culture. The basic aim of mass culture is to divert, amuse, and entertain. Big trials, real and fictional, instruct as well as entertain. They carry messages. This has been a major theme of this book. The messages, to be sure, are often obscure and implicit. The O. J. Simpson trial began as a celebrity trial, a case of murder for passion; it ended up exploring the role of race in criminal justice. Big trials also spread information (and misinformation) about the way the system works. People become familiar with the rhythm of the trial—with juries, defense lawyers, witnesses, cross-examination, the judge's instructions, and so on. Almost everybody can mouth the phrase "beyond a reasonable doubt." Most people are aware, in a general way, of the Miranda warning, and they know that witnesses swear to tell the truth, the whole truth, and nothing but the truth.[56]

Arguably, all this is educational. But media coverage and headline trials give the public a distorted picture; criminal justice is seen through a kind of funhouse mirror. Media coverage of big trials conveys two big messages, which, paradoxically, are inconsistent. They are also misleading. The first message is about a meticulous, careful, delicately balanced system. The courts pay almost excessive attention to due process, and the rights of the defendant are scrupulously protected. Every detail is correct: all the *i*'s are dotted, all the *t*'s crossed. The jury is not just twelve people picked up off the street; potential jurors are screened, probed, prodded, and questioned. Eagle-eyed, aggressive lawyers dominate the trial, zealously guarding the interests of their clients. They sniff out prejudicial or mishandled evidence, improper cross-examination, bad jury instructions, and anything that might harm their client, legally speaking. The lawyers spring up like jacks-in-the box, shouting "I object" when anything seems not quite right. Throughout, the trial preserves the sacred presumption of innocence. All of this seemed obvious to the millions who watched O. J. Simpson on trial.

Yet the second message is quite different: that tricks, smart lawyering, and quirks of procedure can bend and twist the law; that all the maneuvering, the tactics, the objections, on both sides, can pervert the scales of justice. Money buys fancy lawyers, investigators, forensic experts. On cross-examination, clever attorneys can bamboozle anyone who stands in the way of their client. In a real sense, justice is for sale. Truth seems irrelevant. All that matters is the ability to befuddle, fool, or overpower the other side (and, of course, the jury, too). Many of the millions who watched the O. J. Simpson trial also got this message, and perhaps in a stronger form than the first message.

There is some truth in both of these messages. And, for better or for worse, the media influence almost everything in the system. They specifically ignore humdrum, everyday processes. People never learn what is ordinary, typical, or routine and what is not. Only the big, the sensational, the extraordinary is covered by the press and TV.

Do the messages flowing from headline trials affect public attitudes and behavior? In an open society, a society driven by mass media, whatever makes headlines can influence the making and enforcement of law. Scandals, sensations, outrageous events are among the most potent forces that shape legal change.[57] Scandals in the food industry led to the creation of a federal Food and Drug Administration in 1906. The outcry after another scandal in 1938—the death of children from an adulterated drug—goaded Congress into strengthening food and drug laws; from then on no new drug could be marketed without passing stringent clinical tests.[58] Laws on clean air and water owe at least something to smog in Los Angeles and other cities, and also to the tragedy in Donora, Pennsylvania, where the "death fog" (polluted air) in October 1948 brought about darkness at noon, killed 22 people, and made 5,910 people ill.[59] Calamitous oil spills lead to calls for control over drilling in ocean waters. Business scandals can lead to changes in the structure of financial and banking regulation.

But perhaps nowhere do scandals and incidents play as great a role as in the criminal justice system. The impact comes, on the whole, from sensational crimes rather than from sensational trials. One prime example is "Megan's law"[60] and its progeny. A seven-year-old girl, Megan Kanka, was raped and murdered in New Jersey by a man who lived across the street from her. This man was a sex offender with a criminal record, but Megan's family was unaware of this fact. The New Jersey legislature enacted "Megan's Law" in 1994; something similar is now the law in all fifty states. The core idea is that "sex offenders" must register, and that people have a right to know where they live. Under the Pennsylvania law, for example, a "sexually violent predator" must give "written notice" of his whereabouts and his address to neighbors, school districts within a one-mile radius of his home, day-care centers, and colleges within one thousand feet of his home.[61]

A sex offender raped and murdered Jessica Lunsford in 2005. A wave of outrage followed. In response, Florida enacted a law imposing very harsh sentences on sex offenders.[62] The so-called three-strikes law in California (1994) was another draconian law. It essentially imposed a life sentence after three convictions for serious crimes. It, too, arose out of a public outcry, following news of a hideous crime.[63] The 9/11 attacks on the World Trade Center and the Pentagon in 2001 led to passage of the USA PATRIOT Act. A new cabinet position resulted, too, and a raft of new laws and regulations, all part of a "war" on terrorism. There were also a number of terrorist trials.[64]

Charles Lindbergh was a great hero in the 1920s, the first man to fly solo across the Atlantic, in 1927. In 1932, his twenty-month-old son was kidnapped and murdered. After a long investigation, Bruno Richard Hauptmann was arrested and put on trial for this horrific crime. The trial aroused extraordinary interest; H. L. Mencken called it the "greatest story since the Resurrection"; the quote may be apocryphal, but it "shows up in so many sources, always attributed to Mencken, that it seems irrelevant at this point whether he actually said it. He ought to have."[65] Hauptmann was convicted, and on April 3, 1936, at the state prison in Trenton, New Jersey, in the "small, brightly lighted execution chamber" with its "smudged white-washed brick walls," Hauptmann was electrocuted, still insisting he was innocent.[66] Congress, in reaction to the crime (and the huge public outcry), passed a law that made kidnapping a federal crime whenever the kidnapper crossed state lines. Under the law, if seven days passed after the kidnapping, crossing state lines would be *presumed*, and federal authorities could intervene.[67] Many states passed "little Lindbergh" laws of their own. Caryl Chessman, as we mentioned earlier, had technically violated the California law; this violation was the excuse for sentencing Chessman to death.[68] Hinckley's attempt to kill President Reagan and the jury's verdict in his case (not guilty by reason of insanity) were, as we saw, the catalyst for changes in the insanity defense.[69]

13

Instant Celebrity

As we have noted, the rich and famous—in today's world, "celebrities"—are overrepresented in headline trials. Fatty Arbuckle was a Hollywood star; O. J. Simpson was a sports hero, a hall of famer, and a movie personality. Daniel Sickles was a member of Congress. Harry Thaw came from a rich family, and his victim, Stanford White, was a hugely successful architect. Charles Lindbergh was a national hero. Charles Guiteau assassinated an American president.

Other defendants were at least locally prominent. The Bordens, though hardly a household name, were leading citizens of Fall River, Massachusetts. The Walworths, too, were prominent figures in their day. Claus von Bulow was the husband of a rich society woman. In part, the rich and famous can be expected to dominate many big trials, simply because they can afford expensive, flamboyant lawyers. Alan Dershowitz estimated (conservatively, he said) that Claus von Bulow's defense cost well over a million dollars; some of this money, of course, went to Dershowitz himself.[1] Apparently, O. J. Simpson spent over $6 million defending himself in court.[2] The families of Loeb and Leopold, the two young men who killed little Bobby Franks, offered a fortune to Clarence Darrow to try to save these two defendants from the electric chair. Rich and famous clients, too, are in a position to decide, on balance, to run the risk and expense of a full trial; small fry, for the most part, have to settle for whatever they can get through a plea bargain.

Not all headline trials, however, cost the defendants big money. Criminal lawyers thrive on publicity, unlike the dull gray lawyers of Wall Street, who avoid notoriety like the plague. Criminal lawyers have no Fortune 500 companies on retainer. Their clients, by and large, do not provide them with steady business, year in and year out. Criminal lawyers have mostly one-shot clients. They need a constant flow of fresh business. For this reason, they welcome fame, publicity, headlines. Rich and famous clients, of course, will not be charity cases. But if the case is sensational enough, criminal lawyers will step up and volunteer, money or no money, simply to get their name before the public. As Arthur Train wrote in 1912, in celebrated cases, "even if the prisoner has no money to pay the lawyer, the latter is willing to take the case for the advertising he will get out of it."[3] Clara Fallmer was on trial in Oakland in 1897; she had shot and killed her boyfriend, Charlie La Due, who had abandoned her. She was a young girl from a poor family in no position to pay fat fees. My guess is that her lawyers took on her case for virtually nothing.[4]

But in an important sense, all big trials are, or become, celebrity trials. This was, in a way, true as soon as these trials became darlings of the media. Today it is truer than ever. Probably not one person out of a million had heard of Lizzie Borden or Sam Sheppard or Claus von Bulow or Scott Peterson or the Menendez brothers before they became enmeshed in the web of criminal justice. Once they did so, however, they became household names. Most of all, of course, this occurs when the trial is televised. Then it becomes, quite literally, a public show. Other big trials will at least get play on the evening news; a few become subjects of television specials. Headline trials occupy space in the newspapers and, increasingly, on blogs and the web in general.

Today, then, headline trials are a part of celebrity culture. Television can make almost anybody a celebrity, and out of virtually nothing. Indeed, this happens every day, on so-called reality shows, for example. The people on these programs are quite ordinary people. They have no particular talent or virtue, except maybe a bit more than the usual amount of lust for self-promotion. TV makes them famous, at least temporarily. Winners of quiz shows, wannabe singers and dancers who go on "talent" shows, a bachelor who gets to pick a mate, a polygamous family showing off their lifestyle, the "litigants" on shows like *Judge Judy* or *Divorce Court*, airing their dirty linen in public: Television gives all of them a taste of celebrity status and they share in the illusion of familiarity. We see them in television's one-way mirror.[5] We hear them. They talk, they move. Homemade videos, family picnics, antics of cats and dogs, and cute behavior of children posted on YouTube and other websites can have the same effect: And there is always the chance that a video might go "viral" and reach an audience of millions.

In short, television and the Internet magnify celebrity culture. Curiously enough, it does not matter much whether people actually believe what they see on reality TV. In one survey, 25 percent of the people polled thought the programs were complete fiction; 57 percent thought they were distorted. Mostly, the audience doesn't care.[6] Watching television, as Eric Burns has pointed out, is a different experience from going to the movies. Television makes it easy to feel a certain "intimacy," that is, a certain familiarity, in a way the movies never could. Movies, after all, were not seen *live.* In television, however, people can be seen in the flesh. People don't observe men and women on television with "distant veneration." The audience sits in its own living room, bedroom, or rec room, and what they see seems as if it was beamed directly to them. Television personalities become "far more visible in our lives, far more frequent in their appearances," than the stars in the movies.[7] Richard Schickel has used the phrase "imagined intimacy."[8] And what was true of television stars, comedians, musicians, and talk show hosts has become true of *everyone* on television: sports figures, religious leaders, and political personalities; participants in reality shows; people in the news for whatever reason, whether for winning the lottery, committing an awful crime, being the victim of that awful crime, or being the next-door neighbor of the victim or the criminal; or someone exposed to the Ebola virus, or suffering from the results of flood, earthquake, or tornado. Or, indeed, for a starring or supporting role in a headline trial. And because, in our times, every headline trial becomes, in a way, a celebrity trial, it is only natural that the trial proceedings will mesmerize the public. If the defendant (or victim) was a celebrity to begin with—like O. J. Simpson or William Kennedy Smith, the nephew of a president—then so much the better. But even when neither defendant nor victim has celebrity status *beforehand*, the trial itself creates them as celebrities. Lizzie Borden was well known in her community, but she was a complete unknown outside it. The hideous crime in her household blasted away her anonymity and flashed a blinding light on her and her family. When Lizzie was accused of the crime, she moved out of obscurity and onto center stage. She became truly famous—and controversial.

In big trials, all the characters, even those with cameo roles, become celebrities. Before television, they were at best proto-celebrities. But today, just as television can *create* celebrities, so can the headline trial. The defendant, of course, may become a celebrity, but so too may the judge, the lawyers, and the witnesses.[9] During the O. J. Simpson trial, which was televised, millions of people who could not name a Supreme Court justice to save their souls knew, recognized, and were intensely aware of Judge Ito, the lower court judge in Los Angeles who presided over the trial. He had become, overnight, an enormous celebrity. Everybody involved in this trial, even the bit players, became tremendously famous, at least for a while.

There is a certain chicken-and-egg quality to this argument: the big trials both *create* celebrities and *reflect* and *respond* to celebrity society. The twentieth century developed new doctrine about a right to privacy. Protecting this right, managing threats to privacy, parsing the meaning of the right—these are key items on the agenda of modern law and legal policy.[10] Yet, perhaps paradoxically, in our celebrity-driven society, rules and institutions originally designed to protect the privacy and reputation of elites have all but vanished. We think we can and should know everything about the lives of the rich and famous; we think we can peep, so to speak, into their windows. We feel that we have a right to this information: Presidents who have sex with their interns; the love lives of basketball, baseball, and football players; what shoes and robes the Pope wears; the thoughts and feelings of the Queen of England. People in the public eye—so-called public figures—are fair game for photographers and reporters. They have little privacy in fact, and less of a legal right to privacy, than the ordinary citizen has. In Europe, the scale is tilted somewhat differently; there, even a princess can claim some respect for her privacy. Princess Caroline of Monaco, for example, who was plagued by paparazzi, was allowed to suppress photos that showed her shopping, playing tennis, and, at one point, tripping and falling in her bathing suit at a beach club; these photographs, in the opinion of the European Court of Human Rights, served no public interest.[11] Such a case would probably come out differently in the United States. Still, on the whole, the gap between the law in the United States and the law in European countries is not that large; legal and social differences may be slowly diminishing.[12] France and Italy and the rest of Europe are celebrity societies, just like the United States.

In a headline trial—of, O. J. Simpson, for example, or Claus von Bulow or Casey Anthony—the media audience gets to look inside private lives, learns or thinks it learns their secrets, and revels in the scandals and the mysteries. To be sure, conflicting stories are told. The defendant's lawyer is, in a way, his press agent. The prosecution, on the other hand, is engaged in as much character assassination as it can get away with. Or, at times, the tactic is to smear the victim. In the trial of Claus von Bulow, the prosecution described him as a vicious philanderer, a selfish, greedy cad who was quite capable of trying to kill his helpless wife. The defense, for its part, chipped away at the image of Sunny von Bulow; she was weak, addicted, even suicidal, precisely, in other words, the kind of woman who might have mishandled medications and brought her problem on herself. In the Sickles trial, and in other cases of the unwritten law, it is the victim who is smeared as a home wrecker, an adulterer, moral scum. The rules of evidence also make a difference: They act as a kind of censorship board, keeping out whatever is (legally) deemed too inflammatory or prejudicial. But despite all the legal and factual limits, the headline trial still has enough oomph, enough power, enough surprises and revelations, to mesmerize and entrance the public.

14

A Concluding Word

In an age of instant communication, when images and ideas spread around the world in nanoseconds via blogs, tweets, texts, and websites, the headline trial may seem like a kind of dinosaur—a lumbering, awkward form left over from an earlier period. It might seem less important than it was before: as didactic theater, as a vehicle for information, or as an open-air display of basic norms and values of society. The big trial, historically, has had a role in *dramatizing* the rules, whether they were official or unofficial (like the so-called unwritten law). Usually, in a headline trial, a solitary individual was in the dock, but the message could be larger and broader. In colonial Massachusetts, for example, the stocks, the whipping post, and sermons on Sunday helped spread the word about the normative order of Puritan America; so, too, did speeches from the gallows. All of these devices turned rules, roles, norms, and punishments into living, breathing flesh; it made them real, corporeal, effective.

Over the years, the big trial, on the whole, has shifted in function. It is still, of course, public; it is still didactic theater. But since the nineteenth century, it has increasingly come to depend on the media to spread the word, to publicize the proceedings, and to interpret them for the mass audience. Political trials and corruption trials have by no means lost their importance. In many countries, they play a role in suppressing dissent or (to put it more charitably) in enforcing policy. In democratic societies, dissenters can at times make the trial *their* form of didactic theater. Political trials can also be used—nationally and internationally—to bring tyrants to justice. This is the age of the human rights culture—above all, the idea that every human being has certain inherent, immutable, and transcendent rights has given new meaning to one kind of headline trial. The trials that can be traced, ultimately, to Nuremberg, are already important, and these trials, one hopes, have a bright and effective future.

Trials of ordinary crimes—if you can call murder ordinary—evolved along with the media. They may be dismissed as entertainment, but they also have a message. Often, they touch a nerve or dramatize a social problem: race relations, or the changing structure of the family, or, as we argued with regard to the McMartin case, the Boston nanny, or Brooke Astor, deep-seated anxieties about child-care or eldercare in the contemporary world. Trials like Lizzie Borden's served, in the past, to raise larger questions about the nature of bourgeois society. Today, Lizzie's trial would probably still make headlines but with a somewhat different spin. The Borden house is now a bed and breakfast—and a museum. It has a blog, and on the fateful day the public is invited to "get Bizzie with Lizzie" and participate in a re-enactment of the case: "Did she do it? You decide." In short, today, the public is still titillated, still fascinated, but not shocked by any means. It takes a lot more to scandalize the public. No doubt, if the nice man next door keeps body parts in his freezer, or creeps off at night to kill random women, the news will still shock the neighbors. But people know, or think they know, all about psychopaths, serial killers, and the like. They see them on TV.

The mass media play a huge role in public life. We no longer whip transgressors in the public square or gather en masse to see men swing from the gallows. Lynching is history. But the "perp walk," the handcuffs and prison uniforms—along with press releases from the authorities—fill some of the same social space. And private methods—YouTube, social networks—allow ordinary people to play prosecutor, or, if you will, judge and jury. Consider the case of the Korean "dog poop girl." One day in 2005, this woman's dog did its business on the floor of a subway train in Seoul; she refused to clean up the mess. Someone took a photograph, and posted it on the web; thousands saw it. The woman was humiliated and disgraced by the "cyber-posse," which hung a "digital scarlet letter" around her neck. Her life was profoundly affected. This is but one of many lessons about the power of public disclosure and shaming.[1]

The media also filter out what they (or the public) find boring or irrelevant. They help set the national agenda. They define the "boundaries" of interactions. In contemporary society, everything, or almost everything, becomes a *show*. The lines between entertainment and politics, between entertainment and social life, blur almost to the vanishing point. Modern society is celebrity society; people are enthralled and obsessed with the rich and famous, who have become, thanks to the media, *familiar* in a way that was not possible in the past. Headline trials often come out of celebrity life; they also create celebrities. In the age of reality TV, these trials take their place as another version of this art form. Celebrity culture makes it possible to envy and admire the rich and famous, to peek into their houses, eavesdrop on their conversations on late-night talk shows, and see them as (we think) they really are. Gossip magazines—and even mainstream magazines and newspapers—report the doings and misdoings of celebrities. Nothing is censored. Moreover, nothing and nobody is sacred—not the president, not the British royal family, not the Roman Catholic hierarchy.

Today, the social role of headline trials has probably shrunk. Yet public life in society can be compared to a headline trial; much of it takes the form of trial or debate. Candidates for high office are *expected* to debate. These debates, between presidential candidates, for example, have become routine; millions of people watch them on television. In these debates, as in trials, one side wins and one side loses. Instant polling gives out immediate results. The public is the jury. Here public life takes the form (or quasi-form) of a contest, like a hundred-meter dash or an Olympic diving match.

What we might call "political quasi-trials" should also be mentioned here. Congressional committees can hold hearings, call witnesses, and question them. The hearings are usually open to the public; if the subject is newsworthy, reporters will cover the proceedings in detail. Witnesses come equipped with attorneys. At the end of the quasi-trial, the committee may issue a report, make a recommendation, and (at times) issue citations for contempt. In the 1930s the Dies Committee (the House Committee on Un-American Activities), led by Martin Dies, a right-wing congressman from Texas, diligently hunted for subversives. In 1938, for example, the committee called before it Hallie Flanagan, who directed the Federal Theatre Project. Wasn't it true, the committee asked, that the project gave jobs to Communists and produced pro-Communist plays? Flanagan denied all the charges. Congress killed the project anyway.[2]

During the Cold War, the House Un-American Activities Committee (HUAC) carried on this work. The investigations took place in the glare of spotlights. The point was to expose the secret world of un-Americans and to transmit a stern, frightening message about the Communist menace (as the committee saw it). To HUAC, Reds and fellow travelers were everywhere—in every institution, including universities, in the army, in the government, and very definitely in Hollywood. Hollywood cringed as HUAC went on the attack.[3] The Reds lost their jobs and were boycotted. By this time, HUAC had at its fingertips a new and powerful weapon: television. Television also helped to launch the infamous career of Senator Joseph McCarthy.

McCarthy made headlines with his reckless charges against the government, which, in his view, was harboring entire brigades of Communists. He later made news with accusations about a radical army dentist who, McCarthy claimed, posed a serious threat to the Republic. Out of this, and other charges, came the Army-McCarthy hearings, broadcast live on television. Some 80 million people watched the show.

These hearings, a kind of trial by television, actually led to McCarthy's downfall. The climax of the hearings pitted McCarthy against Joseph Welch, who served as counsel for the army. McCarthy launched a collateral attack on Welch; he claimed that a young man in Welch's office, Fred Fisher, had belonged to an organization that McCarthy called a "legal bulwark of the Communist party."[4] Welch was outraged at this allegation and mounted a furious counterattack. His famous line, "Have you no sense of decency, sir, at long last?"—broadcast live to the whole country—somehow sealed McCarthy's fate. The Senate censured him, and his star faded permanently. Television had lifted him up; a quasi-trial on television struck him down.[5]

In 1950 and 1951, a Senate Special Committee ran another television quasi-trial, which proved to be a box-office hit. The committee was charged with investigating organized crime. The chairman was Senator Estes Kefauver of Tennessee. This was at the dawn of the television era; millions watched the hearings, and its cast of character—the senators themselves, but also a motley parade of gangsters, hoodlums, and mobsters—became celebrities, like the characters in a headline trial. One mobster, Frank Costello, objected strenuously to the television cameras. Kefauver accepted his demand: no faces. But then the camera "zeroed in on Costello's hands—wet palms and hairy fingers, crumpling scraps of paper and nervously fiddling with his glasses." The hands became "strangely hypnotic" and made Costello seem even more sinister to the audience of millions.[6] Costello's hands became television stars. The hearings had a certain amount of political impact. The hearings made Kefauver a star; the Democratic Party later nominated him for vice president (he lost).

This is the end of our story of the big trials, a story of changing social norms, of the rise of the media, of the development of a celebrity culture. We began our story with the first uses of the trial as didactic theater, in Puritan New England. Today, celebrity culture, in some ways, makes the whole of society something like a small New England village in the seventeenth century. All of us can watch and see what happens in public life. What has remained constant is the public nature of the trial, its dependence on the media, and its role as didactic theater. Like theater itself, the themes, plots, and issues have changed subtly over time. Like theater, too, much of what we see, or think we see, is illusion.

Notes

Chapter 1. Law and Its Audience

1. David Margolick, "After 474 Days as a Prisoner, He is Free," *New York Times*, October 4, 1995.

2. Whether this is still true in the age of the "war on terrorism" is not so clear. Wartime trials of spies and the like are also something of an exception. During World War II, eight Germans landed on the coast of the United States in 1942; their mission was sabotage. They were caught, tried by a secret military tribunal, and sentenced to death. The Supreme Court of the United States upheld their conviction. Ex parte Quirin, 317 U.S. 1 (1942). Six of the eight were executed. The president commuted the death sentence of two others, who had turned themselves in and helped in the capture of the others.

3. Virginia A. McConnell, *Arsenic Under the Elms: Murder in Victorian New Haven* (Lincoln: University of Nebraska Press, 2005), 68.

4. Michael Macdonald Mooney, *Evelyn Nesbit and Stanford White: Love and Death in the Gilded Age* (New York: Morrow, 1976), 247.

5. There is, of course, an enormous literature on the concept of the rule of law; the meaning given above is only one of the possibilities. See, for example, Brian Tamanaha, *On the Rule of Law: History, Politics, Theory* (Cambridge, UK: Cambridge University Press, 2004).

6. 5 U.S. C.A. § 552 (2012).

7. 5 U.S. C.A. § 553 (2012).

8. See, for example, "Covert Surveillance: 'I have no intention of hiding.... I have done nothing wrong,'" *Guardian* (London), June 10, 2013.

9. After the trial, anybody can ask to see the court files (few do), with some exceptions (juvenile proceedings, for example).

Chapter 2. Open to the Public

1. There is surprisingly little *general* literature on these trials; exceptions include Robert A. Ferguson, *The Trial in American Life* (Chicago: University of Chicago Press, 2007), and Richard L. Fox and Robert W. Van Sickel, *Tabloid Justice: Criminal Justice in an Age of Media Frenzy* (Boulder: Lynne Rienner, 2001). See also Robert Hariman, "Performing the Laws: Popular Trials and Social Knowledge," in *Popular Trials: Rhetoric, Mass Media, and the Law*, ed. Robert Hariman, 17–30 (Tuscaloosa: University of Alabama Press, 1990), 17. I should mention, too, Mary S. Hartman, *Victorian Murderesses* (New York: Schocken Books, 1976). The subtitle of this book is worth citing: "A True History of Thirteen Respectable French and English Women Accused of Unspeakable Crimes." Treatments of media coverage of trials are also valuable; see Fox and Van Sickel, *Tabloid Justice*, and Ray Surette, *Media, Crime, and Criminal Justice: Images, Realities, and Policies*, 3d ed. (Belmont, Calif.: Thomson/Wadsworth, 2007). Of course, if you added together all the books and articles about *particular* headline trials, such as those of Lizzie Borden or Sacco and Vanzetti, and the rest, you would end up with a truly enormous list.

2. See William Haltom and Michael McCann, *Distorting the Law: Politics, Media, and the Litigation Crisis* (Chicago: University of Chicago Press, 2004), 185–226.

3. See, for example, John Denvir, ed., *Legal Reelism: Movies as Legal Texts* (Urbana: University of Illinois Press, 1996). On law and popular culture generally, see Michael Freeman, ed., *Law and Popular Culture* (Oxford: Oxford University Press, 2005); Stewart Macaulay, "Images of Law in Everyday Life," *Law & Society Review* 21 (1987): 185; Lawrence M. Friedman, "Law, Lawyers, and Popular Culture," *Yale Law Journal* 98 (1989): 1,579.

4. The distinction between a felony and a less serious crime (a misdemeanor) varies from state to state. Murder is always a felony, as are rape and armed robbery. In the California Penal Code (section 17) a felony is

defined as a "crime which is punishable with death or by imprisonment in the state prison." All other crimes are "misdemeanors except those offences that are classified as infractions." Infractions are minor crimes. usually punished with fines.

5. There is a large literature on plea bargaining. On its origins, see Lawrence M. Friedman, *Crime and Punishment in American History* (New York: BasicBooks, 1993), 390–393; George Fisher, *Plea Bargaining's Triumph: A History of Plea Bargaining in America* (Stanford: Stanford University Press, 2003).

6. Marc Galanter, "The Vanishing Trial: An Examination of Trials and Related Matters in Federal and State Courts," *Journal of Empirical Legal Studies* 1 (2004): 259; see also Robert P. Burns, *The Death of the American Trial* (Chicago: University of Chicago Press, 2009).

7. See Fisher, *Plea Bargaining's Triumph*, 97, 120. I examined minute books from the 1890s in Leon County, Florida, where the trials were even shorter and more slapdash.

8. Lawrence M. Friedman, "The Day Before Trials Vanished," *Journal of Empirical Legal Studies* 1 (2004): 689.

9. Many books have been written about the Simpson case; see, for example, Janice Schuetz and Lin S. Lilley, eds., *The O. J. Simpson Trials: Rhetoric, Media, and the Law* (Carbondale: Southern Illinois University Press, 1999); Darnell M. Hunt, *O. J. Simpson Facts and Fictions: News Rituals in the Construction of Reality* (Cambridge: Cambridge University Press, 1999); Jeffrey Toobin, *The Run of His Life: The People v. O. J. Simpson* (New York: Random House, 1996).

10. See Friedman, *Crime and Punishment in American History*, 36–41.

11. *Records and Files of the Quarterly Courts of Essex County, Massachusetts*, vol. VIII (1680–1683) (1921), 86–87.

12. *Laws of New Hampshire, vol. 1, Province Period: 1679–1702* (Manchester, NH: John B. Clarke, 1904), 676.

13. Leon deValinger, Jr., etc., *Court Records of Kent County, Delaware, 1680–1705* (Washington, D.C.: American Historical Association, 1959), 167.

14. *Laws and Liberties of Massachusetts* (Cambridge, Mass.: Harvard University Press, 1929 [originally published in 1648]), 3.

15. *Records and Files of the Quarterly Court of Essex County, Massachusetts*, vol. II (Salem: Essex Institute, 1912), 48.

16. Daniel A. Cohen, *Pillars of Salt, Monuments of Grace: New England Crime Literature and the Origins of American Popular Culture, 1674–1860* (Amherst: University of Massachusetts Press, 1993), 20.

17. Cohen, *Pillars of Salt, Monuments of Grace*, 21.

18. Irene Quenzler Brown and Richard D. Brown, *The Hanging of Ephraim Wheeler* (Cambridge, Mass.: Belknap, 2003), 249.

19. Brown and Brown, *The Hanging of Ephraim Wheeler*, 63.

20. Louis P. Masur, *Rites of Execution: Capital Punishment and the Transformation of American Culture, 1776–1865* (New York: Oxford University Press, 1989), 95, 96.

21. But apparently there was still an occasional example of such speeches. When Zephyr Davis was executed, in Chicago in 1888, a minister read Zephyr's "message" to the gathered crowd. Zephyr expressed regret "for all . . . wrongs I have ever done. . . . I am deeply and truly sorry"; he also stated that he had "found forgiveness with God" and he told "all the boys with whom I have ever associated to take warning and always try to do right." Whether Zephyr actually wrote this himself is dubious, however. Elizabeth Dale, *The Rule of Justice: The People of Chicago versus Zephyr Davis* (Columbus: Ohio State University Press, 2001), 96.

22. Masur, *Rites of Execution*, 94.

23. See Lawrence M. Friedman and Robert V. Percival, *The Roots of Justice: Crime and Punishment in Alameda County, California, 1870–1910* (Chapel Hill: University of North Carolina Press, 1983), 305.

24. Elizabeth Dale, *The Chicago Trunk Murder* (DeKalb: Northern Illinois University Press, 2011), 73.

25. Adam Hirsch, *The Rise of the Penitentiary: Prisons and Punishment in Early America* (New Haven: Yale University Press, 1992); Friedman, *Crime and Punishment in American History*, 77–82.

26. Stuart Banner, *The Death Penalty: An American History* (Cambridge, Mass.: Harvard University Press, 2003), 194–196.

27. *Laws of Pennsylvania* (1913), 529.

28. In re Kemmler, 136 U.S. 436 (1890); the Supreme Court upheld this mode of execution. It was "humane," did not constitute "cruel and unusual punishment," and was therefore not forbidden by the constitution.

29. "Far Worse Than Hanging," *New York Times,* August 7, 1890.

30. Ibid.

31. *National Police Gazette,* April 8, 1899. Mrs. Place had killed her stepdaughter, Ida, in a fit of jealousy; she also tried to murder her husband and attempted suicide.

32. George C. Wright, *Racial Violence in Kentucky, 1865–1940* (Baton Rouge: Louisiana State University Press, 1990), 71.

33. See Leon F. Litwack, *Trouble in Mind: Black Southerners in the Age of Jim Crow* (New York: Knopf, 1998); for a vivid description of a lynching, see Sharon F. Davies, *Rising Road: A True Tale of Love, Race, and Religion in America* (Oxford: Oxford University Press, 2010), 153–154.

34. Litwack, *Trouble in Mind*, 289.

35. When Leo Frank was lynched in Georgia, in 1915, "hordes of people made their way to the oak tree where the lifeless figure, with its gaping red throat wound, swayed in the wind. Souvenir hunters tore pieces of cloth from the sleeves of the nightshirt which covered the body, and snipped strands of the rope." But a local judge prevented mutilation and burning of the body. See Leonard Dinnerstein, *The Leo Frank Case* (Athens: University of Georgia Press, 2008).

36. There is a considerable literature on the vigilante movement. For an account of this and related movements, see Richard Maxwell Brown, *Strain of Violence: Historical Studies of American Violence and Vigilantism* (Oxford: Oxford University Press, 1975). Interestingly, Utah lacked a rich history of vigilante action; Utah was a tightly organized society, under the influence of leaders of the Latter Day Saints; it was socially, in other words, quite different from the rest of the West.

37. Thomas A. Dimsdale, *The Vigilantes of Montana, or, Popular Justice in the Rocky Mountains* (reprint, Norman: University of Oklahoma Press, 1953), 194–205.

38. Dimsdale, *Vigilantes of Montana*, 76–78.

39. Dimsdale, *Vigilantes of Montana*, 13.

40. Robert P. Ingalls, *Urban Vigilantes in the New South: Tampa, 1882–1936* (Knoxville: University of Tennessee Press, 1988).

41. Roger D. McGrath, *Gunfighters, Highwaymen, and Vigilantes: Violence on the Frontier* (Berkeley: University of California Press, 1984), 234–242.

42. McGrath, *Gunfighters, Highwaymen, and Vigilantes*, 242.

43. Brown, *Strain of Violence*, 108. This was hardly a unique case of political success. Wilbur Fisk Sanders, who did vigilante service in Montana, was elected one of Montana's senators in 1889. Brown, *Strain of Violence*, 112.

44. For many years, antilynching campaigns foundered on the rock of Southern white intransigence. Action in Congress was consistently thwarted deep into the twentieth century by powerful Southern members of Congress, who sounded the phony but effective battle cry of states' rights.

45. Dimsdale, *Vigilantes of Montana*, 14. Hubert Bancroft's classic account of the San Francisco vigilance committees, *Popular Tribunals* (San Francisco: History Company, 1887) is equally laudatory. On the vigilante movement in general, the fullest account is Brown, *Strain of Violence.*

46. "Mystic Numbers," *San Francisco Chronicle,* December 3, 1894.

47. Michael Feldberg, *The Turbulent Era: Riot and Disorder in Jacksonian America* (New York: Oxford University Press, 1980), 34–35. These riots were "political" in that they were a "social process by which groups compete for . . . material and prestige rewards." Feldberg, *The Turbulent Era*, 34.

48. Feldberg, *The Turbulent Era*, 54–55. "Expressive" riots were "collective violence" used to reinforce group solidarity or to express that solidarity to the outside world. "Recreational" riots were an "outlet" for young people "to release . . . physical and emotional energies." Some of the rioting and hell-raising, according to Feldberg, could be compared to "organized team sports." In this period, too, volunteer fire departments, when they were not fighting fires, seemed to enjoy fighting each other.

49. Feldberg, *The Turbulent Era*, 74.

50. See Elizabeth Dale, *Criminal Justice in the United States, 1789–1939* (Cambridge: Cambridge University Press, 2011). Dale argues that "popular justice" in the broadest sense has been neglected in the literature; historical studies of criminal justice should pay more attention to this phenomenon.

51. On the Tulsa riot, see James S. Hirsch, *Riot and Remembrance: The Tulsa Race War and Its Legacy* (Boston: Houghton Mifflin, 2002), and Scott Ellsworth, *Death in a Promised Land: The Tulsa Race Riot of 1921* (Baton Rouge: Louisiana State University Press, 1982). The Detroit riots were the subject of huge headlines in the press; see "Army Rules Detroit; 23 Die," *Chicago Tribune,* June 22, 1943; Robert Young, "Paratroopers Fight Riot; Restore Law, Order in Detroit, LBJ Says," *Chicago Tribune*, July 25, 1967. On this riot, see Sidney Fine, *Violence in the Model City: The Cavanagh Administration, Race Relations, and the Detroit Riot of 1967* (Ann Arbor: University of Michigan Press, 1989).

52. Les Ledbetter, "San Francisco Tense as Violence Follows Murder Trial," *New York Times*, May 23, 1979. White served a term in prison, was released, and then committed suicide; Robert Lindsey, "Dan White, Killer of San Francisco Mayor, A Suicide," *New York Times*, October 22, 1985.

53. See Seth Mydans, "Verdicts Set Off a Wave of Shock and Anger," *New York Times*, April 30, 1992.

Chapter 3. Political Trials

1. One of the few earlier attempts to classify headline trials has been made by Ray Surette, "Media Trials," *Journal of Criminal Justice* 17 (1989): 293. Surette divides "media trials" into three categories, based on the theme of the trial: "abuse of power and trust," "sinful rich," and "evil strangers." These seem useful, as far as they go, but I think it would make sense to expand the list of categories, and I have tried to do so here.

2. Peter Charles Hoffer, *The Treason Trials of Aaron Burr* (Lawrence: University Press of Kansas, 2008), 1.

3. Indeed, Hoffer is thus able to conclude that "in the end, the Burr trials were not political"; Hoffer, *Treason Trials of Aaron Burr*, 2.

4. Blaine Harden, "2 Guilty in Trade Center Blast," *Washington Post*, November 13, 1997.

5. Katharine Q. Seelye, "Regretful Lindh Gets 20 Years in Taliban Case," *New York Times*, October 5, 2002.

6. For a vivid description of one of these trials, see Simon Sebag Montefiore, *Stalin: The Court of the Red Tsar* (London: Weidenfeld & Nicolson, 2003), 189–193.

7. See, for example, Vadim Z. Rogovin, *Stalin's Terror of 1937–1938: Political Genocide in the USSR* (Oak Park, Mich.: Mehring Books, 2009).

8. "Putin's Victory," *The Economist*, December 30, 2010.

9. In December 2013, Putin unexpectedly released not only Khodorovsky but also the members of the Pussy Riot group—supposedly also for political reasons; he also released members of the crew of a Greenpeace ship who had been imprisoned and charged with piracy. Andrew S. Kramer, "Vast Amnesty by Russians Includes Case of Greenpeace," *New York Times*, December 25, 2013.

10. David M. Herszenhorn, "Dead Lawyer, a Kremlin Critic, Is Found Guilty of Tax Evasion," *New York Times*, July 12, 2013.

11. Andrew Jacobs, "In Sentence of Activist, China Gives West a Chill," *New York Times*, December 26, 2009. The sentence was eleven years in prison. Liu Xiaobo later won the Nobel Peace Prize, but the Chinese government angrily denounced this decision as "blasphemy" and an "insult to the Chinese people." Andrew Jacobs, "China, Angered by Peace Prize, Blocks Celebration," *New York Times*, October 10, 2010.

12. Liz Gooch, "Malaysian Opposition Leader Acquitted in Sodomy Trial," *New York Times*, January 8, 2012. See also "Former Ukraine Prime

Minister Found Guilty of Abuse of Office in 'Show Trial' Verdict Condemned by West," *Daily Mail*, October 11, 2011.

13. The trials—and legal systems, in general—of dictatorial societies are a big subject in themselves. Many modern dictatorships run a kind of dual system: ordinary courts for ordinary cases and special courts or procedures for political cases. So, in Inga Markovits' study of "Lüritz" (the name she gives to a town in East Germany), the district court of the town did not handle "political" offenders; these cases were transferred to a higher, regional court and dealt with there. Inga Markovits, *Justice in Lüritz: Experiencing Socialist Law in East Germany* (Princeton: Princeton University Press, 2010), 93.

14. In 1945, a British bomb hit the building in which Freisler was presiding and put an end to his notorious and murderous career. "Bombing Kills Nazi Judge," *New York Times*, February 8, 1945.

15. See Jim Yardley, "The McVeigh Execution: Oklahoma City," *New York Times*, June 12, 2001.

16. Eleven leaders of the Communist Party were convicted of violating a federal law, the Smith Act, and the convictions were affirmed in Dennis v. United States, 341 U.S. 494 (1951).

17. Quoted in Robert A. Ferguson, *The Trial in American Life* (Chicago: University of Chicago Press, 2007), 233.

18. See the account in William R. Conklin, "Pair Silent to End," *New York Times*, June 20, 1953.

19. Allen Weinstein, *Perjury: The Hiss-Chambers Case* (New York: Knopf, 1978). There is still a lively argument about Hiss and whether he was or was not a Soviet agent; some evidence suggests that he was indeed in the pay of the Soviet Union, at least for a time.

20. "Hiss Convicted in Perjury Case," *Los Angeles Times*, January 22, 1950.

21. See the chapter on the Coplon trials in John Earl Haynes and Harvey Klehr, *Early Cold War Spies* (Cambridge, UK: Cambridge University Press, 2006), 192.

22. *Los Angeles Times*, March 8, 1950.

23. Haynes and Klehr, *Early Cold War Spies*, 207.

24. During the (unpopular) war in Vietnam, the government had trouble winning convictions against draft-evaders, or people who took part in antiwar protests. See the figures given in Presidential Clemency Board, Report to the President (1975, GPO), 46–48.

25. See Shawn Francis Peters, *The Catonsville Nine: A Story of Faith and Resistance in the Vietnam Era* (New York: Oxford University Press, 2012).

26. J. Anthony Lukas, "Seale Put in Chains at Chicago 8 Trial," *New York Times*, October 30, 1969.

27. See Jason Epstein, *The Great Conspiracy Trial* (New York: Random House, 1970). Whether the defendants accomplished what they set out to do is another question. Probably, as one commentator put it, they "were effective in advancing the individual celebrity of the defendants but far less effective in advancing discussion of the Vietnam War." Juliet Dee, "Constraints on Persuasion in the Chicago Seven Trial," in *Popular Trials: Rhetoric, Mass Media, and the Law*, ed. Robert Hariman, 86–103 (Tuscaloosa: University of Alabama Press, 1990), 86, 94.

28. In fact, what the jury decided was that Burr was "not proved to be guilty under this indictment by any evidence submitted to us." Burr demanded, however, that the verdict be recorded as "not guilty," and this was done. Hoffer, *Treason Trials of Aaron Burr*, 171.

29. Bernell Tripp, "The Case of John Brown," in *The Press on Trial: Crimes and Trials as Media Events*, ed. Lloyd Chiasson, Jr., 25–36 (Westport, Conn.: Greenwood, 1997), 25, 34; Charles Joyner, "'Guilty of Holiest Crime': The Passion of John Brown," in *His Soul Goes Marching On: Responses to John Brown and the Harpers Ferry Raid*, ed. Paul Finkelman, 25–36 (Charlottesville: University Press of Virginia, 1995), 296, 314–317.

30. Ironically, the song apparently was not about "the legendary raider of Harpers Ferry" at all but about Sergeant John Brown, a Massachusetts soldier, who died accidentally in 1862. Ferguson, *Trial in American Life*, 151.

31. On Toguri D'Aquino and her trials and tribulations, see Yasuhide Kawashima, *The Tokyo Rose Case: Treason on Trial* (Lawrence: University Press of Kansas, 2013).

32. James Morton Smith, *Freedom's Fetters: The Alien and Sedition Laws and American Civil Liberties* (Ithaca: Cornell University Press, 1956). The law, which went into effect in July 1798, also prohibited anyone from fomenting riots and insurrections.

33. On these prosecutions, see Stanley Elkins and Eric McKitrick, *The Age of Federalism: The Early American Republic, 1788–1800* (New York: Oxford University Press, 1993), 703–711.

34. 40 Stat. 553 (act of May 16, 1918).

35. Abrams v. United States, 250 U.S. 616 (1919). Russian-Jewish immigrants had distributed leaflets, criticizing the president for meddling in the civil war then raging in Russia. Abrams and his colleagues were arrested and tried. They lost their case in the Supreme Court. There was

a famous dissent by Oliver Wendell Holmes, Jr.—even though Holmes had sided with the majority in Schenck v. United States, 249 U.S. 47 (1919), decided a few months earlier, which presented a somewhat similar question. On Abrams, Schenck, and the other cases in this period, see Richard Polenberg, *Fighting Faiths: The Abrams Case, the Supreme Court, and Free Speech* (Ithaca: Cornell University Press, 1987).

36. Whitney v. California, 274 U.S. 357 (1927).

37. Moshik Temkin, *The Sacco-Vanzetti Affair: America on Trial* (New Haven: Yale University Press, 2009). This is only one of the many books on this famous affair and that deal explicitly with the political aftermath of the trial. See also Susan Tejada, *In Search of Sacco and Vanzetti* (Boston: Northeastern University Press, 2012). There are still arguments as to whether either or both of the men were in fact guilty of the crime they were charged with.

38. Felix Frankfurter, *The Case of Sacco and Vanzetti: A Critical Analysis for Lawyers and Laymen* (Boston: Little, Brown, 1927).

39. Temkin, *Sacco-Vanzetti Affair.*

40. See Tejada, *In Search of Sacco and Vanzetti*, 299.

41. Tejada, *In Search of Sacco and Vanzetti*, 288.

42. Temkin, *The Sacco-Vanzetti Affair*, 220.

43. Milton Bracker, "Slain by Partisans: The Inglorious End of a Dictator," *New York Times*, April 30, 1945; Mark Mazower, *Hitler's Empire: How the Nazis Ruled Europe* (New York: Penguin Press, 2008), 503.

44. There is a huge literature on the Nuremberg trials. See Lawrence M. Friedman, *The Human Rights Culture: A Study in History and Culture* (New Orleans: Quid Pro Books, 2011), 145–151; Paul Roland, *The Nuremberg Trials: The Nazis and Their Crimes Against Humanity* (London: Arcturus, 2010); Michael R. Marrus, *The Nuremberg War Crimes Trial, 1945–46* (NewYork: Bedford Books, 1997); Robert E. Conot, *Justice at Nuremberg* (New York: Harper & Row, 1983); Bradley F. Smith, *The Road to Nuremburg* (New York: Basic Books, 1981); Burton C. Andrus, *The Infamous of Nuremberg* (London: Frewin, 1969); Robert K. Woetzel, *The Nuremberg Trials in International Law* (London: Stevens, 1960); August von Knieriem, *The Nuremberg Trials* (Chicago: H. Regnery Co., 1959); and George Creel, *War Criminals and Punishment* (New York: Hutchinson, 1944).

45. Quoted in Christian Delage, *Caught on Camera: Film in the Courtroom from the Nuremberg Trials to the Trials of the Khmer Rouge* (Philadelphia: University of Pennsylvania Press, 2014), 87.

46. Delage, *Caught on Camera*, 63.

47. See George J. Annas and Michael A. Grodin, eds., *The Nazi Doctors and the Nuremberg Code: Human Rights in Human Experimentation* (New York: Oxford University Press, 1992). The most notorious of the doctors, however, Josef Mengele, the "Angel of Death," escaped and lived out his life in South America.

48. Tomaz Jardim, *The Mauthausen Trial: American Military Justice in Germany* (Cambridge, Mass.: Harvard University Press, 2012).

49. See Philip R. Piccigallo, *The Japanese on Trial: Allied War Crimes Operations in the East, 1945–1951* (Austin: University of Texas Press, 1979).

50. See, for example, Tim Maga, *Judgment at Tokyo: The Japanese War Crimes Trials* (Lexington: University Press of Kentucky, 2001).

51. Gerald Steinacher, *Nazis on the Run: How Hitler's Henchmen Fled Justice* (Oxford: Oxford University Press, 2011).

52. On the background, see Homer Bigart, "Trial of Eichmann Opens before Israeli Tribunal," *New York Times*, April 11, 1961. There is a substantial literature on the trial; see Deborah E. Lipstad, *The Eichmann Trial* (New York: Nextbook/Schocken, 2011); Stephan Landsman, *Crimes of the Holocaust: The Law Confronts Hard Cases* (Philadelphia: University of Pennsylvania Press, 2005), 56–109.

53. Ted Morgan, "The Barbie File," *New York Times Magazine*, May 10, 1987.

54. The message was, to say the least, somewhat marred because the Soviet regime was one of the partners in running the trials—a regime second only to the Nazis in bloodiness and oppression.

55. See Friedman, *Human Rights Culture*.

56. Ibid.

57. See Lawrence R. Helfer and Anne-Marie Slaughter, "Toward a Theory of Effective Supranational Adjudication," *Yale Law Journal* 107 (1997): 273; Helen Stacy, *Human Rights for the 21st Century: Sovereignty, Human Rights, Culture* (Stanford: Stanford University Press, 2009).

58. See, for example, Marlise Simons, "10-Year Term for a Serb in War Crimes Called Light," *New York Times*, March 31, 2004.

59. For a trenchant critique of the work of this court, see Thierry Cruvellier, *Court of Remorse: Inside the International Criminal Tribunal for Rwanda* (Madison: University of Wisconsin Press, 2010).

60. Barbara Crossette, "World Criminal Court Is Ratified; Praised by U.N., Opposed by U.S.," *New York Times*, April 11, 2002.

61. On the tribunals, and the ICC, see Stacy, *Human Rights for the 21st Century*, 58–75. "Crimes against humanity" include "systematic" murder

or enslavement of a population, persecution of a "collectivity," apartheid, torture, rape, and enforced disappearance. (Article 7, Treaty of Rome). There is also an elaborate definition of "war crimes."

62. Friedman, *Human Rights Culture*, 154–155.

63. See Rebecca Evans, "Pinochet in London—Pinochet in Chile: International and Domestic Politics in Human Rights Policy," *Human Rights Quarterly* 28 (2006): 207.

64. Kareem Fahim, "Morsi and Muslim Brotherhood Leaders Charged with Inciting Murder," *New York Times*, September 2, 2013.

65. See, for example, Alexander Laban Hinton, ed., *Transitional Justice: Global Mechanisms and Local Realities after Genocide and Mass Violence* (New Brunswick, N.J.: Rutgers University Press, 2010).

66. Christine A. E. Bakker, "A Full Stop to Amnesty in Argentina: the Simon Case," *Journal of International Criminal Justice* 3 (2005): 1, 106; Sam Ferguson, "Argentina's 'Disappeared': Justice at Last or Reneging on Amnesty," *Christian Science Monitor*, December 24, 2009.

67. Alison Bisset, *Truth Commissions and Criminal Courts* (Cambridge, UK: Cambridge University Press, 2012), 75. Each of the types gave rise to a "unique set of issues and challenges as overlapping mandates, interlinked operations, reliance on the same evidence and requirements to access the same witnesses brought them into contact, and sometimes conflict."

68. A policy paper of the ICC, from the Office of the Prosecutor, "endorses" the "role of the other transitional justice mechanisms" and announces that the ICC will "seek to work constructively with them." Bisset, *Truth Commissions and Criminal Courts*, 192.

Chapter 4. Corruption and Fraud

1. This category closely resembles what Ray Surette in "Media Trials," *Journal of Criminal Justice* 17 (1989): 293, calls "abuse of power" and identifies as a major theme of media trials.

2. Basically, there were seven of these Republicans who voted no; they are "recorded in history as the seven martyrs," at least by those who were against the impeachment. Michael Les Benedict, *The Impeachment and Trial of Andrew Johnson* (New York: Norton, 1973), 173.

3. "Clinton Acquitted Decisively; No Majority for Either Charge," *New York Times,* February 13, 1999. A motion to censure the president also failed. Eric Schmitt, "In the End, Senate Passes No Harsh Judgment on Clinton," *New York Times,* February 13, 1999.

4. See Richard B. Lillich, "The Chase Impeachment," *American Journal of Legal History* 4 (1960): 49.

5. Ruth Marcus, "Senate Removes Hastings," *Washington Post*, October 21, 1989.

6. Gerald Gunther, *Learned Hand: The Man and the Judge* (Oxford: Oxford University Press, 1994), 503–515.

7. Sir William Blackstone, vol. 1, *Commentaries on the Laws of England* (Oxford: Clarendon Press, 1765), 178.

8. Edward Banfield, *The Moral Basis of a Backward Society* (Glencoe, Ill.: Free Press, 1958), 10.

9. See Laton McCartney, *The Teapot Dome Scandal* (New York: Random House, 2008).

10. "Fall Found Guilty in Oil Bribe Case; Jury Asks Mercy," *New York Times*, October 26, 1929.

11. Neil A. Lewis, "Alaskan Senator is Guilty Over His Failures to Disclose Gifts," *New York Times*, October 27, 2008; Neil A. Lewis, "Dismissal for Stevens, but Question on 'Innocent,'" *New York Times*, April 11, 2009. Senator Stevens was killed in a plane crash, and one of the federal prosecutors committed suicide; Charlie Savage, "Stevens Case Prosecutor Kills Himself," *New York Times*, September 27, 2010.

12. Monica Davey, "Blagojevich Sentenced to 14 Years in Prison," *New York Times*, December 7, 2011.

13. Susan Saulny, "After Bit Part in Legal Drama, A Blagojevich Tries Reality TV," *New York Times*, June 6, 2009. Ms. Blagojevich explained that she had lost her job and that she needed the money.

14. See Diana B. Henriques and Jack Healy, "Madoff Jailed after Pleading Guilty to Fraud," *New York Times*, March 13, 2009.

15. "Eight White Sox Players are Indicted on Charge of Fixing 1919 World Series," *New York Times*, September 29, 1920.

16. C. J. Hughes, "Ex-Dean Accused of Using Students as Servants," *New York Times*, September 30, 2010; William K. Rashbaum et al., "Fallen Dean's Life, Contradictory to Its Grisly End," *New York Times*, December 10, 2012.

17. See Martin Lowy, *High Rollers: Inside the Savings and Loan Debacle* (New York: Praeger, 1991).

18. "New Act Is Called Boon To Investors," *New York Times*, June 17, 1934.

19. Andrew Jacobs and Chris Buckley, "Chinese Official at Center of Scandal is Found Guilty and Given a Life Term," *New York Times*, September 22, 2013.

Chapter 5. Was Justice Done?

1. See above, at 42–43.

2. There is an enormous literature on this case. A useful summary is George Whyte, *The Dreyfus Affair: A Chronological History* (Basingstoke, UK: Palgrave Macmillan, 2005).

3. See Dan T. Carter, *Scottsboro: A Tragedy of the American South* (Baton Rouge: Louisiana State University Press, 1969).

4. Powell v. Alabama, 287 U.S. 45 (1932). This case played an important role in the development of the right to appointed counsel.

5. See Leonard Dinnerstein, *The Leo Frank Case* (New York: Columbia University Press). Most scholars feel Frank was innocent and that a janitor was the true killer. Ironically, the janitor was black.

6. Theodore Hamm, *Rebel and a Cause: Caryl Chessman and the Politics of the Death Penalty in Postwar California, 1948–1974* (Berkeley: University of California Press, 2001).

7. See, for example, "1,500 Clergy Back Rosenbergs' Plea," *New York Times*, January 15, 1953.

8. William R. Conklin, "Atom Spy Couple Sentenced to Die; Aide Gets 30 Years," *New York Times*, April 5, 1951.

9. "Riots Erupt after White is Convicted of Manslaughter," *Los Angeles Times*, May 22, 1979.

10. On this case, see William F. Lewis, "Power, Knowledge, and Insanity: The Trial of John W. Hinckley, Jr.," in *Popular Trials: Rhetoric, Mass Media, and the Law*, ed. Robert Hariman, 114–132 (Tuscaloosa: University of Alabama Press, 1990), 114.

11. See Robert L. Jackson, "Administration Attacks Insanity Defense," *Los Angeles Times*, July 20, 1982. The federal statute was the Insanity Defense Reform Act of 1984, 98 Stat. 2057, (October 12, 1984); the heart of the law is codified as 18 U.S. C. A. section 17. Under the Idaho Code, Title 18, chapter 2, sec. 18–207, "Mental condition" is "not . . . a defense to any charge of criminal conduct." But there is less here than meets the eye. The same statute states that experts could testify "on the issue of any state of mind which is an element of the offense" [18–207 (3)]. In other words, a defendant cannot plead not guilty by reason of insanity but *can* try to show that he or she did not form the necessary intent for, say, murder, because he or she was, frankly, insane. See also H. J. Steadman et al., "Maintenance of an Insanity Defense under Montana's 'Abolition' of the Insanity Defense," *American Journal of Psychiatry* 146 (1989): 357. The authors argue that describing what Montana did as "abolition" was

simply inaccurate. After the so-called abolition, defendants who might have pleaded not guilty by reason of insanity were usually simply deemed incompetent to stand trial and ended up with indefinite stays in a maximum-security state hospital.

12. *Los Angeles Times*, April 30, 1992.

13. In fact, only two of the five were "Hawaiian"; two were Japanese, and one was part Chinese. On the whole affair, see the account in David E. Stannard, *Honor Killing: Race, Rape, and Clarence Darrow's Spectacular Last Case* (New York: Penguin, 2005).

14. Stannard, *Honor Killing*, 336.

15. Lizette Alvarez and Cara Buckley, "Zimmerman is Acquitted in Trayvon Martin Killing," *New York Times*, July 14, 2013.

16. There is a large literature on this famous incident and what happened afterward. See Arthur F. McEvoy, "The Triangle Shirtwaist Fire of 1911: Social Change, Industrial Accidents, and the Evolution of Common-Sense Causality," *Law and Social Inquiry* 20 (1995): 621; Richard A. Greenwald, *The Triangle Fire, the Protocols of Peace, and Industrial Democracy in Progressive Era New York* (Philadelphia: Temple University Press, 2005).

17. "Indict Owners of Burned Factory," *New York Times*, April 12, 1911.

18. "Triangle Owners Acquitted by Jury," *New York Times*, December 28, 1911.

19. See John C. Esposito, *Fire in the Grove: The Coconut Grove Tragedy and its Aftermath* (Cambridge, Mass.: Da Capo, 2005).

20. See, for example, Keith Schneider, "Jury Finds Exxon Acted Recklessly in Valdez Oil Spill," *New York Times*, June 14, 1994.

21. Reynolds v. United States, 98 U.S. 145 (1879); Sarah Barringer Gordon, *The Mormon Question: Polygamy and Constitutional Conflict in Nineteenth Century America* (Chapel Hill: University of North Carolina Press, 2002).

22. Shawn Francis Peters, *When Prayer Fails: Faith Healing, Children, and the Law* (Oxford: Oxford University Press, 2008).

23. Edward J. Larson, *Summer for the Gods: The Scopes Trial and America's Continuing Debate over Science and Religion* (New York: Basic Books, 1997).

Chapter 6. Tabloid Trials

1. "Thaw Murders Stanford White," *New York Times,* June 26, 1906. The audience, in a panic, rushed for the exits. Thaw said to a policeman, "He deserved it." On the story in general, see Michael Macdonald

Mooney, *Evelyn Nesbit and Stanford White: Love and Death in the Gilded Age* (New York: Morrow, 1976); Gerald Langford, *The Murder of Stanford White* (Indianapolis: Bobbs-Merrill, 1962).

2. Deborah Dorian Paul, ed., *Tragic Beauty: The Lost 1914 Memoirs of Evelyn Nesbit* (Morrisville, N.C.: Lulu Enterprises, 2006), 46.

3. Irvin S. Cobb, *Exit Laughing* (Garden City, N.Y.: Garden City Publishing, 1942), 198–199.

4. Ibid.

5. Mooney, *Evelyn Nesbit and Stanford White*, 257–258.

6. Book after book has presented a "solution" to the mystery of Jack the Ripper. Dozens of people, apparently, have been nominated for the honor of being the actual Jack the Ripper. The mystery writer Patricia Cornwell, for example, claimed to have solved the crime in *Portrait of a Killer: Jack the Ripper; Case Closed* (New York: Putnam's, 2002). Her candidate is an artist, Walter Sickert. But Sickert's guilt seems very unlikely—at least in the opinion of other Jack the Ripper specialists. No theory has won general acceptance, and the trail by now is, of course, extremely cold.

7. Don Terry, "Jeffrey Dahmer, Multiple Killer, Is Bludgeoned to Death in Prison," *New York Times*, November 29, 1994. There is no death penalty in Wisconsin—not officially, at least. A man like Dahmer, however, is probably unlikely to survive to a ripe old age in prison.

8. Adam Higgenbotham, "The Long, Long Life of the Lipstick Killer," *GQ*, May 2008; Steve Mills and Ryan Hagerty, "William Heirens, Known as the 'Lipstick Killer,' Dead," *Chicago Tribune*, March 6, 2012. If indeed Heirens was innocent, his case would be one more illustration of a sad fact: The pressure to "solve" a case that has the public up in arms sometimes leads the police and the prosecutors to cut corners—or worse.

9. See, for example, "Der Kannibale von Rotenburg—Jetzt Rede Ich!," *Bild-Zeitung*, June 19, 2009. See also Guenter Stampf, *Interview with a Cannibal: The Secret Life of the Monster of Rotenburg* (San Francisco: Phoenix Books, 2008); see Lawrence M. Friedman and Nina-Louisa Arold, "Cannibal Rights: A Note on the Modern Law of Privacy," *Northwestern Interdisciplinary Law Review* 4 (2011): 235.

10. On the Jewett case, and its relationship to the media, see Andie Tucher, *Froth and Scum: Truth, Beauty, Goodness, and the Ax Murder in America's First Mass Medium* (Chapel Hill: University of North Carolina Press, 1994).

11. See, on this case, Daniel A. Cohen, "The Murder of Maria Bickford:

Fashion, Passion, and the Birth of a Consumer Culture," *American Studies* 31 (1990): 5.

12. See Colin Wilson and Donald Seaman, *The Serial Killers: A Study in the Psychology of Violence* (London: W. H. Allen, 1990).

13. See Vincent Bugliosi, *Helter Skelter: The True Story of the Manson Murders* (New York: Norton, 1974).

14. For example, Scott Peterson was accused of murdering his pregnant wife, and convicted. Carolyn Marshall, "Jury Finds Scott Peterson Guilty of Wife's Murder," *New York Times*, November 13, 2004. Peterson had a mistress, and this was presumed to be part of his motive. He was sentenced to death and is now on death row in California.

15. On the Clara Fallmer trial, see Lawrence M. Friedman and Robert V. Percival, *The Roots of Justice: Crime and Punishment in Alameda County, California, 1870–1910* (Chapel Hill: University of North Carolina Press, 1981), 239–244.

16. A full treatment is Carole Haber, *The Trials of Laura Fair: Sex, Murder, and Insanity in the Victorian West* (Chapel Hill: University of North Carolina Press, 2013); see also Gordon Morris Bakken and Brenda Farrington, *Women Who Kill Men: California Courts, Gender, and the Press* (Lincoln: University of Nebraska Press, 2009), 19–39.

17. See Nat Brandt, *The Congressman Who Got Away with Murder* (Syracuse: Syracuse University Press, 1991). The "unwritten law" flourished in the late nineteenth and early twentieth centuries; on this point, see Lawrence M. Friedman and William E. Havemann, "The Rise and Fall of the Unwritten Law: Sex, Patriarchy and Vigilante Justice in the American Courts," *Buffalo Law Review* 61 (2013): 997.

18. On this meaning of the "unwritten law," see Robert M. Ireland, "The Libertine Must Die: Sexual Dishonor and the Unwritten Law in the Nineteenth-Century United States," *Journal of Social History* 23 (1992): 27; Hendrik Hartog, "Lawyering, Husbands' Rights and the 'Unwritten Law' in Nineteenth-Century America," *Journal of American History* 84 (1997): 67; Martha Merrill Umphrey, "The Dialogics of Legal Meaning: Spectacular Trials, the Unwritten Law, and Narratives of Criminal Responsibility," *Law and Society Review* 33 (1999): 393; Friedman and Havemann, "Unwritten Law."

19. The story is told in Edward Ball, *The Inventor and the Tycoon* (New York: Doubleday, 2013). The tycoon in question was Leland Stanford, who sponsored Muybridge's photographic work. The murder trial is prominently featured in the book; see pp. 166, 199, 279.

20. "Saved by Unwritten law," *Atlanta Constitution*, January 19, 1908.

21. "Unwritten Law Saves," *Washington Post*, May 13, 1900. The wife, a "woman of refinement and considerable beauty," testified for the defense, "substantiating" the defense "at the cost of her own good name."

22. On this case, see Bill Neal, *Sex, Murder, & the Unwritten Law: Gender and Judicial Mayhem, Texas Style* (Lubbock: Texas Tech University Press, 2009), 18–39.

23. "Widowed Bride Tells Her Pathetic Story to Save Her Brothers," *Atlanta Constitution*, February 28, 1907.

24. Ibid.

25. "Unwritten Law in His Charge, Although Not Specially Mentioned by Judge Harrison," *Atlanta Constitution*, March 6, 1907; on the testimony (on both sides of the issue) relating to the "emotional insanity" of the brothers, see "Made Insane by the Wrong Done Sister," *Atlanta Constitution*, March 3, 1907.

26. "Strother Boys Freed and Judge Approves Verdict of the Jury," *Atlanta Constitution*, March 8, 1907.

27. *Los Angeles Times*, February 9, 1909.

28. Ball, *The Inventor and the Tycoon*, 199.

29. Rosemary Gartner and Jim Phillips, "The Creffield-Mitchell Case, Seattle, 1906: The Unwritten Law in the Pacific Northwest," *Pacific Northwest Quarterly* 94 (2003): 69, 79. The case in question was the murder of Franz Creffield, leader of a small, deviant religious sect. The killer was a man who thought Creffield had either slept with or intended to sleep with the killer's sister. The case is recounted in more detail in Jim Phillips and Rosemary Gartner, *Murdering Holiness: The Trials of Franz Creffield and George Mitchell* (Vancouver: University of British Columbia Press, 2003).

30. In the Thaw trial, the prosecution tried to argue that Evelyn Nesbit, even at sixteen, was hardly as innocent as she made out—she already had a career on stage, as a "Floradora girl." But this argument seemed to have no real impact.

31. Karen Halttunen, "'Domestic Differences': Competing Narratives of Womanhood in the Murder Trial of Lucretia Chapman," in *The Culture of Sentiment: Race, Gender, and Sentimentality in Nineteenth-Century America*, ed. Shirley Samuels, 39–57 (New York: Oxford University Press, 1992), 39, 44.

32. For a discussion of the origins and social meaning of this image of women, see Nancy Scott, "Passionlessness: An Interpretation of Victorian Sexual Ideology, 1790–1850," *Signs* 4 (1978): 219.

33. In the celebrated trial of Laura Fair, in 1871, mentioned previously, the stereotypes were reversed: Laura, a much-married woman, and the victim's mistress, was portrayed as an evil, seductive monster and hardly a real woman at all, while the victim was portrayed as a weak man, easily led astray by this jezebel. See Haber, *The Trials of Laura Fair*, chap. 2. Laura was sentenced to death, but the California Supreme Court reversed and she was acquitted at the second trial. At this trial, the major issue was the insanity plea; Laura herself did not testify and her character (or lack of character) was not at the forefront of the case.

34. "Unwritten Law Liberates Woman," *Chicago Tribune*, January 29, 2008. See Carolyn Ramsey, "Domestic Violence and State Intervention in the American West and Australia, 1860–1930," *Indiana Law Journal* 86 (2011): 185, especially 222–231; Carolyn Ramsey, "Intimate Homicide: Gender and Crime Control, 1880–1920," *University of Colorado Law Review* 77 (2006): 101.

35. Jeffrey S. Adler, "'I Loved Joe, But I Had to Shoot Him': Homicide by Women in Turn-of-the-Century Chicago," *Journal of Criminal Law and Criminology* 92: 867, 882–883; Marianne Constable, "Chicago Husband-Killing and the 'New Unwritten Law,'" *Triquarterly* 124 (2000): 85.

36. Adler, "'I Loved Joe, But I Had to Shoot Him,'" 883.

37. The case was extensively covered by the *New York Times*, often on the front page. See, for example, Russell Porter, "Defense Opens Case, Says Sander Will Testify Air Followed Death," *New York Times*, March 3, 1950; Russell Porter, "Sander Acquitted in an Hour; Crowd Outside Court Cheers," *New York Times*, March 10, 1950.

38. See Friedman and Havemann, "Unwritten Law," 1,044–1,049.

Chapter 7. Celebrity Trials

1. On celebrity trials, see Gini Graham Scott, *Homicide by the Rich and Famous: A Century of Prominent Killers* (Westport, Conn.: Praeger, 2005).

2. Jim Fisher, *The Lindbergh Case* (New Brunswick: Rutgers University Press, 1987).

3. Gail Collins, *Scorpion Tongues: Gossip, Celebrity, and American Politics* (New York: William Morrow, 1998), 85–87.

4. Collins, *Scorpion Tongues*, 88.

5. See Ruth Brandon, *The Life and Many Deaths of Harry Houdini* (New York: Random House, 1993).

6. Samantha Barbas, *Movie Crazy: Fans, Stars, and the Cult of Celebrity* (New York: Palgrave, 2001), 16–17.

7. For the story of this dubious genre, see Anthony Slide, *Inside the Hollywood Fan Magazine: A History of Star Makers, Fabricators, and Gossip Mongers* (Jackson: University Press of Mississippi, 2010).

8. Douglas B. Craig, *Fireside Politics: Radio and Political Culture in the United States, 1920–1940* (Baltimore: Johns Hopkins University Press, 2000), 154–156. Roosevelt "paid close attention to public reaction" to these broadcasts, and he received "avalanches of mail" sparked by these "chats." Craig, *Fireside Politics*, 156.

9. Lawrence M. Friedman, *Guarding Life's Dark Secrets* (Stanford: Stanford University Press, 2007), 226.

10. Ellis Cashmore, *Celebrity/Culture* (New York: Routledge, 2006), 7.

11. On the privacy rights of "public figures," see Diane L. Zimmerman, "Requiem for a Heavyweight: A Farewell to Warren and Brandeis's Privacy Tort," *Cornell Law Review* 68 (1983): 291; Friedman, *Guarding Life's Dark Secrets*, 220–225.

12. There is a considerable literature on the O. J. Simpson trial. See, for example, Jeffrey Toobin, *The Run of His Life: The People v. O. J. Simpson* (New York: Random House, 1996); Darnell M. Hunt, *O. J. Simpson Facts and Fictions: News Rituals in the Construction of Reality* (Cambridge, UK: Cambridge University Press, 1999). Simpson is currently in jail, serving a long sentence on charges unrelated to the double killing.

13. A full account is in Greg Merritt, *Room 1219: The Life of Fatty Arbuckle, the Mysterious Death of Virginia Rappe, and the Scandal that Changed Hollywood* (Chicago: Chicago Review Press, 2013); see also David A. Yallop, *The Day the Laughter Died: The True Story of Fatty Arbuckle* (New York: St. Martin's Press, 1976).

14. Merritt, *Room 1219*, 223–227.

15. "Arbuckle is Not Guilty, Jurors Decide Quickly," *Los Angeles Times*, April 13, 1922. See Merritt, *Room 1219*, 268.

16. Paul Thaler, *The Watchful Eye* (Westport, Conn.: Praeger, 1994), 38.

17. Did the trial, with its lurid publicity—and Kennedy's acquittal—act to "discourage . . . rape victims from reporting the crime?" In Palm Beach County, we are told, "the number of reported rapes dropped dramatically" between the time of the incident and the actual trial; but nothing is said about what happened afterward. Thaler, *Watchful Eye*, 40. It is possible that any impact or influence was transient.

18. Vincent Bugliosi, *Helter Skelter: The True Story of the Manson Murders* (New York: Norton, 1974).

19. Edward Steers, Jr., *Blood on the Moon: The Assassination of Abraham Lincoln* (Lexington: University Press of Kentucky, 2001), 211–226; Michael W. Kauffman, *American Brutus: John Wilkes Booth and the Lincoln Conspiracies* (New York: Random House, 2004), 342–370.

20. Charles Rosenberg, *The Trial of the Assassin Guiteau: Psychiatry and Law in the Gilded Age* (Chicago: University of Chicago Press, 1968).

21. Clinicians in the twentieth century who studied the case tended to agree that Guiteau was a "paranoid schizophrenic." Rosenberg, *The Trial of the Assassin Guiteau*, xiii.

22. "Assassin Czolgosz Is Executed at Auburn," *New York Times*, October 30, 1901.

23. John Kaplan, *The Trial of Jack Ruby* (New York: MacMillan, 1965).

24. "Zangara Given Death Penalty," *Los Angeles Times*, March 11, 1933.

25. See p. 66, supra, and notes 10–11.

Chapter 8. Mystery and Identity

1. Susan M. Drucker and Janice Platt Humold, "The Claus von Bulow Retrial: Lights, Camera, Genre?" in *Popular Trials: Rhetoric, Mass Media, and the Law*, ed. Robert Hariman, (Tuscaloosa: University of Alabama, 1990), 133.

2. Alan M. Dershowitz, *Reversal of Fortune: Inside the von Bulow Case* (New York: Random House, 1985).

3. Dershowitz, *Reversal of Fortune*, 245. The book is a full account of the case, told, of course, from Dershowitz's standpoint.

4. See, for example, Edward D. Radin, *Lizzie Borden: The Untold Story* (New York: Simon & Schuster, 1961). Radin claims that Lizzie was innocent and implicates Bridget Sullivan, the Bordens' Irish maid. It seems to me, though, that the most likely solution is the obvious one: Lizzie was guilty of the crime.

5. Discussed in Fred Graham, "Sheppard—Fair Trial Issue Raised," *New York Times*, November 21, 1965. The Supreme Court mentions this in its opinion in Sheppard v. Maxwell, 384 U.S. 333 (1966).

6. Cynthia L. Cooper and Sam Reese Sheppard, *Mockery of Justice: The True Story of the Sheppard Murder Case* (Boston: Northeastern University Press, 1995), 91–93. The co-author was Sheppard's son. The book argues, of course, that Sheppard was completely innocent.

7. *Sheppard*, 384 U.S. 333 (1966).

8. "Sheppard Freed in Wife's Killing at 2d Trial After 9 Years in Jail," *New York Times*, November 17, 1966.

9. Cooper and Sheppard, *Mockery of Justice*. See Fox Butterfield, "New Clues in an Old Murder Case," *New York Times*, February 5, 1997. Cooper and Sheppard argue that a window-washer, who had worked at the house and who was later convicted of murdering an old widow, was the real killer. Some people also think that Dr. Sheppard's story inspired a popular television series, "The Fugitive," and the movie "The Fugitive," which was based on the television series.

10. For an account of this case, see Martin L. Friedland, *The Death of Old Man Rice: A True Story of Criminal Justice in America* (New York: New York University Press, 1994).

11. *New York Times*, November 28, 1912.

12. See "Was It Murder?" *Stanford Magazine*, January-February 2000; available at http://www.stanfordalumni.org/.

13. People v. Lamson, 1 Cal. 2d 648, 36 P. 2d 361. On death row, Lamson wrote a book, *We Who Are About to Die: Prison as Seen by a Condemned Man*, which was later published, in 1936.

14. Ludovic Kennedy, *Crime of the Century* (New York: Penguin, 1996).

Chapter 9. The Worm in the Bud

1. There is an enormous literature about the Lizzie Borden case, which has also been the subject of at least one opera and ballet. I have particularly relied on Cara W. Robertson's study, "Representing 'Miss Lizzie': Cultural Convictions in the Trial of Lizzie Borden," *Yale Journal of Law and the Humanities* 8 (1996): 350.

2. Quoted in Robertson, "Representing 'Miss Lizzie,'" 414.

3. Robertson, "Representing 'Miss Lizzie,'" 416. See also A. Cheree Carlson, *The Crimes of Womanhood: Defining Femininity in a Court of Law* (Urbana: University of Illinois Press, 2009), 85–110.

4. I take the phrase from Ronald Pearsall, *The Worm in the Bud: The World of Victorian Sexuality* (London: Weidenfeld and Nicolson, 1969).

5. The trial is discussed in Ian C. Pilarczyk, "The Terrible Haystack Murder: The Moral Paradox of Hypocrisy, Prudery and Piety in Antebellum America," *American Journal of Legal History* 41 (1997): 25. Many people did think, however, that Avery was responsible for Cornell's death; Avery lost his ministry. William G. McLoughlin, in "Untangling the Tiverton Tragedy: The Social Meaning of the Terrible Haystack Murder of 1833," *Journal of American Culture* 7 (1984): 75, agrees that a way of life was on

trial, but suggests that it was not only the clergyman but also the "factory girl" who was at the emotional core of the case. Was she a good, hard-working girl, one of the new army of women in the textile mills, or was she someone whose life represented a betrayal of respectable womanhood?

6. Karen Halttunen, "'Domestic Differences': Competing Narratives of Womanhood in the Murder Trial of Lucretia Chapman," in *The Culture of Sentiment: Race, Gender, and Sentimentality in Nineteenth-Century America*, ed. Shirley Samuel (New York: Oxford University Press, 1992), 55. The true villain, according to the defense, was an impostor who had taken her in, duped her, stole her money and (by marrying her after her husband died) stolen her respectability as well. Interestingly, in *his* trial, he was convicted of the murder of her husband.

7. Virginia A. McConnell, *Arsenic Under the Elms: Murder in Victorian New Haven* (Lincoln: University of Nebraska Press, 1999), 115.

8. Richard K. Sherwin, *When Law Goes Pop: The Vanishing Line between Law and Popular Culture* (Chicago: University of Chicago Press, 2000), 98.

9. Hal Higdon, *Leopold and Loeb: The Crime of the Century* (New York: Putnam, 1975).

10. Kirk Johnson, "Trial Opening for Chambers in Park Killing," *New York Times*, January 4, 1988. The story goes on to say: "Whether or not Miss Levin and Mr. Chambers belonged in that category, they have come to represent it in the minds of many."

11. Kirk Johnson, "Chambers, With Jury at Impasse, Admits lst-Degree Manslaughter," *New York Times*, March 26, 1988.

12. Tom Cullen, *The Mild Murderer: The True Story of the Dr. Crippen Case* (London: Penguin Books, 1989).

13. On this trial, see Helen Thomson, *Murder at Harvard* (Boston: Houghton Mifflin, 1971).

14. A great deal has been written about the Salem trials. See Paul Boyer and Stephen Nissenbaum, *Salem Possessed: The Social Origins of Witchcraft* (Cambridge, Mass.: Harvard University Press, 1974), and Carol F. Karlsen, *The Devil in the Shape of a Woman: Witchcraft in Colonial New England* (New York: Norton, 1987).

15. Another, less likely, interpretation is that the movie is a metaphor for witch hunts: People think they see Communists under every bush, and they treat ordinary people, who somehow arouse their suspicion, as if they were aliens from outer space (or from the Soviet Union).

16. On these trials, see Debbie Nathan and Michael Snedeker, *Satan's Silence: Ritual Abuse and the Making of a Modern American Witch Hunt*

(New York: Basic Books, 1995); Paul and Shirley Eberle, *The Abuse of Innocence: The McMartin Preschool Trial* (Buffalo: Prometheus, 1993).

17. There is a huge literature on McCarthy and McCarthyism. See, for example, Ellen Schrecker, *Many Are the Crimes: McCarthyism in America* (Boston: Little, Brown, 1998); Arthur J. Sabin, *Red Scare in Court: New York vs. the International Workers' Order* (Philadelphia: University of Pennsylvania Press, 1993); and Arthur J. Sabin, *In Calmer Times: The Supreme Court and Red Monday* (Philadelphia: University of Pennsylvania Press, 1999); see also Thomas Doherty, *Cold War, Cool Medium: Television, McCarthyism, and American Culture* (New York: Columbia University Press, 2003).

18. See n. 14 supra.

19. See "Nanny, Accused of Murdering Baby, Enters Not Guilty Plea," *New York Times*, February 14, 1997.

20. Quoted from Paula Fass, a history professor, in Carey Goldberg, "Trial of Au Pair Reveals Unease in U.S. Society," *New York Times*, November 19, 1997.

21. Jonathan Bignell, *An Introduction to Television Studies*, 2d ed. (London: Routledge, 2008), 129. Bignell argues that "Nannies from Hell" encouraged its audience to "stigmatise and fear the young and often exploited care workers who appear . . . only as the perpetrators of disturbing crimes." This also lent weight to "conservative definitions of femininity"; the mothers "employing the nannies vowed to stay at home and care for their own children," spreading the ideology that "mothers who work outside the home are both irresponsible and unnatural."

22. Wendy Ruderman and Marc Santora, "Two Children Slain at Home in City; Nanny Arrested," *New York Times*, October 26, 2012.

Chapter 10. The Reason Why

1. Richard L. Fox and Robert W. Van Sickel, *Tabloid Justice: Criminal Justice in an Age of Media Frenzy* (Boulder: Lynne Rienner, 2001).

2. The trial is dealt with in Virginia A. McConnell, *The Adventuress: Murder, Blackmail and Confidence Games in the Gilded Age* (Kent, Ohio: Kent State University Press, 2010). The passage about the crowd is at p. 75. At the end of the trial, Minnie was acquitted. There were real questions in the case, about innocence and guilt. And the age and beauty of the defendant—and the identity of the victim, the mayor—gave the case its lurid glow.

3. Elizabeth Dale, *The Chicago Trunk Murder: Law and Justice at the Turn of the Century* (DeKalb: Northern Illinois University Press, 2011).

4. See Mark A. Weitz, *The Sleepy Lagoon Murder Case: Race Discrimination and Mexican-American Rights* (Lawrence: University Press of Kansas, 2010). The judge's attitude toward the young Mexican defendants seemed extremely hostile; they were convicted on the shakiest of evidence, but the conviction was reversed on appeal.

5. See Dan T. Carter, *Scottsboro: A Tragedy of the American South* (Baton Rouge: Louisiana State Press, 1969); the case in question was Powell v. Alabama, 287 U.S. 45 (1932).

6. Jeffrey Toobin, *The Run of His Life: The People vs. O. J. Simpson* (New York: Random House, 1996), 101–103.

7. Sarah Anne Hughes, "Nancy Grace, Trial Watchers React to Casey Anthony Verdict," *Washington Post*, July 6, 2011.

8. Lizette Alvarez, "Casey Anthony Not Guilty in Slaying of Daughter," *New York Times*, July 5, 2011; "Not since . . . O. J. Simpson . . . has the nation diverged so greatly from a jury. . . . Anger was apparent as people demanded to know why the jurors would allow this death to go unpunished." Jonathan Turley, "Anthony Case: Hate the Facts, Not the Jury," *USA Today*, July 12, 2011.

9. On neonaticide, see Lawrence M. Friedman, "Dead on Arrival," manuscript in possession of the author.

10. Seth Mydans, "The Other Menendez Trial, Too, Ends With the Jury Deadlocked," *New York Times*, January 29, 1994. On the retrial, the two brothers were convicted. "Menendez Brothers Sentenced to Life in Prison," *New York Times*, July 3, 1996

11. Meryl Gordon, "The New Astor Court," *Vanity Fair* (September 2009). This "morality play," a "marvelous distraction," was a "story about money that everyone could understand." Brooke Astor had been "universally beloved"; her funeral "drew such large crowds that Fifth Avenue was briefly shut down." But now, in court, "the final years of her life were being deconstructed," her "medical records" revealed, and details of her lavish lifestyle exposed to an eager media audience of millions.

12. A medical parole, we are told, is granted when a person is "so physically or cognitively debilitated or incapacitated" that they are no longer a "danger to society." Russ Beuttner, "Deemed Too Sick, Astor Son is Paroled," *New York Times*, August 23, 2013. Marshall died in 2014. Robert P. McFadden, "Anthony Marshall, 90, Astor Son Who was Convicted in Estate Scandal, Dies, *New York Times*, Dec. 2, 2014.

Chapter 11. Who Are We?

1. There were, of course, exceptions. In the Loeb-Leopold case, the two defendants admitted their guilt; the sole issue was whether they would get the death penalty. And cases of the "unwritten law" are open and shut with regard to the facts of the case, as we have pointed out.

2. F. James Davis, *Who is Black? One Nation's Definition* (University Park: Pennsylvania State University Press, 1991), 13.

3. The extreme definition of blackness made it possible, in rare cases, for somebody to "pass" in the other direction. Clarence King, a distinguished nineteenth-century scientist, member of a prominent family, had a second, secret identity; he lived with a black woman, Ada Todd, fathered children with her, and "passed" as a light-skinned black man who worked as a porter and steelworker. The two identities were hermetically sealed from each other. Martha A. Sandweiss, *Passing Strange: A Gilded Age Tale of Love and Deception Across the Color Line* (New York: Penguin, 2009).

4. The device had been used before, in Lydia Maria Child's novel *A Romance of the Republic* (Boston: Ticknor and Fields, 1867); on this book, see Shirley Samuels, "The Identity of Slavery," in *The Culture of Sentiment: Race, Gender, and Sentimentality in Nineteenth-Century America*, ed. Shirley Samuels (New York: Oxford University Press, 1992), 157, 168–171.

5. Daniel J. Sharfstein, *The Invisible Line: Three American Families and the Secret Journey from Black to White* (New York: Penguin, 2011).

6. See Annette Gordon-Reed, *The Hemingses of Monticello: an American Family* (New York: Norton, 2008).

7. James M. O'Toole, *Passing for White: Race, Religion, and the Healy Family, 1820–1920* (Amherst: University of Massachusetts Press, 2002).

8. Earl Lewis and Heidi Ardizzone, *Love on Trial: An American Scandal in Black and White* (New York: Norton, 2001); see also, A. Cheree Carlson, *The Crimes of Womanhood* (Urbana: University of Illinois Press, 2009) 136–155; Ariela Julie Gross, *What Blood Won't Tell: A History of Race on Trial in America* (Cambridge, Mass.: Harvard University Press, 2008).

9. Rohan McWilliam, *The Tichborne Claimant: A Victorian Sensation* (London: Hambledon Continuum, 2007).

10. Mark Twain, *Following the Equator: A Journey Around the World*, vol. 1 (New York: Harper & Bros., 1906 edition) 156–157.

11. Peter Kurth, *Anastasia: The Riddle of Anna Anderson* (Boston: Little, Brown, 1983).

12. Margot Finn, Michael Lobban, and Jenny Bourne Taylor, "Afterword," in *Legitimacy and Illegitimacy in Nineteenth-Century Law, Literature and History,* ed. Finn, Lobban, and Taylor, 173–174 (Houndmills, UK: Palgrave MacMillan, 2010). Illegitimacy, of course, killed the right to inherit. Thus nineteenth-century novels often posed the question: Who is the rightful heir? It figured, for example, in Anthony Trollope's *Lady Anna* (1874) and *Mr. Scarborough's Family* (1883).

13. See Laura Peters, *Orphan Texts: Victorian Orphans, Culture and Empire* (Manchester: Manchester University Press, 2000).

14. Rohan McWilliam, "Unauthorized Identities: The Impostor, the Fake and the Secret History in Nineteenth-Century Britain," in *Legitimacy and Illegitimacy,* 67, 81–84.

15. The case for his innocence is spelled out in Yoram Sheftel, *The Demjanjuk Affair: The Rise and Fall of a Show-Trial* (London: V. Gollancz, 1994).

16. This is treated in Heinrich Wefing, *Der Fall Demjanjuk: Der letzte Grosse NS-Prozess* (Munich: C.H. Beck, 2011).

17. Lawrence M. Friedman, *Guarding Life's Dark Secrets: Legal and Social Controls over Reputation, Propriety, and Privacy* (Stanford: Stanford University Press, 2007).

18. The adultery was almost certainly real enough, but the jury failed to agree and Beecher won his case, at least by default. On this celebrated trial, see Richard Wightman Fox, *Trials of Intimacy: Love and Loss in the Beecher-Tilton Scandal* (Chicago: University of Chicago Press, 1999).

19. Friedman, *Guarding Life's Dark Secrets.*

20. Thus blackmail became a crime in the nineteenth century—punishment for those who might want to besmirch the reputation of elites. See Friedman, *Guarding Life's Dark Secrets,* 81–100; see also 132–133.

21. A similar idea may help explain why the media, for so long, were willing to practice self-censorship. Despite "yellow journalism" and the blatant behavior of the mass-circulation newspapers, which wallowed in scandal, there was in fact a good deal of self-censorship—with regard, for example, to the health of national leaders. President Grover Cleveland was secretly operated on for cancer; not a word of this was reported by the press. See Matthew Algeo, *The President Is a Sick Man* (Chicago: Chicago Review Press, 2011). Franklin Roosevelt's health problems were also mostly hidden; he was never seen in a wheelchair, and his serious decline at the end of his presidency was never revealed. See Hugh C. Gallagher, *FDR's Splendid Deception* (New York: Dodd, Mead, 1985); Steven Lomazow and Eric Fettmann, *FDR's Deadly Secret* (New York:

PublicAffairs, 2009). The British newspapers similarly never reported on Edward VII's entanglement with an American divorcee until very late in the game. President Kennedy's womanizing was also never reported. All of this, of course, is gone with the wind. Today, every presidential sniffle is broadcast from the rooftops. In Britain, any reticence about reporting the goings-on of the royals has similarly vanished.

22. A. Cheree Carlson, *The Crimes of Womanhood: Defining Femininity in a Court of Law* (Urbana: University of Chicago Press, 2009), 110. And in the sensational trial of Laura Fair, in 1871, the prosecution argued that Laura was not a real woman, that she was "manly" (not intended as a compliment), and that she was not a woman of purity, delicacy, and piety but an evil she-devil in effect. See Carole Haber, *The Trials of Laura Fair* (Chapel Hill: University of North Carolina Press, 2013), 49–78.

23. There is a similar theme, in a way, in Oscar Wilde's novel *The Picture of Dorian Gray* (1891); the picture, which reflects Gray's vile and criminal personality, grows old and hideous; on the surface, Gray remains young and fresh in appearance.

24. Robert N. Bellah et al., *Habits of the Heart: Individualism and Commitment in American Life,* 3d ed. (Berkeley: University of California Press, 2008).

25. On this, see Lawrence M. Friedman, "True Detective," in *Studies in Law, Politics, and Society,* Susan S. Silbey and Austin Sarat, eds., 14: 9 (Bingley, UK: Emerald Group Publishing Limited, 1994); Lawrence M. Friedman and Issachar Rosen-Zvi, "Illegal Fictions: Mystery Novels and the Popular Image of Crime," *UCLA Law Review* 48 (2001): 1,411. There is a sizeable literature on the history and analysis of this genre. See, for example, T. J. Binyon, *Murder Will Out: The Detective in Fiction* (Oxford: Oxford University Press, 1989); Julian Symons, *Bloody Murder* (Harmondsworth, UK: Viking, 1985); Carl D. Malmgren, *Anatomy of Murder: Mystery, Detective and Crime Fiction* (Bowling Green, Ohio: Bowling Green State University Popular Press, 2001); Haia Shpayer-Makov, *The Ascent of the Detective: Police Sleuths in Victorian and Edwardian England* (Oxford: Oxford University Press, 2011). It is always possible to find some book or story from earlier times and places, that is, before the nineteenth century, and (in hindsight) point to this book or story as a "mystery," thus laying claim to some sort of parentage. But, realistically speaking, this is a genre that arose in the first half of the nineteenth century, and its popularity dates from the middle and the end of the century.

26. Raymond Paul, *Who Murdered Mary Rogers?* (Englewood Cliffs, N.J.: Prentice-Hall, 1971), 1.

27. The case and the newspaper coverage are dealt with in Andie Tucher, *Froth and Scum: Truth, Beauty, Goodness, and the Ax Murder in America's First Mass Medium* (Chapel Hill: University of North Carolina Press, 1994).

28. See Daniel Stashower, *The Beautiful Cigar Girl: Mary Rogers, Edgar Allan Poe, and the Invention of Murder* (New York: Dutton, 2006), 287–308. Mary Rogers may have died as a result of a botched abortion, but this leaves the strangulation unexplained. Another treatment of the case is Amy Gilman Srebnick, *The Mysterious Death of Mary Rogers: Sex and Culture in Nineteenth-Century New York* (New York: Oxford University Press, 1995). See also Raymond Paul, *Who Murdered Mary Rogers?* (Englewood Cliffs, N.J.: Prentice-Hall, 1971).

29. The novel was published under the pseudonym of Charles Felix. A modern edition was published in 2012.

30. See, for example, Michael Lesy, *Wisconsin Death Trip* (New York: Pantheon, 1973); Cheri L. Farnsworth, *Murder and Mayhem in St. Lawrence County* (Charleston, S.C.: History Press, 2010).

31. The author of this book confesses that he is also a member of this large, unruly cohort of writers who have published "mysteries." My "detective" is a suburban lawyer who specializes in wills and trusts, Frank May. The "Frank May Chronicles" are set in the San Francisco Bay area.

32. James D. McCabe, Jr., *Lights and Shadows of New York Life; or the Sights and Sensations of the Great City* (New York: Farrar, Straus and Giroux, 1970), 316.

33. A Supplement to the *OED* quotes the term from a Louisiana newspaper in 1849; Herman Melville's novel, *The Confidence Man: A Masquerade,* was published in 1857.

34. Helen Campbell, *Darkness and Daylight, or Lights and Shadows of New York Life* (Hartford, Conn.: N.p., 1896), 728–729.

35. Karen Halttunen, "'Domestic Differences': Competing Narratives of Womanhood in the Murder Trial of Lucretia Chapman," in *The Culture of Sentiment: Race, Gender, and Sentimentality in Nineteenth-Century America,* ed. Shirley Samuel (New York: Oxford University Press, 1992), 39. See also Karen Halttunen, *Confidence Men and Painted Woman: A Study of Middle-Class Culture in America, 1830–1870* (New Haven: Yale University Press, 1982).

36. "A Rank Skin," *National Police Gazette,* June 19, 1880

37. Official Secrets Act, 52 & 53 Vict. ch. 52 (1889).

38. David A. T. Stafford, "Spies and Gentlemen: The Birth of the British Spy Novel, 1893–1914," *Victorian Studies* 24 (1981): 489.

39. On precursors in England, see Angus McLaren, *Sexual Blackmail: A Modern History* (Cambridge, Mass.: Harvard University Press, 2002).

40. *New York Times,* January 14, 1916.

41. On the rise of the police force, see Lawrence M. Friedman, *Crime and Punishment in American History* (New York: BasicBooks, 1993), 67–71.

42. This is from an account (no doubt exaggerated) of the work of detectives; see George S. McWatters, *Knots Untied: Or, Ways and By-Ways in the Hidden Life of American Detectives* (Hartford, Conn.: J. B. Burr and Hyde, 1873), 648–649. McWatters adds that the "criminal classes" have become "so cunning . . . that the ordinary officers of the law cannot surprise or entrap them." McWatters, *Knots Untied,* 650. There was a rich literature in the nineteenth century about detectives, some of it written by men like McWatters, who had been a detective. See also Haia Shpayer-Makov, *The Ascent of the Detective: Police Sleuths in Victorian and Edwardian England* (Oxford: Oxford University Press, 2011).

43. Angus McLaren, *A Prescription for Murder: The Victorian Serial Killings of Dr. Thomas Neill Cream* (1993). The defendant did not take the stand. Indeed, in the nineteenth century, in capital cases, defendants did not take the stand in England. His lawyer mounted a rather spirited, but futile defense—never mentioning, however, a possible insanity plea. Only after the guilty verdict was this notion advanced, but unsuccessfully. McLaren, *A Prescription for Murder,* 54–60.

44. Darnell M. Hunt, *O. J. Simpson Facts and Fictions* (Cambridge, UK: Cambridge University Press), 196. The same man talked about a "conspiracy to bring down prominent black men"; Hunt, *O. J. Simpson,* 210.

45. One of the wilder theories claimed that a white supremacist group did the killings and then proceeded to frame O. J. Simpson in order to incite a race war. Simpson was "targeted for this nefarious plot" because his wife, Nicole, was a "race traitor," a white woman who married an African American. Hunt, *O. J. Simpson,* 40.

46. In Scotland, there is an alternative to "not guilty": "not proven." The defendant escapes punishment, but there is a cloud over his head. This was a key plot device in Wilkie Collins' novel, *The Law and the Lady* (London: Chatto & Windus, 1875).

47. *New York Times,* February 11, 1997.

Chapter 12. Enter the Media

1. On this affair, see Patricia Cline Cohen, *The Murder of Helen Jewett* (New York: Alfred A. Knopf, 1998).

2. See Andie Tucher, *Froth and Scum: Truth, Beauty, Goodness, and the Ax Murder in America's First Mass Medium* (Chapel Hill: University of North Carolina Press, 1994).

3. Crime was not the only subject of cheap, sensational newspapers. There was a brief flurry of "flash" newspapers in the 1840s specializing in news about brothels, prostitutes, and the sporting life. See Patricia Cline Cohen, Timothy J. Gilfoyle, and Helen Lefkowitz Horowitz, *The Flash Press: Sporting Male Weeklies in 1840s New York* (Chicago: University of Chicago Press, 2008). The *National Police Gazette* also featured sports news, especially about boxing.

4. See, for example, *Trial for the Murder of Mr. White* (Salem: Ives & Ives, 1830), ii; *Trial of Prof. John W. Webster* (1850), available at http://openlibrary.org/.

5. On the rise of the "yellow press," see, for example, Helen MacGill Hughes, *News and the Human Interest Story* (Chicago: University of Chicago Press, 1940), especially chap. 9, "Sensationalism and the Yellow Press."

6. For an example of a "sob sister" at work, see Giles Fowler, *Deaths on Pleasant Street: The Ghastly Enigma of Colonel Swope and Doctor Hyde* (Kirksville, Mo.: Truman State University Press, 2009), 162ff., on the work of Winifred Black.

7. See Trevor D. Dryer, "'All the News that's Fit to Print': the *New York Times*, 'Yellow' Journalism, and the Criminal Trial 1898–1902," *Nevada Law Journal* 8 (2008): 541, 568.

8. On this case, see Paul Collins, *The Murder of the Century: The Gilded Age Crime That Scandalized a City & Sparked the Tabloid Wars* (New York: Crown, 2011).

9. *New York Times*, August 2, 1898.

10. See, for example, Nicole Rafter, *Shots in the Mirror: Crime Films and Society* (Oxford: Oxford University Press, 2000). Chapter 4, pp. 93–115, deals specifically with courtroom movies.

11. She was acquitted; see Lawrence M. Friedman, *Guarding Life's Dark Secrets* (Stanford: Stanford University Press, 2007), 216–219; Gabrielle Darley (who became a Mrs. Melvin), sued the moviemakers in a notable California case, Melvin v. Reid, 121 Cal. App. 285, 297 Pac. 91 (1931).

12. *12 Angry Men* (United Artists, 1957). This famous movie, of course, never actually shows the trial: all of the action takes place in the jury room.

13. *Anatomy of a Murder* (Columbia Pictures, 1959).

14. Stig Hjarvard, "The Mediatization of Society: A Theory of the Media as Agents of Social and Cultural Change," *Nordicom Review* 29, no. 2 (2008): 105, 113.

15. Gianpetro Mazzoleni and Winfried Schulz, "'Mediatization' of Politics: A Challenge for Democracy?" *Political Communication* 16 (1999): 247, 250.

16. Richard L. Fox and Robert W. Van Sickel, *Tabloid Justice: Criminal Justice in an Age of Media Frenzy* (Boulder: Lynne Rienner, 2001), 3. They define "tabloid justice" as including three elements. First, the "educational function of the press is undermined by its entertainment role" (this is hardly new, however); second, a "frenzy of media activity . . . envelops . . . legal proceeding"; and third, an "attentive public . . . witnesses these legal travails and uses them as a means by which to understand and assess the criminal justice process." Fox and Van Sickel, *Tabloid Justice*, 4–5.

17. Fox and Van Sickel, *Tabloid Justice*, 54.

18. See the discussion supra, p. 99–100.

19. Greg Merritt, *Room 1219: The Life of Fatty Arbuckle, the Mysterious Death of Virginia Rappe, and the Scandal that Changed Hollywood* (Chicago: Chicago Review Press, 2013), 82.

20. Richard Ford has made this argument about the more recent case of the "Jena 6." Six black teenagers were accused of assaulting a white student at a high school in Jena, Louisiana, in December 2006. The trials themselves, which took place later, were hardly protracted or sensational in themselves. But then the "Jena 6" began to get national attention. The media portrayed their trial as a classic case of discrimination against African Americans in criminal justice. The defendants were pictured as fine, upstanding young men, in a community of redneck bigots. Race discrimination in criminal justice is real enough, but the case of the "Jena 6" was badly distorted. The actual situation was more nuanced and ambivalent. On closer inspection, a lot of the bias and bigotry fades away, and it becomes increasingly difficult to identify heroes and villains. Richard Thompson Ford, *Rights Gone Wrong* (New York: Farrar, Straus and Giroux, 2011), 3–9; Richard Thompson Ford, "The Wrong Poster Children: Why the Jena 6 protests have gone awry," *Slate*, September 24, 2007, available at http://www.slate.com.

21. White's defense was diminished capacity, and a key point was his severe depression. At one point, a psychiatrist did mention in passing that eating lots of junk food may be a sign of depression, and might aggravate depression. See Carol Pogash, "Myth of the 'Twinkie Defense,'" *San Francisco Chronicle*, November 23, 2003.

22. Christian Delage, *Caught on Camera* (Philadelphia: University of Pennsylvania Press, 2014), explores this in detail.

23. Ray Surette, *Media, Crime, and Criminal Justice: Images, Realities, and Policies*, 3d ed. (Belmont, Calif.: Thomson/Wadsworth, 2007), 135.

24. 381 U.S. 532 (1965).

25. This is a quote from Robert D. Macfadden, "Billie Sol Estes, Texas Con Man Whose Fall Shook Up Washington, Dies at 88," *New York Times*, May 14, 2013.

26. Warren felt that the "televising of criminal trials is inherently a denial of due process." 381 U.S. at 552 (Warren, J. concurring). Four justices dissented. Justice Stewart, one of the dissenters, thought that, although "the introduction of television into a courtroom is . . . an extremely unwise policy" and "detracts from the inherent dignity of a courtroom," he and others of his colleagues were "unable to escalate this personal view into a *per se* constitutional rule." 381 U.S. at 601–02 (Stewart, J. dissenting).

27. Chandler v. Florida, 449 U.S. 560 (1981).

28. Bert Pryor et al., "The Florida Experiment: An Analysis of On-the-Scene Responses to Cameras in the Courtroom," *Southern Speech Communication Journal* 45 (1979): 12. Not everybody thought cameras were harmless; as to whether the use of TV cameras was "a desirable practice," 50.9 percent said yes, 24 percent said no, and 25 percent were uncertain. Jurors were even less certain: 43 percent thought cameras were desirable, 21 percent thought not, and 35 percent were uncertain. Pryor et al., "The Florida Experiment," 21.

29. Sheppard v. Maxwell, 384 U.S. 333 (1966).

30. The statutes and rules are collected in *MLRC 50-State Survey: Media Privacy and Related Law 2011–2012* (New York: Media Law Resource Center, 2011).

31. Kyu Ho Youm, "Cameras in the Courtroom in the Twenty-First Century: The U.S. Supreme Court Learning From Abroad?" *Brigham Young University Law Review* 6 (2012): 1,989.

32. Adam Liptak, "Bucking a Trend, Supreme Court Justices Reject Video Coverage," *New York Times*, February 18, 2013. A few federal appellate courts do allow cameras at appellate arguments; and in 2011 the

Judicial Conference authorized a three-year experiment, but only for civil cases, and only with the consent of the judge and both parties. Kyu Youm, "Cameras in the Courtroom," 2003.

33. Kyu Youm, "Cameras in the Courtroom."

34. Paul Thaler, *The Watchful Eye: American Justice in the Age of the Television Trial* (Westport, Conn.: Praeger, 1994), 34.

35. Millions of Americans watch daytime "judge" shows; in recent years, "Judge Judy" has been the most popular daytime television program. But hers are small cases, civil cases. "Judge Judy" is not really a judge, of course (though she once was); and these "cases" are even further removed from reality than evening trial dramas. See Lawrence M. Friedman, "Judge Judy's Justice," *Berkeley J. of Entertainment and Sports Law* 1 (2012): 124.

36. Thaler, *The Watchful Eye*, 116.

37. Thaler, *The Watchful Eye*, 118, 186.

38. Ray Surette thinks courts welcomed television as a way to counterbalance "negative public perceptions" of the work of the courts; see Surette, *Media, Crime, and Criminal Justice*, 136. The cameras "would show impartial justice [and] fair procedure." Meanwhile, the "seamy backstage of the criminal justice process" (such as plea bargaining) "would go unseen."

39. See the discussion in Harold Mendelsohn and H. T. Spetnagel, "Entertainment as a Sociological Enterprise," in *The Entertainment Function of Television*, ed. Percy H. Tannenbaum (Hillsdale, N.J.: Erlbaum Associates, 1980), 13.

40. Neil Postman, *Amusing Ourselves to Death: Public Discourse in the Age of Show Business* (New York: Viking, 1985), 87. He goes on to say: "No matter what is depicted or from what point of view, the overarching presumption is that it is there for our amusement and pleasure." Ibid.

41. Leo Bogart, "Television News as Entertainment," in *The Entertainment Function of Television*, 209. The Internet—through websites, blogs, social networks, and the like—may, in the future, supplant TV as the main source of news. Arguably, this is already happening.

42. Kurt Andersen, "The Culture Industry, 'Entertainer-in-Chief,'" *New Yorker*, February 16, 1998.

43. Robert N. Bellah et al., *Habits of the Heart: Individualism and Commitment in American Life*, 3d ed. (Berkeley: University of California Press, 2007), 150.

44. *The Godfather*, directed by Francis Ford Coppola, appeared in 1972 and was spectacularly successful; *The Godfather: Part II* appeared in 1974.

"The Sopranos" was a much-admired television series that ran between 1999 and 2007.

45. Nicole Rafter, *Shots in the Mirror: Crime Films and Society* (Oxford: Oxford University Press, 2000), 9–10.

46. Jack Katz, "What Makes Crime 'News'?" *Media, Culture & Society* 9 (1987): 47.

47. The story is told in Geoffrey O'Brien, *The Fall of the House of Walworth: A Tale of Madness and Murder in Gilded Age America* (New York: Henry Holt and Co., 2010).

48. O'Brien, *The Fall of the House of Walworth*, 188.

49. *Los Angeles Times*, September 24, 1921. According to this story, a witness, Alfred Demnacher, testified about the "drinking party" in the hotel and described the dying woman with her clothing torn off.

50. Douglas Perry, *The Girls of Murder City: Fame, Lust, and the Beautiful Killers who Inspired Chicago* (New York: Viking, 2010).

51. "Queen for a Day" ran from 1945 to 1964, on radio and television, and was extremely popular; so, too, was "Candid Camera," which lasted from the late 1940s to 2004. "Major Bowes' Amateur Hour" was a radio staple from 1934 to 1945; it was replaced by "The Original Amateur Hour," which lasted in various forms until 1992.

52. James D. Livingston, *Arsenic and Clam Chowder: Murder in Gilded Age New York* (Albany: State University of New York Press, 2010).

53. "New T.V. Spots Assail Dukakis on Furloughs," *Associated Press*, October 21, 1988.

54. See, for example, the discussion in Franklin Zimring, *The City that Became Safe: New York's Lessons for Urban Crime and Its Control* (Oxford: Oxford University Press, 2012).

55. Terrorist attacks may be an exception; or at least people might think so.

56. The reference, of course, is to Miranda v. Arizona, 384 U.S.436 (1966), which insisted, among other things, that a person who has been arrested and is going to be questioned has to be told about the right to remain silent.

57. On the meaning and social importance of scandal, see Ari Adut, *On Scandal: Moral Disturbances in Society, Politics, and Art* (Cambridge, UK: Cambridge University Press, 2008).

58. Carol Ballentine, "Sulfanilamide Disaster," *FDA Consumer Magazine*, June 1981.

59 "Smog Linked to 18 Deaths in Day and Hospital Jam, in Donora,

Pa.," *New York Times*, October 31, 1948. The death toll later rose; see "Steel Company Pays $235,000 to Settle $4,643,000 in Donora Smog Death Suits," *New York Times*, April 18, 1951.

60. This law, passed originally in 1994, was a response to the murder of young Megan Kanka. The law is NJSA 2C:7–1ff.

61. See *United States Department of Justice National Sex Offender Public Website*, available at http://www.nsopw.gov/Core/PublicRegistrySites.aspx. The provision of the Pennsylvania law cited is 42 Pa. C. S. sec. 9798 (B). The neighbors have to be given this notice "within five days after information of the sexually violent predator's release date and residence has been received by the chief law enforcement officer, and within seven days to the others." 42 Pa. C. S. sec. 9798 (C).

62. See "5 Years After Jessica Lunsford's Death, Florida Revisits Sex-Offender Laws," *Miami Herald*, February 24, 2010. Jessica's Law is codified at Florida Statute 800.04.

63. Cal. Penal Code, sec. 667. The Supreme Court upheld this statute in Ewing v. California, 538 U.S.11 (2003). The three-strikes law has since been modified by Proposition 36 (2012), which cut down somewhat on the harshness of the law.

64. USA PATRIOT Act, Public Law 107–56, October 26, 2001. Among the trials was the trial of John Walker Lindh, mentioned above at p. 32.

65. Alex Kozinsky and Robert Johnson, "Of Cameras and Courtrooms," *Fordham Intellectual Property, Media, and Entertainment Law Journal* 20 (2010): 1107, 1133; a typical reference to this quote is Alfred N. Delahaye, "The Case of Bruno Hauptmann," in *The Press on Trial: Crimes and Trials as Media Events*, ed. Lloyd Chiasson, Jr., 117–130 (Westport, Conn.: Greenwood, 1997), 117, though, as always, without citation of a source.

66. Russell B. Porter, "Hauptmann Put to Death for Killing Lindbergh Baby," *New York Times*, April 3, 1936.

67. 18 U.S. Const. § 1201.

68. See Theodore Hamm, *Rebel and a Cause: Caryl Chessman and the Politics of the Death Penalty in Postwar California 1948–1974* (Berkeley: University of California Press, 2001).

69. See above, p. 66.

Chapter 13. Instant Celebrity

1. Dershowitz, *Reversal of Fortune* (New York: Random House, 1986), 253. Dershowitz felt that this case "may well have been the most expensive prosecution in history against a single individual." The prosecution probably spent more than the defense; the prosecution also had "access to more free services." On the other hand, "state salaries are lower than private fees." What was unusual about this case was that Sunny's family members—who were enormously rich—used their private money and influence to help the state bring charges against Claus. Dershowitz, *Reversal of Fortune*, 256.

2. Darnell Hunt, *O. J. Simpson Facts and Fictions* (Cambridge, UK: Cambridge University Press), 26.

3. Arthur Train, *Courts and Criminals* (New York: Scribner, 1926), 66.

4. On the Fallmer trial, see Lawrence M. Friedman and Robert V. Percival, *The Roots of Justice: Crime and Punishment in Alameda County, California, 1870–1910* (Chapel Hill: University of North Carolina Press, 1981), 239–244.

5. Lawrence M. Friedman, "The One-Way Mirror: Law, Privacy, and the Media," *Washington University Law Quarterly* 82 (2004): 319.

6. Laurie Ouellette and Susan Murray, "Introduction," in *Reality TV: Remaking Television Culture*, 2d ed., ed. Susan Murray and Laurie Ouellette, 1–20 (New York: New York University Press, 2009), 6.

7. Eric Burns, *Invasion of the Mind Snatchers: Television's Conquest of American in the Fifties* (Philadelphia: Temple University Press, 2010), 48–49.

8. Richard Schickel, *Intimate Strangers: The Culture of Celebrity* (Garden City, N.Y.: Doubleday, 1985).

9. But, interestingly, never the members of the jury; they have to remain largely anonymous in order to play their proper role.

10. There is, of course, a huge literature on the right of privacy. The starting point is conventionally taken to be the classic article, Samuel D. Warren and Louis D. Brandeis, "The Right of Privacy," *Harvard Law Review* 4 (1890): 193. See also Jeffrey Rosen, *The Unwanted Gaze: The Destruction of Privacy in America* (New York: Random House, 2000); Lawrence M. Friedman, "The Eye that Never Sleeps: Privacy and Law in the Internet Era," *Tulsa Law Review* 40 (2005): 561–578; Daniel J. Solove, *Understanding Privacy* (Cambridge, Mass.: Harvard University Press, 2008).

11. Von Hannover v. Germany, App. No. 59320/00, 40 Eur. H. R. Rep. 1 (2005); see also James Q. Whitman, "The Two Western Cultures of Privacy: Dignity Versus Liberty," *Yale Law Journal* 113 (2004): 1,151.

12. See, for example, Michaels v. Internet Entertainment Grp., Inc., 5 F. Supp 2d 823, 839 (C.D. Cal. 1998), where the court said that "newsworthiness is defined broadly to include not only matters of public policy, but any matter of public concern, including the accomplishments, everyday lives, and romantic involvements of famous people." In Europe, deference to elites still seems to survive; and courts, at least, are sometimes willing to express a sense of limits. What the public is interested in is not necessarily in the public interest. The same seems to hold in Japan; see Noriko Kitajima, "The Protection of Reputation in Japan: A Systematic Analysis of Defamation Cases," *Law & Social Inquiry* 37 (2012): 89.

Chapter 14. A Concluding Word

1. Jonathan Krim, "Subway Fracas Escalates into Test of the Internet's Power to Shame," *Washington Post*, July 7, 2005.

2. See Milly S. Barranger, *Unfriendly Witnesses: Gender, Theater, and Film in the McCarthy Era* (Carbondale: Southern Illinois University Press, 2008), 4–8.

3. John Joseph Gladchuk, *Hollywood and Anticommunism: HUAC and the Evolution of the Red Menace, 1935–1950* (London: Routledge, 2007).

4. Eric Burns, *Invasion of the Mind Snatchers: Television's Conquest of America in the Fifties* (Philadelphia: Temple University Press, 2010), 184.

5. Burns, *Invasion of the Mind Snatchers*, 366.

6. Thomas Dohert, "Frank Costello's Hands: Film, Television, and the Kefauver Crime Hearings," *Film History* 10 (1998): 359, 361–362.

Index